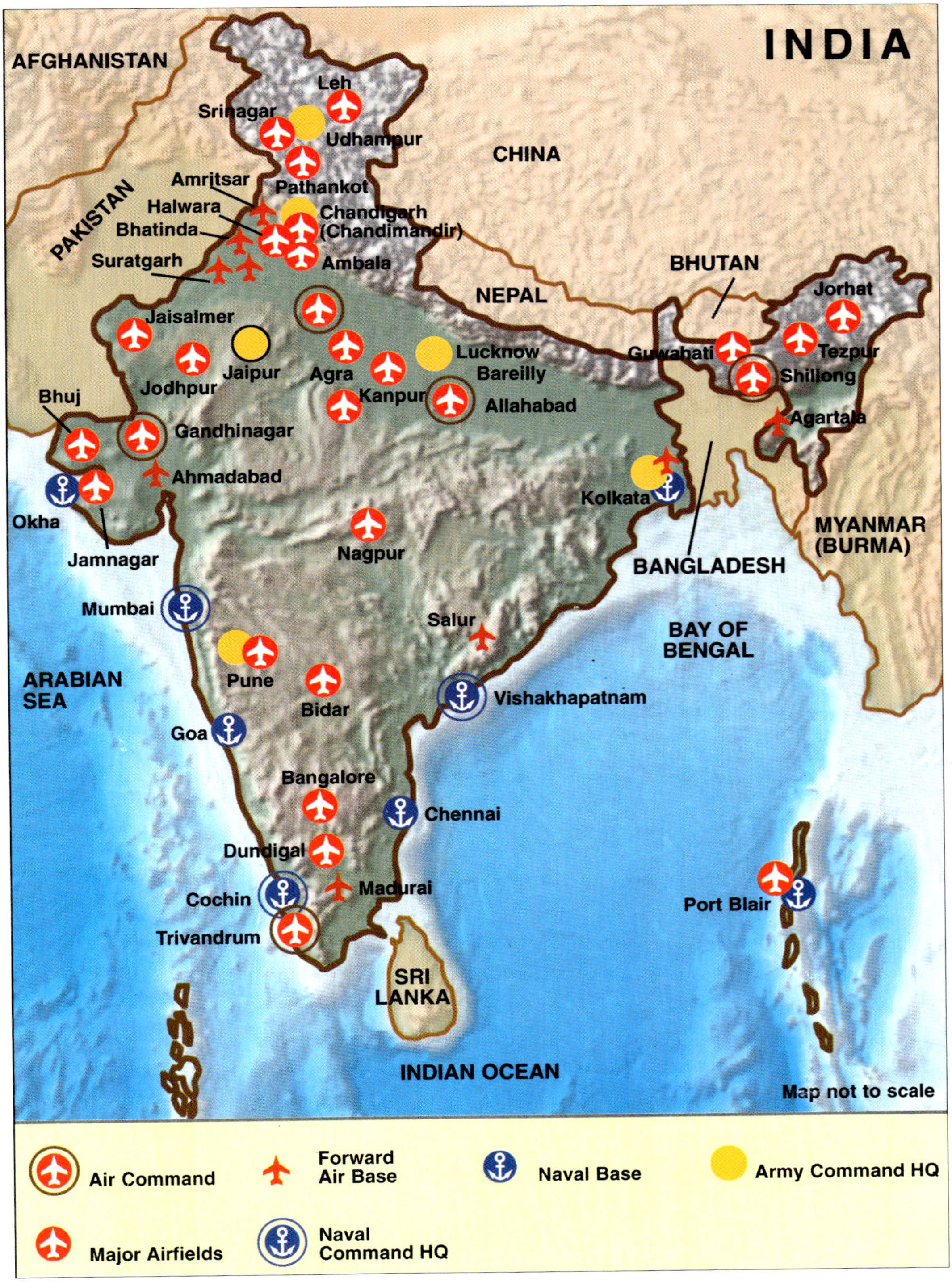

Source: Asian Strategic and Military Perspective by RSN Singh

Indian Armed Forces

INDIAN ARMED FORCES

Capt Bharat Verma

Vice Admiral (Retd) GM Hiranandani,
PVSM, AVSM, NM, PhD

Air Marshal (Retd) BK Pandey,
PVSM, AVSM, VM

Lancer * New Delhi * Olympia Fields IL
www.lancerpublishers.com

LANCER PUBLISHERS

Published in the United States
by Lancer Publishers,
a division of Lancer InterConsult, Inc.
19900 Governors Drive, Suite 104
Olympia Fields IL 60461

Published in India
by Lancer Publishers & Distributors
2/42 (B) Sarvapriya Vihar
New Delhi-110016

© Lancer Publishers 2008

All rights reserved. No part of this publication
may be reproduced, stored in a retrieval system or transmitted,
in any form or by any means, electronic, mechanical, photocopying,
recording or otherwise, without the prior permission of the publishers.
For additional information, contact Lancer Publishers.

Printed at Sona Printers, New Delhi.
Printed and bound in India.

ISBN: 0-9796174-2-1   978-0-9796174-2-3

Online Military Bookshop
www.lancerpublishers.com

Contents

Introduction
By Bharat Verma — xi

Acronyms and Abbreviations — xvi

INDIAN ARMY
Captain Bharat Verma

1. Historical Overview — 1
2. Role of the Armed Forces — 5
3. The Command and Control Structure of the Army — 8
   - The Rank Structure — 8
   - The Chain of Command — 10
   - Field Formations — 13
   - Static Formations — 15
4. Branches of the Army — 18
   - The Infantry — 18
   - The Armoured Corps — 22
   - The Artillery — 23
   - Army Air Defence — 26
   - Army Aviation Corps — 28
   - Corps of Engineers — 28

	Corps of Signals	30
	Rashtriya Rifles	31
	Army Service Corps	32
	Army Ordnance Corps	33
	Corps of Electronics and Mechanical Engineers	34
	Army Medical Corps	35
	Minor Corps/Services	36
	The Territorial Army	37
5.	A Glimpse of Life in the Army	39
	Life in a Peacetime Location	39
	Unit Institutes	41
	Life in Field Areas	43
	High Altitude Areas	45
6.	Traditions and Customs of the Service	47
	Battle Cry	48
	Battle Honour	50
	Gallantry Awards	50
	War Medals	52
	Distinguished Service Medals	52
7.	Recruitment in the Army	56
	Officers' Selection System	56
	Women's Special Entry Scheme	58
	Recruitment of Other Rank	60
	Pay and Allowances	62
8.	A Brief History of the Wars and Conflicts after Independence	65
	The First Indo-Pak War, 1947-48	65
	The Sino-Indian War, 1962	67
	The Second Indo-Pak War, 1965	68
	The Third Indo-Pak War, 1971	70
	The Proxy War	71

INDIAN NAVY
Vice Admiral GM Hiranandani, PVSM, AVSM, NM, PhD

9.	India's Maritime Background	73

	In the Millennia Prior to the Europeans	73
	European Contests for Naval Dominance of the West Coast	74
	European Contests for Naval Dominance of the East Coast	74
	The Maratha Navy in the 17th and 18th Centuries	75
	The Anglo-French Contests on the East Coast 1740 to 1815	76
	British Supremacy in the Indian Ocean after 1815 until 1947	77
10.	**The Navy's Development after Independence in 1947**	**79**
	The Acquisition of Ships from Britain	79
	After China's Intrusion in 1962	79
	The Leander Frigate Project	80
	The Changeover to Russian Naval Acquisitions	80
	The 1965 War	80
	The Arrival of the Russian Acquisitions	82
	The Acquisition of British Anti-submarine Helicopters	82
	The Acquisition of Russian Anti-ship Missiles	83
	The 1971 War	84
	Operations in the Arabian Sea	84
	Operations in the Bay of Bengal	84
	Lessons of the 1971 War	85
	Indo-Russian Interaction in Indigenous Warship Design	86
	The Acquisition and Indigenous Construction of German SSK Submarines	86
11.	**Contemporary Naval Warfare**	**88**
	Surface Ships	88
	Innovation in Warship Design and Indigenous Research & Development	89
	India's Warship Building Yards	90
	Post-Independence Acquisition of Mazagon Docks Limited and Garden Reach Workshops	91
	Goa Shipyard Limited	91
	Submarines & Anti-submarine Warfare	92
	Stealth and Snorting	92
	Submarine Tactics	93
	Anti-submarine Tactics	93
	Sound Propagation under the Sea	93
	MRASW Aircraft	94
	Anti-submarine Ships and their ASW Helicopters	94
	Submarine Search and Kill (SSK) Submarines	95

	The Navy's Submarine Arm	96
	The Role of the Navy's Air Arm	96
12.	Naval Operations after 1971	98
	Operations in Support of the Indian Peace-Keeping Force (IPKF) in Sri Lanka	98
	Operations in Support of the Maldivian Government in 1988	98
	Patrols along the Gujarat and Maharashtra Coasts	99
	Deployments in Support of the United Nations Humanitarian Operations in Somalia, September 1993 to December 1994	99
	Anti-militant Operations in the Andaman Islands	100
	Deployment of the Fleet in the North Arabian Sea during the Kargil War 1999	100
	Deployment of the Fleet in the North Arabian Sea in 2002 after Terrorists' attack on Indian Parliament in December 2001	100
	Assistance rendered by the Navy in Peacetime	101
13.	The Foreseeable Future	103
14.	The Indian Navy Today	105
	Command and Control	105
	Base Support	106
	Training	106
15.	Career Opportunities	108
	Executive Branch	108
	Engineering Branch	108
	Electrical Branch	109
	Education Branch	109
16.	Officers' Entry	110
	Terms and Conditions	113
	Sailors' Entry	114
	Artificers	114
	Seaman Branch	114
	Engineering Branch	115
	Electrical Branch	115
	Logistics Cadre	115
	Medical Branch	115

	Sailors for the Submarine Arm and the flight crew of the Naval Air Arm	115
	List of Recruiting Offices	116

INDIAN AIR FORCE
Air Marshal BK Pandey, PVSM, AVSM, VM

17.	The History of the Indian Air Force	119
	Foundation	119
	Decade of the Sixties	120
	Liberation of Bangladesh	121
	Post-1971: Emergence of a Regional Power	121
	Lessons of Kargil	122
18.	Roles of the IAF	124
	Force Structure	124
	Integrated HQ of MoD (Air Force): Organizational Structure	125
	Air Command Headquarters	126
	Wing/Station	127
	Squadron	127
19.	Types of Air Operations	129
	Air Defence	129
	Weapons of Air Defence	129
	Long Range Strike	130
	Offensive Air Support	131
	Aerial Reconnaissance	132
	Air Transport Operations	132
	Electronic Warfare	132
	Training Philosophy	133
20.	IAF: Meeting the Challenges of the Twenties	135
	Planning for Modernization of the IAF	135
	Conflict and the Developing World	135
	Sino-Indian Relations	136
	Indo-Pak Confrontation	137

	India as a Regional Power	138
	Security Environment in the Twenties	139
	Aerial Reconnaissance	140
	Strategic & Tactical Strike Capability	140
	Air Defence	141
	Strategic & Tactical Airlift Capability	142
	Battlefield Strike	143
	In-flight Refuelling	143
	Exploitation of Space	143
	Training	144
	Technological Revolution	144
21.	**Officers' Cadre: Rank Structure**	**146**
	Entry Conditions: Officers' Cadre	147
	Induction of Women in the Officers' Cadre	147
	Branches	147
	Entry Criteria: Officers' Cadre	148
22.	**Personnel Below Officers' Rank / Airmen Cadre**	**152**
	The PBOR	152
	Entry Criteria	153
	Trade Structure : PBOR (Airmen)	154
	Airmen Selection Centres in India	155

INDIAN COAST GUARD
Vice Admiral GM Hiranandani, PVSM, AVSM, NM, PhD

23.	**The Coast Guard**	**157**
	The Coast Guard Act-1978	157
	The Maritime Zones of India (Regulation of Fishing by Foreign Vessels) Act-1981	158
	Coast Guard Resources	159
	Regional Organization	159
	Activities	160

Introduction

Bharat Verma
Editor, Indian Defence Review

The Security Environment

Today, India is ringed by turbulent states - Pakistan (land boundary with India 3,310 kms in the northwest), Nepal (land boundary with India 1,751 kms in the north), Bangladesh (land boundary with India 4,095 kms in the southeast) and Myanmar (land boundary with India 1,463 kms in the northeast). Turbulence has percolated through India's porous borders in the form of arms and narcotics to finance insurgents, militants, terrorists and religious fundamentalists.

India remains Pakistan's primary target and operating ground for Islamic fundamentalists and terrorist groups who infiltrate through Jammu & Kashmir (J&K), Nepal and Bangladesh and carry out anti-Indian activities with impunity.

Nepal is vulnerable to China's influence. Its extremists have linkages with the People's War Group (PWG) in India. In its bid to expand its influence, the PWG has carved a corridor ringing the states of Andhra Pradesh–Madhya Pradesh–Chhatisgarh–Orissa–West Bengal–Jharkhand–Bihar as shown in the map.

This endless internal turbulence in India is also inter-linked with external factors. To the North, India shares a 3,440-km long border with China, which can pose the entire spectrum of conventional, nuclear and missile threats. It can also influence and use as proxy India's neighbours to weigh India down in every possible way.

In short, India's 14,058-km long land frontier is impacted by a perpetually hostile or semi-hostile environment. Indian security stands threatened by demographic assault, arms and drug smuggling, and the safe havens that the insurgents have in India. Fundamentalist-religious groups in Bangladesh under Pakistani tutelage, West Asian finance and China's patronage have synergized sufficiently to add to India's security headache.

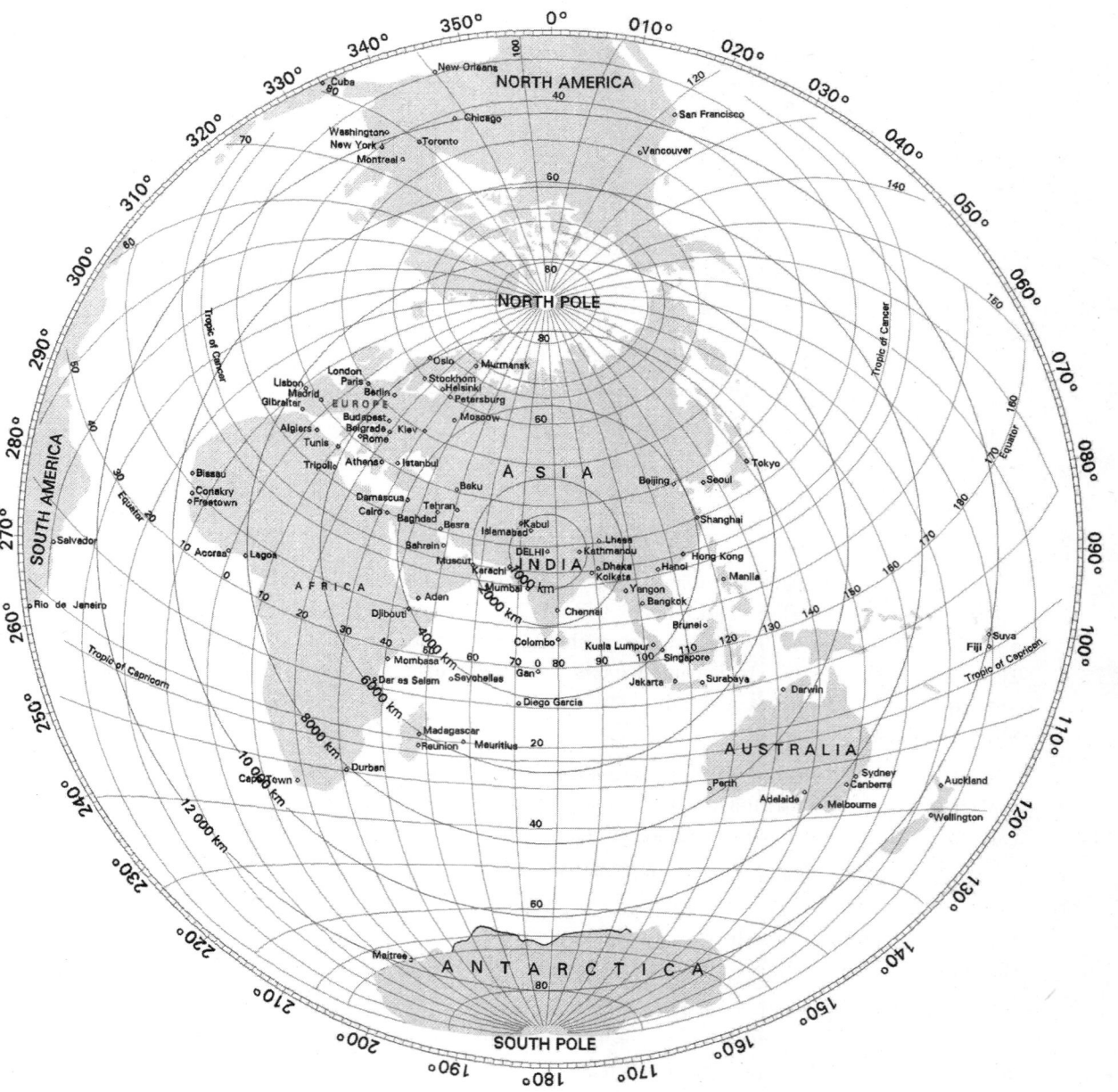

An equidistant map of the world centred on Delhi showing true bearings & distance from Delhi.

Scale 1 : 45 5 00 000 • Projection : Lambert Azimuthal Equidistant (Oblique Aspect) • Origin : Delhi • Latitude 28°35'N • Longitude 77°13'E • Read off the value on the graduated circle to get the true bearing to the nearest degree, of well known places radially from Delhi. Examples :- True bearings from Delhi to San Francisco, Tokyo, Cape Town and Moscow are 015°, 065°, 226°, and 325°, respectively.

• Excerpted from *Transition to Eminence : The Indian Navy 1976-1990* by Vice Admiral GM Hiranandani.

The grim reality is that the unending turbulence will continue to afflict our land and sea frontiers and airspace.

The Indian Temperament

By nature, the average Indian is highly individualistic and an entrepreneur. In every endeavour, his calculation is simply based on, "What's in it for me?" He does not have the time or the inclination to actively get involved with the intricacies of the nations' security.

This kind of entrepreneurial society requires a steel frame of military, naval and air power to ensure that India's accommodative temperament and societal characteristic of gentleness remains protected from the turbulent violence that assaults the values of our democratic polity.

India's Armed Forces

On attaining Independence in 1947, India inherited possibly the best instrument of war in Asia - a fine battle-ready military machine with a formidable reputation of winning wars in distant lands. Britain had employed it skilfully for over a century to sustain her empire and treasured it as the jewel in its crown.

In the years after Independence, India's Army has been unendingly deployed for internal policing tasks to cope with the complex security situation. This deployment has kept the Union of India physically intact. But it is sad that 60 years after Independence, the stability of India still depends directly on the stability of the Indian Army. Field Marshal Wavell who was India's British Viceroy in 1946, was prophetic when he said "... the stability of the Indian Army may perhaps be a deciding factor in the future of India."

Making India's Armed Forces Younger

For a number of reasons, and despite considerable efforts, the Armed Forces remain short of the manpower they need. It is imperative that this manpower shortage be removed speedily before the system buckles under the ageing profile of its leadership. There is only one viable strategy to attract the kind of talent that is needed and that is to assure military personnel of assured lateral induction into the para-military and police forces, the intelligence services and the civil administration.

Unfortunately, a consensus has not been achieved that "Lateral Induction" is the best way to attract India's young but savvy population to the tough profession of arms where risk-to-life is an everyday affair.

Major benefits will accrue from Lateral Induction. First, the transfer of highly disciplined, trained and skilled manpower to the civil set-up will contribute towards the creation of a 'discipline culture' the country. Second, the superior training standards of lateral inductees will aid civil and para-military forces in combating terrorism and internal violence.

However, placing a large segment of a young Army on the land borders cannot entirely ensure security of India. There are two aspects to it.

First, if a football team defends only its half of the field, it is certain that an adversary determined to create mischief, short of going to war, will create opportunities for its irregular forces *(jihadis)* to score goals through infiltration, smuggling and creeping invasion. The hostile environment that impacts India's long frontiers requires that the role of military power to defend strategic frontiers must be firmly embedded in India's foreign policy.

The second aspect is the need for political will to project the power of Armed Forces beyond the Indian subcontinent to secure the sea-lanes for external trade and ensure the security of imported energy supplies.

India's Place in Asia

India's geo-strategic location with its 7,500 kms long peninsular coastline jutting into the Indian Ocean makes India a continental as well as a maritime power.

India impacts directly on East, West and Central Asia. As a rising economic power dependent almost entirely on foreign energy supplies, a time may come when India has to project its military power to protect and preserve the energy resources from Central and West Asia, and Africa. For India, with its pacifist temperament, this may sound imperial. But without a ruthless winning attitude, India's multi-religious and multi-cultural society cannot survive endless undermining by disaffected elements.

The world has already recognised that with its democratic institutions, its liberal philosophy and its unique strategic location, India's influence will extend beyond South Asia and directly affect Asia's well-being.

Dovetailing Foreign-Economic-Military Objectives

A nation's foreign policy is dependent primarily on the strength of its economic and military power. The ability and the will to wield military power ruthlessly, to defend and advance national interests, when combined with the capacity and resolve to create wealth, constitute the proven route for every aspirant seeking recognition as an eminent power.

India has the potential and the prerequisites of becoming a great power within the next few decades, provided it can dovetail its foreign, economic and military objectives and mainstream its military power.

The crucial question is whether India will be a surrogate power or be a 'great power'?

Ostensibly, our national objectives are to have a peaceful neighbourhood. What should be the strategy to achieve it? Statements like a "Stable and secure neighbours are in India's interest" are well-meant. The fundamental question however is – "Will India's neighbours ever be stable and secure?" Appeasement of neighbours cannot constitute a strategy for any country.

India's larger objective in Asia is to emerge as a geo-economic hub that can integrate and influence its extended neighbourhood through mutually beneficial economic linkages and military relationships. As a benevolent power that has no external territorial interests, India is uniquely located - geographically and culturally to play this role effectively. India's free media can be intelligently harnessed to further these national objectives and develop the complementarities that influence Asia.

To attain eminence in Asia, India needs to move simultaneously on three axes. These are India–West Asia, India–Southeast Asia and India–Central Asia. Of these, the critical one is the India-Afghanistan-Iran-Russia axis. Today, Russia is reacting firmly to intruders into its neighbourhood. Her economic and military resurgence presents an opportunity for a relationship which would lend stability to the region.

Moreover, as the second largest consumer of oil and gas in Asia, the assurance of uninterrupted energy supplies is a vital factor in India's security calculus. By 2010, a substantial amount of oil and gas will be sourced from Central Asia. This resource-rich region will succumb to fundamentalist-religious Talibanisation if India and like-minded countries do not pre-empt it. In such an eventuality, American oil corporations will be expelled, particularly with the Chinese gaining ground and occupying positions that could dictate the future agenda in Central Asia. It is therefore timely for American capitalists to join hands with Indian counterparts in joint ventures.

In the favourable geo-political scenario now emerging, India's strategy must be to strengthen existing friendly relationships while developing mutually advantageous new relationships,

Acronyms and Abbreviations

A&N	Andaman and Nicobar
AAC	Army Aviation Corps
AAD	Army Air Defence
AAM	Air-to-Air Missile
AC	Ashoka Chakra
ACAS	Assistant Chief of Air Staff
ACC	Army Cadet College
ACM	Air Chief Marshal
AD	Air Defence
ADC	Army Dental Corps
ADGES	Air Defence Ground Environment Scheme
ADS	Air Defence Ship
AEC	Army Education Corps
ALG	Advanced Landing Ground
ALH	Advanced Light Helicopter
AMC	Army Medical Corps
AOA	Air Officer-incharge of Administration
AOC	Army Ordnance Corps
AOC	Air Officer Commanding
AOC-in-C	Air Officer Commanding-in-Chief
AOM	Air Officer-incharge of Material
AOP	Air Officer-incharge of Personnel
APO	Army Post Office
APS	Army Postal Services
APTC	Army Physical Training Corps
AREN	Army Radio Engineering Network
ASC	Army Service Corps
ASCON	Army Static Switched Communication Network

ASW	Anti-Submarine Warfare
AVSM	Ati Vishisht Seva Medal
AWACS	Airborne Warning and Control System
BAI	Battlefield Air Interdiction
BAS	Battlefield Air Support
BISNC	British India Steam Navigation Company
BRO	Border Roads Organisation
BRO	Branch Recruiting Office/Officer
BVR	Beyond Visual Range
CAC	Central Air Command
CAS	Chief of Air Staff
CDS	Chief of Defence Staff
CDS	Combined Defence Services
CEE	Common Entrance Examination
CIF HQ	Counter-Insurgency Force HQ
C-in-C	Commander-in-Chief
CMP	Corps of Military Police
CNS	Chief of Naval Staff
COAS	Chief of Army Staff
CoP	Chief of Personnel
COMINT	Communication Intelligence
CoM	Chief of Material
DCAS	Deputy Chief of Air Staff
DCNS	Deputy Chief of Naval Staff
DGFS & I	Director General incharge of Flight Safety and Inspection
EAC	Eastern Air Command
EEZ	Exclusive Economic Zone
ELINT	Electronic Intelligence
EME	Electronics and Mechanical Engineers
EW	Electronic Warfare
FOC-in-C	Flag Officer Commanding-in-Chief
FONA	Flag Officer Naval Aviation
FOSM	Flag Officer Submarine
GCI	Ground Control Interception
GRSE	Garden Reach Shipbuilders and Engineers
GSL	Goa Shipyard Limited
GTO	Group Testing Officer
HQ (s)	Headquarter (s)
ICV	Infantry Combat Vehicle

IED	Improvised Explosive Device
IFG	Indian Field Gun
IHQ of MoD	Integrated Headquarters of Ministry of Defence
IHQ of MoD (Navy)	Integrated Headquarters of Ministry of Defence (Navy)
IMA	Indian Military Academy
INS	Indian Naval Ship
IOC	Indian Oil Corporation
IPKF	Indian Peace-Keeping Force
J & K	Jammu and Kashmir
JAG	Judge Advocate General
JCO	Junior Commissioned Officer
KC	Kirti Chakra
LCA	Light Combat Aircraft
LoC	Line of Control
MBRL	Multi-Barrel Rocket Launcher
MC	Maintenance Command
MDL	Mazagon Dock Limited
MI Room	Medical Inspection Room
MNS	Military Nursing Service
MoD	Ministry of Defence
MRASW Aircraft	Maritime Reconnaissance and Anti-Submarine Warfare Aircraft
MRCA	Multi-Role Combat Aircraft
MVC	Maha Vir Chakra
NCO	Non-Commissioned Officer
NDA	National Defence Academy
NM	Nausena Medal
NOIC	Naval Officer-in-Charge
OEM	Original Equipment Manufacturer
ONGC	Oil and National Gas Commission
OPV	Offshore Patrol Vessel
Orbat	Order of Battle
ORP	Operational Readiness Platform
OTA	Officers' Training Academy
P&O	Peninsular and Orient
PBOR	Person Below Officers' Rank
PC	Permanent Commission
PoK	Pakistan Occupied Kashmir
PVC	Param Vir Chakra
PVSM	Param Vishisht Seva Medal

PWG	People's War Group
RIAF	Royal Indian Air Force
RR	Rashtriya Rifles
RVC	Remount and Veterinary Corps
SAC	Southern Air Command
SAM	Surface-to-Air Missile
SAR	Synthetic Aperture Radar
SASO	Senior Air Staff Officer
SATA	Surveillance and Target Acquisition
SC	Shaurya Chakra
SM	Sena Medal
SMSO	Senior Maintenance Staff Officer
SOA	Senior Officer incharge Administration
SOS	Save Our Souls
SSB	Service Selection Board
SSC	Short Service Commission
SSK	Submarine Search and Kill
SSM	Surface-to-Surface Missile
SWAC	South Western Air Command
SYSM	Sarvottam Yudh Seva Medal
TAT	Thematic Appreciation Test
TC	Training Command
UAV	Unmanned Aerial Vehicle
UYSM	Uttam Yudh Seva Medal
VA	Vital Area
VCAS	Vice Chief of Air Staff
VCNS	Vice Chief of Naval Staff
VDS	Variable Depth Sonar
VP	Vital Point
VrC	Vir Chakra
VSM	Vishisht Seva Medal
WAC	Western Air Command
WAT	Word Associate Test
YSM	Yudh Seva Medal

Indian Army
by
Captain Bharat Verma

Bharat Verma was commissioned into 69 Armoured Regiment in 1972. Later, he set up the first dedicated military publishing house in India in 1983. Today, the Lancer Publishers is rated as "India's premier publishing house on strategic affairs" (Asia Times Online). He is also the Editor of Indian Defence Review.

1
Historical Overview

The Indian Army has its origin in the armed guards of the East India Company, a company of merchants from Britain. These guards were required for protection of the company's factories and warehouses. Initially, these were all Englishmen but gradually Indians too were enrolled. To begin with, the company carried out trade from Madras, Bombay, Surat and Calcutta. As the company expanded with conquests, more and more Indian soldiers were enlisted. Gradually steps were taken to unite various units or groups from Madras, Bombay and Bengal to form an unified Army.

In 1902, when Lord Kitchener took over as Commander-in-Chief (C-in-C) of the army it was further reorganized as a new regular force. By 1914, at the time of the outbreak of the World War I, the strength of the Indian Army had reached approximately 1,50,000. By the time the World War II had started in 1939, the strength of the army had risen to 1,89,000. In 1947, with the partition of the country, two-thirds of the strength remained with India and one-third went away to Pakistan. On the eve of our Independence the strength of the undivided army was nearly 25,00,000.

Indian soldiers have served all over the world during the British regime. They fought from China in the east to France and Africa in the west, during 1914-18 and 1939-45 in the two World Wars. They scripted many victories with their valour and sacrifice in numerous battlefields in China, Iraq, Africa, Italy, France and Burma. The secret of success of the Indian Army has been its unflinching sense of duty, discipline and traditions of valour.

In August 1947, the subcontinent was plunged in a great turmoil due to widespread communal riots and movement of refugees. This situation created major administrative problems and the army had to step in to control the situation. A special Army Command was set up to 'keep the peace' while the partition proceeded. This command functioned under Major General T. E. Rees with effect from 1 August 1947 and an ad hoc force -the Punjab Boundary Force with its Headquarters (HQ) at Lahore was formed. This force consisted of undivided mixed units with a high proportion of British officers. The charter of command gave Major General Rees control of troops in both the dominions. He was made responsible to both the governments, through the Supreme Commander and the Joint Defence Council. One Brigadier each from the Indian and the Pakistan Armies was appointed as adviser to Major General Rees. The forces under the command of this HQ had to go into action in all major towns in Punjab. The fanatical mobs struck back with fury and many soldiers sustained serious injuries. The army, however, managed to carry out its task with great impartiality throughout the communal frenzy which prevailed in the country during the partition.

On 15 January 1948, Lieutenant General K. M. Cariappa became the first Indian C-in-C. 15 January is now celebrated every year as 'Army Day'. On this occasion the Chief of the Army Staff (COAS) takes the salute at the Army Day Parade in the Delhi Cantonment. This is a grand parade which is held just before the Republic Day Parade.

The rulers of some princely states were reluctant to join the new Indian dominion and many had to be coaxed by threat of force. The army was yet to reorganize after its division when the call came from Junagadh and Hyderabad. The Indian Army consolidated our position in these states without bloodshed, which then became parts of the Indian dominion.

The Maharaja of Kashmir did not make up his mind till October 1947 as he wanted to remain independent as long as possible. However, in October 1947 when Pakistan sent a large body of tribesmen to invade and occupy various parts of J&K, the Maharaja was compelled by the circumstances to ask for India's intervention. As the Government of India was unwilling to send troops to Kashmir until the state acceded to India, the Maharaja acceded to the Indian Union on 27 October 1947. The first troops landed at the Srinagar airfield on 27 October 1947 in Dakotas (small aircraft carrying about 20 troops each). To be precise initially only a few companies (strength of one company is normally about 100) landed on a dusty and improvised airstrip at Srinagar. The raiders would have reached Srinagar before our troops landed there had they not wasted time in plunder, murder and rape in Baramulla.

Some gallant actions were fought by a handful of infantrymen on the outskirts of Srinagar, which saved the day for India. To commemorate the indomitable spirit of infantrymen, 27 October is now celebrated every year as 'Infantry Day'.

The war raged in J&K from October 1947 to January 1949. It ended in a proud victory for our army and Pakistan failed to capture Jammu or Srinagar. However, a premature cease-fire was accepted by our Government which enabled Pakistan to hold on to large parts of J&K state. These areas under Pakistan's occupation are called Pak Occupied Kashmir (POK) and the Northern Areas.

From 1948 to 1962, Indian Army contingents did a number of peacekeeping assignments outside the country, in Korea, Gaza (Egypt) and Congo (Central Africa) on behalf of the United Nations and earned great honour for the country.

In 1962, when China attacked India, the Indian Army was rushed to fight the enemy on the icy heights of the Himalayas for which it was ill-equipped and ill-prepared. It resulted in a crushing defeat which compelled the politicians to change their attitude of neglect towards the armed forces.

Yet another reminder came in 1965, when Pakistan attacked our territory in the Rann of Kutch (Gujarat) and later invaded in J&K. The Indian Army repulsed all Pakistani attacks and went on the offensive in the Punjab where our troops reached within a few miles of Lahore (an important Pakistani city). It was now proved beyond doubt that India needed a well-trained and well-equipped army to take on its adversaries. Once the army was properly trained and equipped, it defeated Pakistan decisively in 1971 and helped in the creation of Bangladesh. After 1971, the supremacy of the Indian Army was fully established in the subcontinent and no enemy has dared attack us openly since then.

Stung by colossal defeat and loss of face, Pakistan adopted an innovative strategy of waging a proxy war against India. Pakistan's intelligence agency –the ISI and the army set up many camps where anti-India elements were indoctrinated, trained and armed. These included misguided youths from Punjab, J&K, PoK and a large number of foreign mercenaries. The aim of Pakistan was to *'bleed India through thousand cuts.'* Since 1989, Indian Army has been in the forefront in fighting the nefarious design of Pakistan. Insurgency in Punjab was comprehensively defeated. The religious fervour and mass appeal of Pak-sponsored *jihad* in J&K has been effectively blunted and the people of J&K do not take Pakistani propaganda seriously.

In 1999, Pakistan Army clandestinely infiltrated in areas along the line of control (LoC) and occupied important heights opposite Kargil in Ladakh. The grand aim of this (mis)adventure was to sever Kargil and Leh from the rest of India. Infiltrators were driven out by Indian Army and Air Force who fought relentlessly for many days inflicting heavy causalities on the enemy. During Kargil conflict media played an important role. It reported every action in real time, galvanising domestic and international opinion against Pakistan. Perhaps for the first time Indian public received first-hand account of valour and sacrifices of our valiant *Jawans*, while defending the sovereignty of the Nation.

It will not be wrong to say that if we did not have such a steadfast, efficient and patriotic army it would have been difficult to save our country from foreign invaders. Our army is the ultimate insurance policy to safeguard our freedom as it stands guarantee against disintegration of the country, whether planned by our enemies from outside or from within. From Nagaland, Manipur, Mizoram, Tripura and Assam in the east to Kashmir in the north and Punjab in the west, the Indian Army has stood firm as a rock against the attempts to divide and weaken the country.

A sort of *'code of honour'* has come down to us from our great commanders and soldiers of the past. It is a matter of great pride that whenever India has been attacked or threatened, the Indian Army has stood by its unwritten code of *Duty, Honour and Country*. The tradition of never to surrender to the enemy or to circumstances has remained ingrained in our Army which has resolute soldiers who are ever ready to do their duty unto death without hesitation.

The main characteristics of Indian soldiers are:

- *Valour and Sacrifice.*
- *Fidelity, Honour and Courage.*
- *Integrity, Honesty and Discipline.*
- *Determination.*
- *Non-discrimination.*
- *Comradeship.*

2
Role of the Armed Forces

The primary or main role of the Indian Armed Forces is *to defend our country from the external and internal aggression*. To achieve this task the Nation has to maintain a large standing army, navy and air force - trained and suitably equipped with weapons and equipments - ever ready to deal with the enemies on land, sea and air. Battle worthiness and readiness of the armed forces is very important, as unlike in sports, *'there are no runners-up in war'*- there are only victors and the vanquished. Hence, the training, equipping, administration and morale of the armed forces is a sacred responsibility of the politicians, the bureaucrats, the generals and above all - the countrymen.

As we all know, the armed forces are also required to restore peace and order within the country whenever required by the government. Thus, the secondary role of the armed forces is *to provide aid to civil authorities whenever required due to internal problems or natural calamities.* It is evident that if we use the armed forces too frequently for internal security duties their primary role may get neglected.

Internal security tasks can only be undertaken by the armed forces when they are not engaged in their primary role of defending the country's borders. The armed forces are not specially organized or equipped for such tasks, so they have to reorganize and temporarily shed their heavy weapons and equipments as these are not required in carrying out tasks in aid to civil authorities.

To fulfill the primary role the army, navy and air force have been divided into several branches or departments. Those which are required to go in close combat with the enemy on land, on the seas and in the air form the 'combat elements'. Those who support these troops in combat are called 'supporting arms' and 'services'. The service branches carry out administrative and supply jobs.

Main Branches of the Armed Forces

Army

Infantry
Armour } Combat arms.

Artillery
Corps of Engineers
Corps of Signals
Army Air Defence (AAD)
Army Aviation Corps (AAC)
Intelligence Corps } Combat support arms.

Army Service Corps (ASC)
Army Ordnance Corps (AOC)
Corps of Electronics and
Mechanical Engineers (EME) } Logistic services for support of the war effort.

Army Medical Corps (AMC)
Army Dental Corps (ADC)
Military Nursing Service (MNS) } To treat the sick and the wounded.

Army Postal Service (APS) — Postal department of the army.
Army Education Corps (AEC) — To run schools and educate soldiers.
Remount and Veterinary Corps (RVC) — To treat sick or wounded animals and breed animals.

Judge Advocate General (JAG) — Military justice department.
Corps of Military Police (CMP) — To maintain discipline.
Army Physical Training Corps (APTC) — To maintain standard of physical fitness and sports in the army.

Military Farms — To produce milk and provide fodder for animals on farms.

Navy

Executive Branch
Engineering Branch
Electrical Branch
Education Branch
Medical Branch

Combat aviation arms/Submarine.

Indian Army

Air Force

Flying Branch   Pilots and Navigators.
Technical Branches   Aeronautical engineering,
                                        Electronics, Mechanical.

Ground Duty Branches
Administration and Logistic Branch
Accounts Branch
Meteorological Branch
Education Branch
Medical and Dental Branch

Ranks: Officers

Officers' ranks of the three services are given below:-

Army	Air Force	Navy
Field Marshal	Marshal of the Air Force	Admiral of the Fleet
General	Air Chief Marshal	Admiral
Lieutenant General	Air Marshal	Vice Admiral
Major General	Air Vice Marshal	Rear Admiral
Brigadier	Air Commodore	Commodore
Colonel	Group Captain	Captain
Lieutenant Colonel	Wing Commander	Commander
Major	Squadron Leader	Lieutenant Commander
Captain	Flight Lieutenant	Lieutenant
Lieutenant	Flying Officer	Sub Lieutenant

Ranks: Personnel Below Officers' Rank (PBOR)

Ranks of the PBOR of Army, Navy and Air Force are given below:

Army	Air Force	Navy
Subedar/Risaldar Major	Master Warrant Officer	Master Chief Petty Officer (First Class)
Subedar/Risaldar	Warrant Officer	Master Chief Petty Officer (Second Class)
Naib Subedar/Risaldar	Junior Warrant Officer	Chief Petty Officer
Lance Havildar/Daffadar	Sergeant	Petty Officer
Naik	Corporal	Leading Seaman
Lance Naik	Leading Aircraftsman	Seaman I
Sepoy	Airman	Seaman II

3
The Command and Control Structure of the Army

The Rank Structure

The COAS is the rank of a General. His badges of rank, which he wears on his shoulders, are crossed sword and baton; a star and State Emblem (the Ashoka Lions). Rank structure of the army from top to bottom is as follows:-

Ranks	Appointments
General	The COAS.
Lieutenant General	Vice Chief of Army Staff (VCOAS), General Officer Commanding-in-Chief (GOC-in-C), Principal Staff Officers, Senior Staff Officers, Corps Commanders and Departmental Heads.
Major General	Divisional Commanders, Area Commanders and Staff Officers.
Brigadier	Brigade Commanders, Sub-Area Commanders, Centre Commandants, Staff Officers, etc.
Colonel	Unit Commanders and Staff Officers.
Lieutenant Colonel / Major	Company Commanders and Junior Staff Appointments.
Captain / Lieutenant	Appointments in a Company or equivalent.
JCO (Junior Commissioned Officer)	Platoon Commanders.

NCO (Non-Commissioned Officer)	Section Commanders.
Jawan or Sepoy	Combat soldiers.

Indian Commissioned officers hold commission as Class 1 government official. The rank structure of JCOs, NCOs and Jawans is given below:

The JCOs

These officers are granted Junior Commissioned ranks. They are equivalent to Class 2 gazetted officers. The rank structure and appointments are as under: -

Subedar Major / Risaldar Major	Administrative jobs.
Subedar / Risaldar Naib Subedar / Naib Risaldar	Platoon or Troop Commanders.

The JCOs in supporting services also hold clerical and special technical appointments for which they are especially trained and groomed.

The NCOs

These are non-gazetted officers and form the backbone of the fighting forces. The structure of this rank is as under: -

Company Havildar Major Squadron Daffadar Major Company Quarter Master Havildar Squadron Quarter Master Daffadar	Administrative appointments for command and control.
Havildar / Daffadar Lance Havildar / Daffadar Naik Lance Naik	Section/Detachment Commander. (A Section is of 10 men.)

Jawans

This is a term applied to a majority of soldiers who have not yet attained the NCO's status. They are called Sepoy/Sowar/Paratrooper/Grenadier/Rifleman depending up on their arms/service or trade. A jawan wears the same dress as a JCO or NCO except that he has no rank on his sleeve or shoulder. However, the name of the regiment/service is generally worn on the shoulder.

The chain of command and orders starts from the top rank in a unit (or formation) and goes right down to a jawan. The jawans play a major role in training in peace, and they are on the hottest forefront in war.

The Chain of Command

The President of India is the Supreme Commander of the armed forces. However, all orders and instructions are issued to the COAS by the Union Cabinet through the Ministry of Defence (MoD). Thus, the army is under the control of the civil government and does not act on its own. The Raksha Mantri is responsible for all matters related to the defence of the country. The MoD deals on a day-to-day basis with the Integrated Headquarters of MoD Army [IHQ of MoD (Army)] located in New Delhi. All service HQs are now an integral part of the MoD. All actions to implement government policies and directions are passed by the COAS through his principal staff officers and technical advisers to the lower formations (see Fig. 3.1)

Fig. 3.1: The Chain of Command

The Army HQ issues directives and commands to all branches (Arms and Services) through their departmental heads and through the seven Command HQs located in following places:-

- Northern Command   Udhampur (J&K)
- Western Command   Chandigarh
- Central Command   Lucknow
- Eastern Command   Kolkata
- Southern Command   Pune
- South Western Command   Jaipur
- Army Training Command   Shimla

(Not given in order of seniority)

The area of responsibility of each command HQs is indicated by its location. The command boundaries and the number of formations under each command depend on the operational requirement in war and peace. Command boundaries do not follow state boundaries. For example, the area of responsibility of the Central Command extends over Uttar Pradesh, Uttrakhand, part of Bihar and Jharkhand; Chattisgarh and Madhya Pradesh. Each command HQ is headed by a senior Lieutenant General who is appointed as the GOC-in-C. He is also sometimes called the Army Commander, since he commands a large number of army formations and units which constitute a large Army Group. Commands are also called as Armies such as, Eastern, Western, Central, Southern, South Western and Northern Army.

Various commanders in the army are authorised to fly certain types of flags on their vehicles and official residences. Details about the vehicle flags are given below:

Army Vehicle Flags

The Indian Army's insignia is two crossed swords and the State Emblem –the Ashoka lions. Traditionally the colour of the Army is scarlet red which is used in all flags, pennants and unit colours. Senior army officers are authorised to fly flags and display stars on their official vehicles.

A general, lieutenant general, major general and brigadier display four, three, two and one star on their vehicles. Vehicle flags are of different size and pattern for each rank, for example, general and lieutenant generals fly a rectangular flag; the major generals use a swallow-tailed flag; while the brigadiers fly a tri-angular pennant.

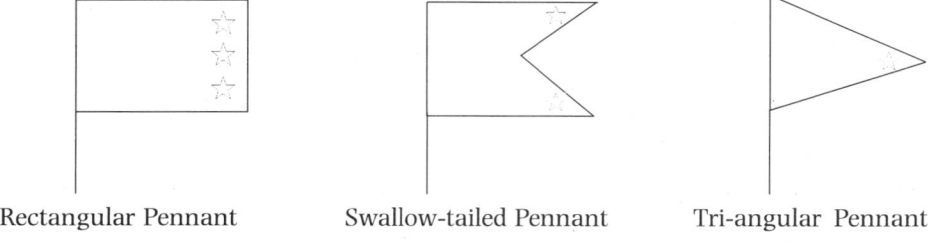

Rectangular Pennant   Swallow-tailed Pennant   Tri-angular Pennant

The details of vehicle flags are as under:-

Field Marshal	A red flag with crossed batons surrounded by a single wreath of five lotus flowers on each side with the State Emblem on the top and five stars beneath the lotus wreath.
The COAS	A red rectangular flag with the National Flag superimposed in the first quarter next to the staff; crossed swords with the State Emblem and four stars in the fly.
The VCOAS	A red rectangular flag horizontally divided into three equal portions - scarlet, black and scarlet; crossed swords and State Emblem in golden colour are placed in the centre of the flag. There is Army HQ insignia in the first quarter of the flag next to the staff and three stars in the fly.
Principal Staff Officer	Rectangular scarlet flag with crossed swords in yellow; Dharma Chakra between the upper half of the swords and three stars in the fly.
Lieutenant General on Staff	Rectangular scarlet flag with crossed swords and three stars in the fly.

Commands

GOC-in-C	Rectangular flag horizontally divided into three equal portions, scarlet, black and scarlet with Command insignia in the middle. State Emblem in the first quarter next to the staff and three stars in the fly.
Chief of Staff	Rectangular flag horizontally divided into three equal portions - scarlet, black and scarlet with Command insignia and three stars in the fly.

Corps

Corps Commander	Rectangular flag horizontally divided into three equal portions - scarlet, white and scarlet with Corps insignia and three stars in the fly.
Major General on Staff	Swallow-tailed flag divided into three equal portions

Areas and Divisions

GOC Area, GOC Division — scarlet, white and scarlet with Corps insignia and two stars in the fly.

Swallow-tailed red flag with formation sign and two stars in the fly.

Sub-areas and Brigades

Independent Brigade Red tri-angular pennant with formation sign and a star in the fly.

Commander Brigade

Independent Sub-area

Commander Sub-area

Independent Artillery Brigade

Corps Artillery Brigade

Commander Artillery

AAD Brigade

Commander Engineer Brigade

Training Establishments and Schools of Instruction

All training establishments and regimental centres have their own insignia which are used on their flags, but the basic pattern of the flag remains same. Some of the training establishments are given below:-

Commandant National Defence College	Rectangular maroon flag with tri-services insignia with three stars in the fly.
Commandant DSSC	Rectangular maroon flag with Defence Services Staff College (DSSC) insignia with three stars in the fly.
Commandant NDA	Rectangular maroon flag with NDA crest with three stars in the fly.
Commandant IMA	Rectangular red flag with IMA crest with three stars in the fly.

Field Formations

The Corps

Each command HQ has two or three corps under its command. A corps is a large HQ responsible for a zone within the jurisdiction of a command HQ For example, HQ Northern Command has three corps zones - one in Jammu area and the other two in the Kashmir Valley and Ladakh. A corps HQ has three or more army divisions under its command and control. Generally, the orgnization followed in the army is a three-tiered system i.e. a formation will have three subordinate formations or a unit will have three sub-units. Accordingly, the organization of supporting arms and services has been tailored. However, the number of subordinate formations and units under any formation always depends up on the operational requirement and is not a mathematical distribution.

Fig. 3.2: Corps and Subordinate Formations and Units

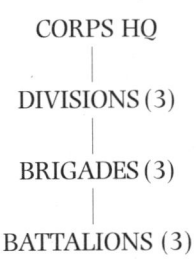

CORPS HQ
|
DIVISIONS (3)
|
BRIGADES (3)
|
BATTALIONS (3)

A corps HQ can shift from sector to sector or even to another command depending on the operational requirements. Those formations which are designed to be mobile and have transportable weapons and equipments are called Field Formations. Corps HQ is the highest field formation in the army. Corps are further catagorised in to 'Holding Corps' and 'Strike Corps'. A strike corps is an offensive formation organized to launch an offensive inside the enemy territory, while the holding corps is a defensive formation organized for defensive roles. Indian Army has three strike corps and 10 holding corps.

The Divisions

An army division is the largest striking force in the field. A division is commanded by a Major General who is appointed as its General Officer Commanding or GOC. There are following five types of army divisions catering to various operational needs:-

- Infantry Division
- Mountain Division
- Armoured Division
- Mechanized Division
- Artillery Division

A division has a balanced component of arms and services to fight a war in a given terrain. In the high Himalayas, where the armoured or mechanized formations have limited or nil employability, infantry-based mountain divisions operate. While in the Punjab or Rajasthan or

Gujarat infantry, armoured and mechanized divisions will be needed. A division has three or more brigades under its command and control. The various brigades and major units under an infantry division are indicated in Fig. 3.3.

Fig. 3.3: Organization of an Infantry Division

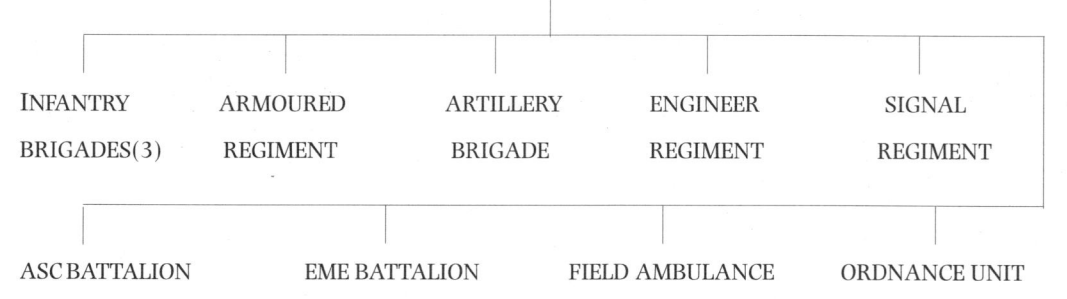

```
                            DIVISIONAL HQ
    ┌───────────┬───────────┬───────────┬───────────┐
 INFANTRY    ARMOURED    ARTILLERY    ENGINEER     SIGNAL
 BRIGADES(3) REGIMENT    BRIGADE      REGIMENT     REGIMENT

    ┌───────────┬───────────┬───────────┐
 ASC BATTALION  EME BATTALION  FIELD AMBULANCE  ORDNANCE UNIT
```

The Brigades

A brigade is the smallest fighting formation of the army. Its commander is a Brigadier. Brigades are of following types:-

- Infantry Brigade.
- Mountain Brigade.
- Armoured Brigade.
- Mechanized Brigade.
- Airborne or Parachute Brigade.
- Artillery Brigade.
- Engineer Brigade.
- Army Air Defence Brigade.

Brigades normally have three battalions/regiments under their command. A brigade, which is not a part of any division and is organized to function independently, is called an Independent Brigade. Such brigades are provided with additional supporting arms (artillery, engineers, signals) and services (ASC, AOC, EME, AMC) units to enable these to operate independently.

Static Formations

Command HQ controls all static formations in the areas of its jurisdiction. A static formation is the one whose role is purely administrative and is responsible for a specified area. A static HQ primarily deals with internal security duties or employment of troops during natural calamities.

The highest static HQ is an Area HQ. It is commanded by a Major General, who is like a divisional commander and is called GOC. See Fig. 3.4.

Fig. 3.4: Static Formations of the Indian Army

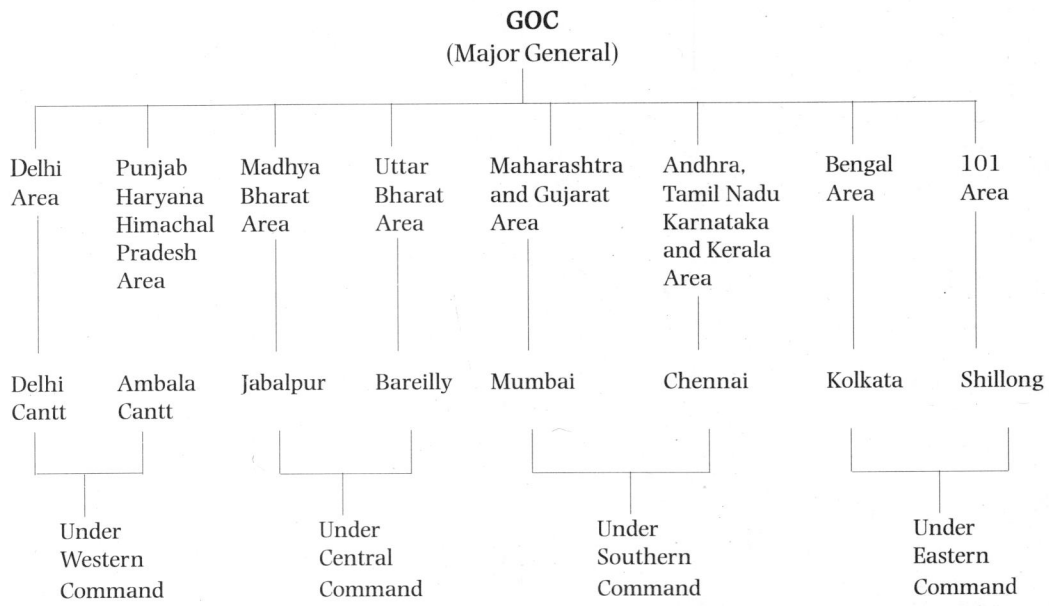

AREA HQs
GOC
(Major General)

Delhi Area	Punjab Haryana Himachal Pradesh Area	Madhya Bharat Area	Uttar Bharat Area	Maharashtra and Gujarat Area	Andhra, Tamil Nadu Karnataka and Kerala Area	Bengal Area	101 Area
Delhi Cantt	Ambala Cantt	Jabalpur	Bareilly	Mumbai	Chennai	Kolkata	Shillong
Under Western Command		Under Central Command		Under Southern Command		Under Eastern Command	

Each area may have a sub-area under its command which is commanded by a Brigadier. Some sub-areas are designated as Independent Sub-areas, when they are not under the jurisdiction of an Area HQ but directly under the command HQ for example, sub-areas in J&K and Rajasthan.

The main role of a static formation is administration, which includes execution of construction projects like accommodation and other facilities and water works; distribution of government funds for works and the control of static supply depot and other administrative units required in military stations and cantonments. The area and sub-area HQs keep in direct touch with civilian authorities of the state or region where they are located. In addition, each big station has a Station HQ which runs the administration of a station or a cantonment. All citizens/civilians can approach the area, sub-area or station HQ for any help or necessary information required from the army. When active field formations, army divisions or brigades move out for operational or other duties the administration of the cantonments is carried out unhindered by the static HQs for support and protection. You will find that the army has a well laid out command and control structure from top to bottom. To recollect:

- The President is the Supreme Commander of the Armed Forces.
- All orders are issued to the army by the MoD.

- The COAS, who is the top boss of the army, passes down various instructions and orders through Army HQ staff. He commands and controls the army through command HQ.
- Command HQs are regional, Northern, Western, Central, Eastern, Southern and South Western.
- There are corps HQs under each command HQ which are field formations meant for war. Each corps has few army divisions under command.
- Areas and sub-areas are static HQs.
- The organization of the IHQ (Army) is at Appendix.

4
Branches of the Army

Arms and Services

The Army has been organized, equipped and trained to be self-contained in all respects and not to depend on local sources, as this would cause inconvenience to the civil population. To achieve self-sufficiency, the army has all the elements in its organisation to move and feed the soldiers, to supply the essential stores, to repair or replace the equipments even in the most remote and far-flung areas. The army can look after it's wounded or sick in the deserts or jungles or the glacial heights of the mighty Himalayas. No wonder, sometimes it is said that the army is like a 'state within a state'.

The main branches of the army as mentioned in the "Role of the Armed Forces" are dealt with a greater detail here. Although, the various arms and services have been assigned seniority due to diverse historical reasons and traditions, the 'combat or the teeth' elements need to be explained first for ease of understanding of the supporting role of other branches and services.

The Infantry

THE INFANTRY
THE ULTIMATE

The so-called "Foot Soldier" forms the largest fighting component of the army. The infantry is known as the "Queen of the Battle" because it is the foot soldier who holds the captured territory or a town. Infantry consists of combat soldiers who fight the enemy - man to man. The infantry is carried to the battlefield in aircrafts, ships, trains, motor transport, infantry combat vehicles etc. or advances on foot to establish contact with the enemy.

The basic organisation of the infantry is a battalion, which has six companies. (Fig.4.1) It has its own supporting (heavy) weapons and a limited increment of motor transport. The individual infantryman carries assault rifle or light machine gun, and grenades which can easily be carried in mountains, deserts, jungles or plains. An infantry *Jawan* can reach, survive and operate in all kinds of terrains, unlike the machines, however versatile they may become.

Fig 4.1: Organization of an Infantry Battalion

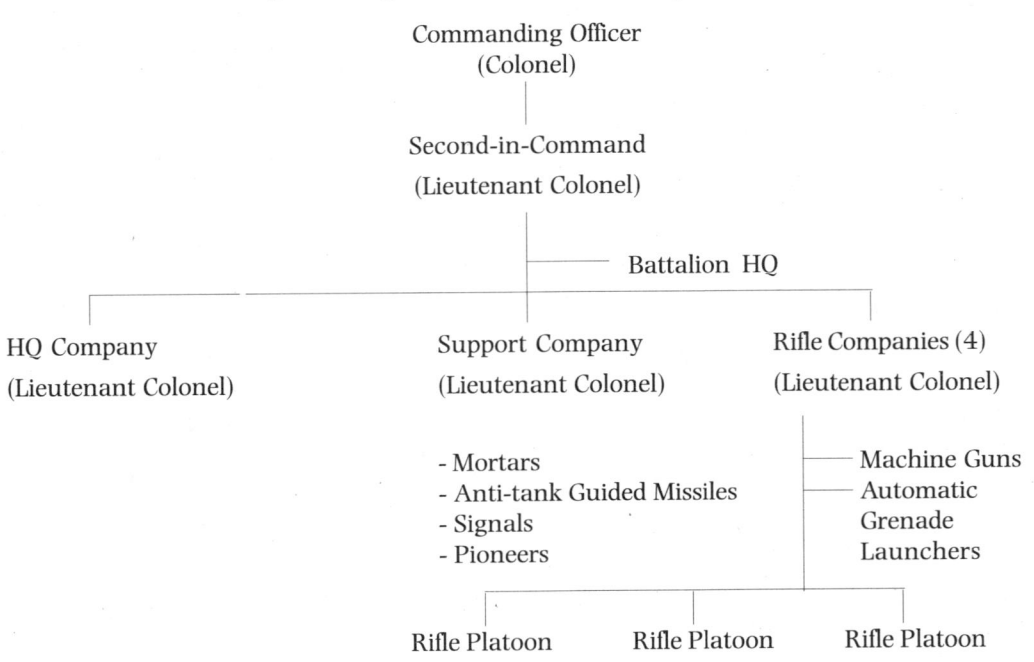

```
                    Commanding Officer
                        (Colonel)
                            |
                    Second-in-Command
                    (Lieutenant Colonel)
                            |
                    ─── Battalion HQ
   ┌────────────────────────┼────────────────────────┐
HQ Company            Support Company          Rifle Companies (4)
(Lieutenant Colonel)  (Lieutenant Colonel)     (Lieutenant Colonel)
                                                     │
                      - Mortars                ── Machine Guns
                      - Anti-tank Guided Missiles ── Automatic
                      - Signals                      Grenade
                      - Pioneers                     Launchers
                   ┌──────┼──────┐
              Rifle Platoon  Rifle Platoon  Rifle Platoon
```

In the present-day army, a part of the infantry is mechanized. These infantrymen are provided with light armour-plated Infantry Combat Vehicles (ICVs) to move forward and engage the enemy with heavy weapons till they dismount close to the enemy position and destroy him. There is also a kind of specialized infantry called the Parachute or Airborne Infantry. These soldiers drop in enemy rear areas by parachutes from the aircraft provided by the air force. They carry with them all the weapons and equipment necessary to fight the enemy on the ground. Then there are some specialized units of the infantry called Special Forces. These highly trained units operate in the rear of enemy troops and destroy targets deep in the enemy country.

To summarize, the infantry is organised as under:-

Infantry Units. Foot soldiers, transported by air or by normal transport to the battlefield, whether for defensive or offensive operations.

Mechanized Infantry. Carried in ICVs which are light armour-plated fitted with heavy weapons like cannons and heavy machine guns. Characteristics of ICVs (BMP Series) some of them are used by Mechanized Infantry in Indian Army are appended at Table 4.1.

Table 4.1: Characteristics of ICVs

ICV	Weight	Range	Crew and Troops	Armaments
BMP-I	13.5 Tons	600 kms	3+8	73 mm smooth bore gun, AT-3 Sagger ATGM, 7.62 mm machine gun.
BMP-II	14.3 Tons	600 kms	3+7	30 mm cannon, 7.62 mm machine gun, AT-4 Spigot and AT-5 Spandrel ATGM.
BMP-III	18.7 Tons	600 kms	3+7	100 mm Gun, AT-10 Stabber ATGM, 30 mm auto cannon, 7.62 mm machine gun.

Parachute Infantry. Specially trained to drop from the air in the rear of the enemy positions.

Special Units. Special Forces units trained to carry out the job of attacking targets deep into enemy territory, or behind the enemy frontline.

Each infantry unit forms part of a larger group called a Regiment. (see Table 4.2) A regiment has a number of battalions grouped together which have certain common features such as:

- A common training centre for recruitment and training.
- A distinguishing cap badge, crest and colour of berets and belts.
- Common class composition as passed down by tradition, for example, Kumaoni or Mahar or Sikh Regiments.
- Uniform training for recruits, for example, mechanized or parachute training.

Table 4.2: Regiments of the Infantry

Regiment	Training Centre
THE BRIGADE OF GUARDS	Kamptee, Maharashtra
THE PARACHUTE REGIMENT	Bangalore, Karnataka
THE MECHANIZED INFANTRY	Ahmednagar, Maharashtra
THE PUNJAB REGIMENT	Ramgarh, Jharkhand
THE MADRAS REGIMENT	Wellington, Tamil Nadu
THE GRENADIERS	Jabalpur, Madhya Pradesh
THE MARATHA LIGHT INFANTRY	Belgaum, Karnataka
THE RAJPUTANA RIFLES	Delhi Cantonment
THE RAJPUT REGIMENT	Fatehgarh, Uttar Pradesh
THE SIKH REGIMENT	Ramgarh, Jharkhand
THE JAT REGIMENT	Bareilly, Uttar Pradesh

THE SIKH LIGHT INFANTRY	Fatehgarh, Uttar Pradesh
THE DOGRA REGIMENT	Faizabad, Uttar Pradesh
THE GARHWAL RIFLES	Lansdowne, Garhwal Hills, Uttrakhand
THE KUMAON REGIMENT	Ranikhet, Uttrakhand
THE ASSAM REGIMENT	Shillong, Meghalaya
THE BIHAR REGIMENT	Danapur Cantonment, Bihar
THE MAHAR REGIMENT	Saugor, Madhya Pradesh
THE JAMMU AND KASHMIR RIFLES	Jabalpur, Madhya Pradesh
THE SCOUTS	
• LADAKH SCOUTS	Leh (J&K)
• GARHWAL SCOUTS	Lansdowne
• KUMAON SCOUTS	Ranikhet
THE NAGA REGIMENT	Ranikhet (a part of Kumaon Centre)
THE JAMMU AND KASHMIR LIGHT INFANTRY	Srinagar, J&K
THE GORKHA BRIGADE	
• 1st GORKHA RIFLES	Sabatu, Himachal Pradesh
• 3rd GORKHA RIFLES	Varanasi, Uttar Pradesh
• 4th GORKHA RIFLES	Sabatu (Combined with 1st Gorkha Rifles)
• 5th GORKHA RIFLES	Shillong, Meghalaya
• 8th GORKHA RIFLES	Varanasi (combined with 3rd Gorkha Rifles)
• 11th GORKHA RIFLES	Lucknow, Uttar Pradesh

It should be noted that a regiment is like a parental home or a joint family whose sons or daughters after growing up find jobs (deployed) all over India in the fighting formations and seldom serve in one station. However, parental ties are maintained through well-defined regimental traditions, customs and patterns of uniforms. The centre is responsible for reinforcing battalions to make up the deficiency in manpower caused due to retirements and casualties. Regimental centres also carry out recruitment for the regiment. Each battalion provides a training team to the centre to train the recruits. The centre commandant invites all battalion commanders of his regiment every two years for a conference to discuss various regimental matters. Regular reunions are held in which old retired officers and pensioners are also called so that younger officers and men can meet the old war veterans of the regiment. Regimental affiliations are very strong and loyalty to the regiment is fierce. All this helps in maintaining the fighting traditions of the army.

The Armoured Corps

In ancient times the pride of armies rested on chariots and horsed cavalry. The cavalry with its soldiers mounted on well-bred horses was highly mobile and swift. The cavalry could outflank foot soldiers and cut off their retreat. The shock effect of a massed cavalry charge at full gallop was tremendous and the infantry and other less mobile forces were destroyed by these swift manoeuvres.

The British initially raised two *Risalahs* or troops or Indian Cavalry and gradually increased the strength over a period of time. The present Regiments of the Armoured Corps are the descendants of the horsed cavalry. Now cavalrymen are mounted on tanks instead of horses. During the World War I, the trench warfare proved to be a kind of stalemate for the warring sides. The British secretly developed an armour-plated, tracked and armed vehicle, which could negotiate anti-infantry obstacles with impunity. It was named as "water carrier" and later on came to be known as "tank". It was first used in the Battle of Somme on 15 Sep 1916 and later on in the Battle of Cambrai in large numbers. Tank has space for 3 or 4 troops inside and it can fire on the enemy while on the move. Nowadays, tanks are equipped with a heavy gun, machine guns and missile and state-of-the-art systems such as global positioning systems, night-vision and night-firing devices; and computerized sighting and firing devices. As only a few infantry weapons have an effect on a tank, it can attack ground troops with little harm to itself. In a war in the plains (or desert) the side which can mass or use armour in greater numbers is likely to be the winner. Tanks have steel tracks instead of wheels, similar to those in dozers and road-building machines. These tracks enable the tank to go cross-country at high speeds and turn quickly in any direction.

Many anti-tank weapon systems have been developed to defeat the armour. These are hand-held, vehicle-mounted and even fired from the air by helicopters. Infantry defends itself against tanks with the help of hand-held rocket/missile launchers. In today's battlefield tanks cannot roam about with impunity.

Armoured corps is the senior most and a highly coveted arm of the army and it has great traditions of valour and daring. The armoured corps men wear black berets and overalls, which has become a mark of distinction.

The training centre for all armoured units or regiments is at Ahmednagar, Maharashtra. There are over 60 Armoured Regiment in the army. Some of the old armoured regiments are:

- 1st Horse (Skinners Horse).
- 2nd Lancers.
- 3rd Cavalry.
- 4th Horse (Hodson's Horse).
- 7th Light Cavalry.
- 8th Cavalry.
- 9th Horse (Deccan Horse).
- 14th Horse (Scinde Horse).
- 15th Lancers.
- 16th Light Cavalry.
- 17th Horse (Poona Horse).
- 20th Lancers.
- Central India Horse.

The organization of an armoured regiment is illustrated in Fig. 4.2.

Fig. 4.2: Organization of an Armoured Regiment

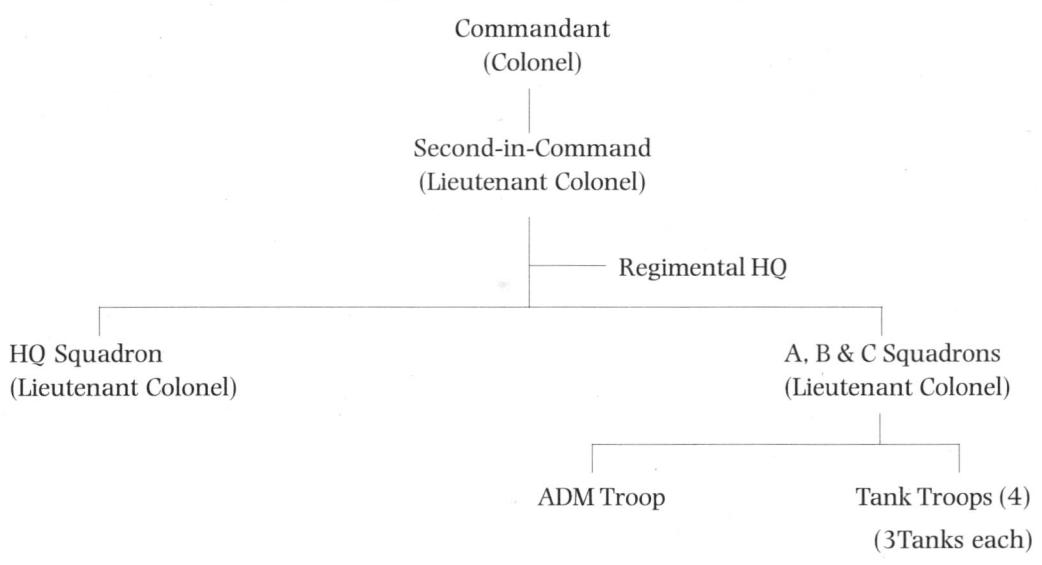

```
                    Commandant
                    (Colonel)
                        |
                Second-in-Command
                (Lieutenant Colonel)
                        |———————— Regimental HQ
         ———————————————————————————
         |                         |
    HQ Squadron              A, B & C Squadrons
  (Lieutenant Colonel)       (Lieutenant Colonel)
                                   |
                         ——————————————————
                         |                |
                     ADM Troop      Tank Troops (4)
                                    (3 Tanks each)
```

There are 45 tanks is an armoured regiment. Armoured regiments of Indian Army are mainly equipped with T-90 or T-72 or T-55 tanks. Selection of a type of tank primarily depends up on the task of the armoured regiment. Characteristics of few tanks used by Indian Army are given in Table 4.3.

Table 4.3: Battle Tanks of the Indian Army

Tank	Weight	Range	Armament	Crew
T-55	48 Tons	500 kms	105 mm main gun, one machine gun, one anti-aircraft gun.	Four
T-72(Ajeya)	44.5 Tons	550 kms	125 mm main gun, one machine gun, one anti-aircraft gun.	Three
T-90(Bhishma)	46.5 Tons	550 kms	125 mm smooth bore main gun, one machine gun, one anti-aircraft gun. Fires Refleks laser-guided anti-tank missiles from the main gun.	Three
Arjun	58.5 Tons	200 kms	120 mm main gun, one machine gun, one anti-aircraft gun.	Four

The Artillery

The Regiment of Artillery handles big guns, rockets and missiles of the army. You must have noticed big cannons mounted on the forts. These cannons when fired at the enemy caused tremendous shock effect and panic in the rank and file, leading to stampede and confusion. The guns in olden days were of two types – the heavier ones, which were permanently mounted on the forts and, the lighter ones, which were towed by horses, bullocks and even elephants. Some armies had even lighter guns which could be mounted on the camel back. In fact, lighter guns often won the day for a king as these could be moved and fired at the vulnerable flank of the enemy.

Mughal King Babur introduced artillery in the battlefields of India. He won the two most decisive battles of his military career – the Battle of Panipat (1526) against Ibrahim Lodi and the Battle of Kanwah (1527) against Rajput confederacy led by Rana Sangram Singh due to his artillery and founded the Mughal Empire. In both the battles, Babur's opponents did not possess a single piece of artillery.

In 1748, the East India Company raised first Company of Artillery. Later the Regiment of Artillery was raised on 28 September 1827. This day is now celebrated as 'Gunners' Day'.

The Regiment of Artillery is the largest regiment of the army. Unlike the infantry where soldiers and officers of each regiments wear different insignias and accoutrements, Gunners use a common badge and uniform. Artillery soldiers are better qualified than the others as they have to handle a lot of sophisticated equipment. The Regiment of Artillery has its training centres at Devlali (Maharashtra) and Golconda (Andhra Pradesh). Artillery units are called 'Regiments' just as infantry units are known as 'Battalions'.

Present-day artillery fires shells, rockets and missiles which burst on impact on the target or in the air. The ranges of the guns have tremendously improved over the years. The guns being a heavy weapon are towed by powerful vehicles while some guns can also move on their own, known as 'Self-Propelled Artillery'. The latter can 'shoot and scoot' – meaning capable of shifting the location quickly after firing at the enemy.

Main role of the Artillery is to destroy or neutralize enemy's positions and weapons by accurate fire assaults.

Artillery guns bring down 'indirect' fire on a target - meaning that the gun crew does not see the target while firing. The adjustment of fire is done by 'observers' who observe the target from a vantage point such as a tree, building, hill top and even a helicopter. Observers 'correct' the fire by giving corrections in terms of distances to gun crew, to bring it on the target. Such observers are men of intelligence and daring as they move with the tanks and infantry during an attack for providing fire support to own troops.

The artillery is divided in to following branches:-

- Field Branch.
- Surveillance and Target Acquisition (SATA) Branch.

The units of field branch artillery are equipped with various types of mortars, guns, rocket launchers, etc. The SATA branch deals with equipments such as radars, unmanned aerial vehicles

(UAVs) and meteorological devices for collecting information about enemy and meteorological conditions.

Field branch artillery units are further catagorized as under:-

- Light Regiments: Units equipped with 120 mm Mortars.
- Field Regiments: Units equipped with 105 mm Indian Field Guns (IFG)
- Medium Regiments: Units equipped with 130 mm and 155 mm Medium Guns.
- Rocket Regiments: Units equipped with BM 21 GRAD Multi-barrel Rocket Launchers (MBRLs).
- Missile Groups: Units holding Surface-to-Surface Missiles(SSMs).

A brief characteristic of the weapon systems by Indian Artillery is given in Table 4.4.

Table 4.4: Weapon Systems of Indian Artillery

Weapon System	Maximum Range	Ammunition/ Warhead	Remarks
120 mm Mortar	6.5-8.9 km	High Explosive, Smoke and Illumination.	Towed by a truck. Can be transported by helicopter and mules.
105 mm IFG	17.2 km	High Explosive, Smoke and Illumination.	Towed by a truck. Can be transported by an aircraft and helicopter.
130 mm Gun	27.5 km	High Explosive.	Towed by a KRAZ truck.
155 mm FH 77B (Bofors)	24 km	High Explosive, Smoke and Illumination.	Towed by a SCANIA truck. Can also 'shoot and scoot'.
BM 21 GRAD (MBRL)	20.4 km	High Explosive.	Towed by a URAL truck. Fires 40 rockets in 20 seconds.
Prithvi Missile	150 km	High Explosive.	Transported on a TATRA truck. Can carry a nuclear warhead also.

The basic organization of a Field Regiment is as given in Fig. 4.3.

Fig 4.3: Organization of a Field Regiment

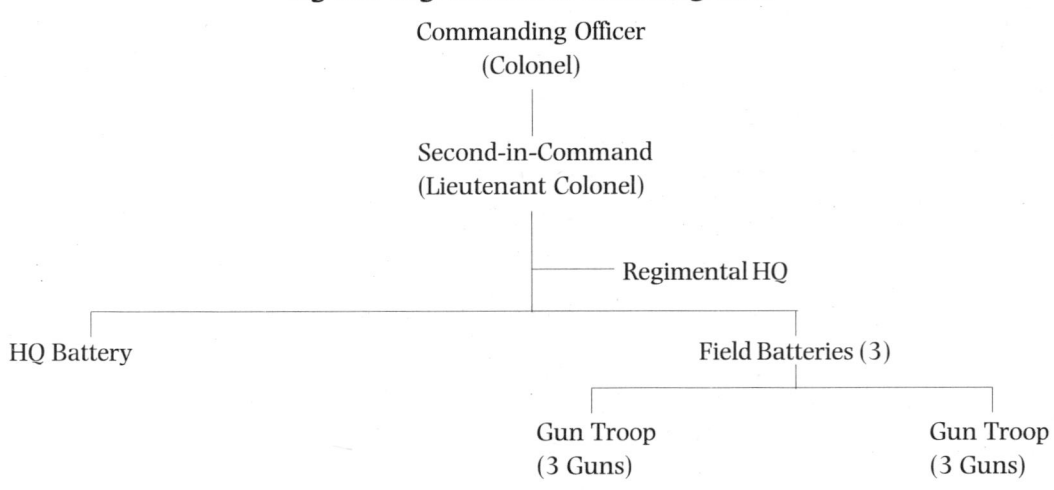

```
              Commanding Officer
                  (Colonel)
                      |
              Second-in-Command
              (Lieutenant Colonel)
                      |
                      ├────── Regimental HQ
         ┌────────────┴────────────┐
     HQ Battery              Field Batteries (3)
                           ┌─────────┴─────────┐
                       Gun Troop           Gun Troop
                       (3 Guns)            (3 Guns)
```

Army Air Defence

Till 1993, Artillery (Air Defence) was a branch of Regiment of Artillery. Thereafter, it was formed into a separate corps and was christened as Corps of Army Air Defence (AAD). The AAD functions in conjunction with the air force to defend country's airspace. During war the air defence units deploy themselves in such a manner to protect vital installations and military targets from enemy air attacks. Some units also accompany mechanized forces during an offensive in to enemy territory.

AAD is a technical arm as it operates a host of air defence guns, surface-to-air missiles (SAMs), radars, communication equipments and other military hardware. The AAD units are known as 'Regiments' and are catagorized on the basis of type of weapon systems and their degree of mobility in the battlefield.

Organization of an Air Defence (AD) Regiment is given in Fig. 4.4.

Fig. 4.4: Organization of an AD Regiment

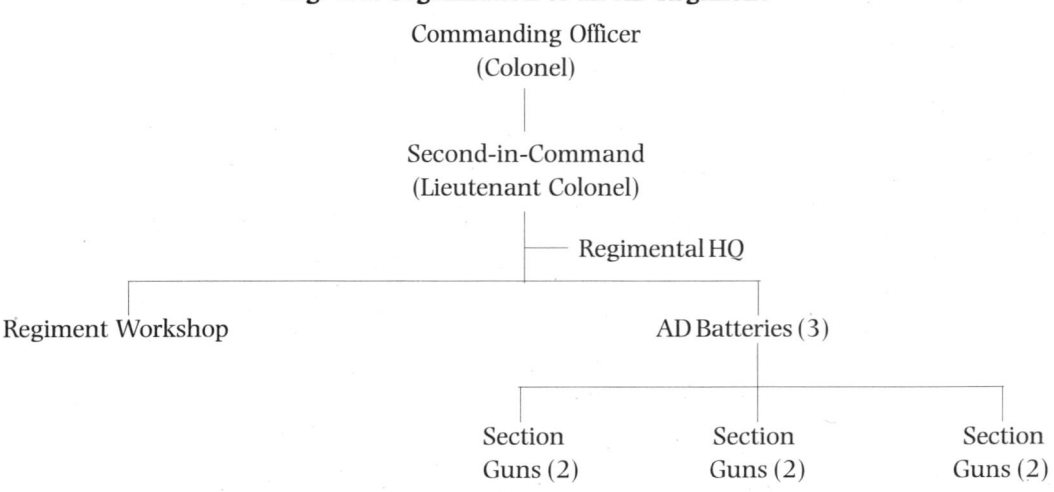

```
           Commanding Officer
              (Colonel)
                 |
          Second-in-Command
          (Lieutenant Colonel)
                 |
                 ├── Regimental HQ
                 |
      ┌──────────┴──────────┐
Regiment Workshop      AD Batteries (3)
                             |
              ┌──────────────┼──────────────┐
           Section         Section        Section
           Guns (2)        Guns (2)       Guns (2)
```

Note: The batteries may hold single or mixed type of AD weapons.

Characteristics of some of the AD weapons held by the army are given in Table 4.5.

Table 4.5: Characteristics of the AD Weapons

Weapon System	Maximum Range	Warhead	Remarks
L-70 Gun	3.5 km	High Explosive.	Single-barrel gun.
ZU-23-2 (Twin)	2.5 km	High Explosive, Incendiary, Armour Piercing and Tracer.	Twin-barrel gun.
ZSU-23-4 (Schilka)	2.5 km	High Explosive, Incendiary, Armour Piercing and Tracer.	Four-barrel gun.
SAM 7 (Strela)	2.8 km – 4.2 km	High Explosive.	Man-portable SAM.
SAM 14 (Igla)	3.0 km – 3.5 km	High Explosive.	Man-portable SAM.
SAM 13 (Strela)	5.0 km	High Explosive.	Self-propelled SAM.
SAM 8 (OSA-AK)	10 km	High Explosive.	Self-propelled SAM.
SAM 6 (KWADRAT)	5.0 km – 24 km	High Explosive.	Self-propelled SAM.
Tungushka	2.5 km – 10 km (Missile) 0.2 km – 4 km (Gun)	High Explosive, Armour Piercing and Incendiary.	Self-propelled gun-missile system.

Army Aviation Corps

In 1986, the aviation arm of Indian Army was founded under the Regiment of Artillery with some light helicopters transferred from Indian Air Force. It was then known as 'Air Observation Post' whose main job was to observe and correct artillery fire; and carry out aerial surveillance of the battlefield.

The Army Aviation Corps (AAC) is now organized into Reconnaissance and Observation Squadrons and Flights and operates over 200 helicopters of *Cheetah, Chetak* and Advanced Light Helicopter (ALH) variety. In fact, the AAC operates the largest number of light helicopters in India.

The AAC Centre is at Nasik (Maharashtra). Army aviation training, which was previously carried out at the School of Artillery at Devlali (Maharashtra), is now carried out at an independent Combat Air Training School, also at Devlali.

Corps of Engineers

The Army Engineers are builders as well as destroyers. They build bridges, roads, embankments, airfields and water supply facilities to enable the army to move and fight. They destroy the enemy's or our own facilities to halt the enemy's advance into our territory. Engineers also lay mines to block the enemy's advance or lift mines to enable our troops to advance. They build fortifications, such as bunkers for our troops and demolish those of the enemy. Engineers also carry out survey and mapping of field areas.

The Engineers are organized in units according to their tasks. Those who work forward are the field units or the Field Park units (which carry equipment). The equipment they hold ranges from graders, tractors, to bridging and mine lifting stores. By tradition the Corps of Engineers is divided into three Groups - the Madras Engineering Group and Centre at Bangalore, the Bengal Engineering Group and Centre at Roorkee and the Bombay Engineering Group and Centre at Kirkee. All Engineers wear the same cap badge and have a common regimental crest. Engineers are also called as 'Sappers'.

| Madras Engineering Group | Bengal Engineering Group | Bombay Engineering Group |

Engineer units are known as 'Regiments'. Units are organized into 'basic field units' – those which render support to field formations i.e. brigades, divisions and corps and 'specialist units' – those which carryout special tasks such as bridging, minefield clearing, bomb disposal, survey and mapping etc. Orgnization of an Engineer Regiment and Engineer Bridging Regiment is given at Fig. 4.5 and Fig. 4.6 respectively.

Fig. 4.5: Organization of an Engineer Regiment

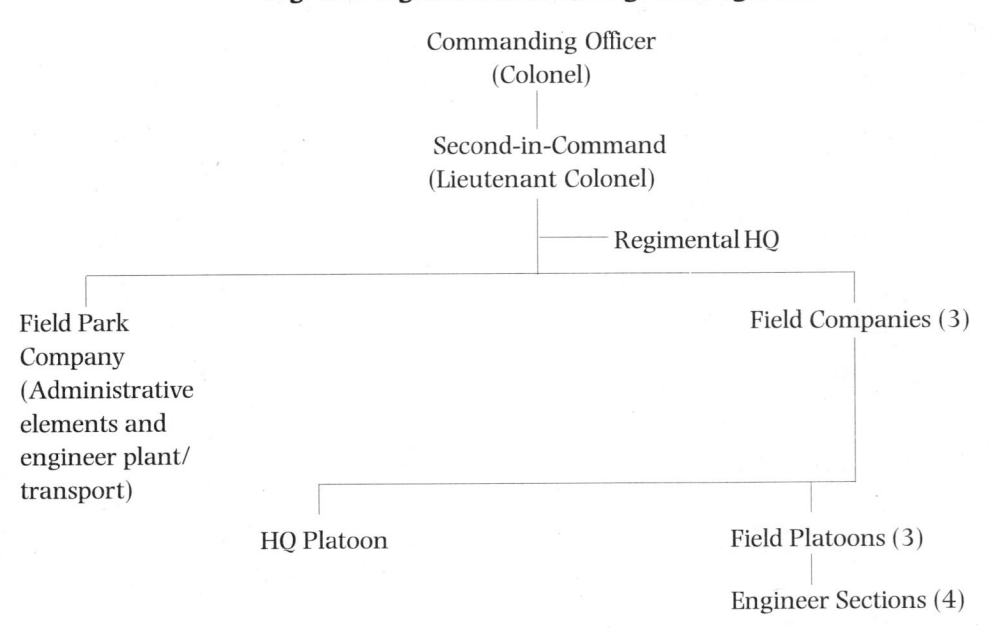

```
                    Commanding Officer
                        (Colonel)
                            |
                    Second-in-Command
                   (Lieutenant Colonel)
                            |
                            ├────── Regimental HQ
          ┌─────────────────┴─────────────────┐
    Field Park                          Field Companies (3)
    Company
    (Administrative
    elements and
    engineer plant/
    transport)
                    ┌───────────────────┴─────┐
                HQ Platoon              Field Platoons (3)
                                              |
                                      Engineer Sections (4)
```

Fig.4.6: Organization of an Engineer Bridging Unit

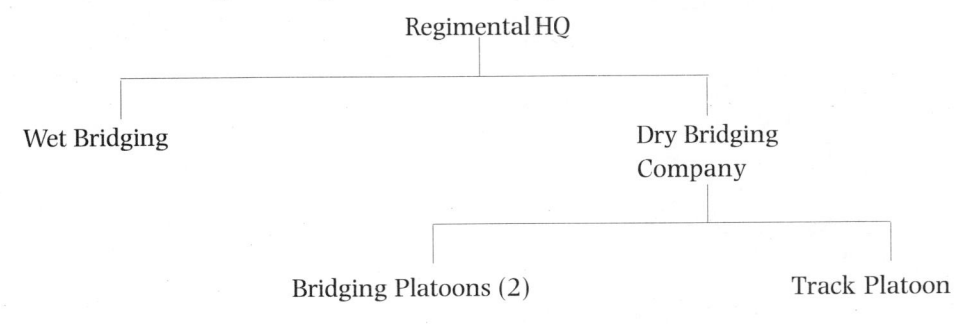

```
                        Regimental HQ
                              |
              ┌───────────────┴───────────────┐
         Wet Bridging                    Dry Bridging
                                           Company
                                   ┌──────────┴──────────┐
                           Bridging Platoons (2)    Track Platoon
```

Branches of the Army   29

The main tasks performed by Sappers in war and peace are:

- Laying of minefields and obstacles, and carrying out demolitions.
- Neutralizing the Improvised Explosive Devices (IEDs) and bombs in counter-insurgency operations and during peacetime.
- Constructing defences, airstrips and helipads.
- Establishing water supply facilities.
- Taking concealment and deception measures to hide troops from enemy air and ground surveillance.
- Constructing roads and tracks.
- Assisting in river crossing operations.
- Survey and cartographic tasks.
- Manning and controlling Military Engineering Services (MES) in cantonments (which are like the PWD).
- Controlling the Border Roads Organization (BRO) which plans and constructs roads in border areas.

The Corps of Signals

The telecommunication network of today is a complex interconnection between a variety of heterogeneous switching systems. Telecommunication architecture of a field army consists of electromechanical and electronic, direct and common control, and hard-wired and stored programme controlled sub-systems. The first and foremost prerequisite of a fighting force in war is a good, all-weather, secure and reliable communication system. Communication systems help in ensuring good command and control, intelligence gathering, battlefield surveillance, fire support, troops' movement, and administration and logistics in a given combat zone. Its importance can be gauged from the fact that the communication infrastructure of a nation is always vulnerable to the evil designs of its enemies - either by overt or covert means.

The Corps of Signals provides radio and line communication for the army in the field and co-ordinates the overall communication systems. Signals have established a special grid system of communication – Army Radio Engineering Network (AREN) and Army Static Switched Communication Network (ASCON) which provides a reliable and responsive network along the country's Northern and Western borders. The Signals are organised into following types of units, which are task and requirement specific:-

- Army HQ Signal Regiment
- Divisional Signal Regiment
- Signal Intelligence Units
- Air Support Signal Units
- Corps Engineering Signal Regiments
- Command Signal Regiment
- Corps Operating Units
- Composite Signal Regiments
- Electronic Warfare Units

The basic organization of a Divisional Signal Regiment is illustrated in Fig 4.7.

Fig. 4.7: Organization of a Divisional Signal Regiment

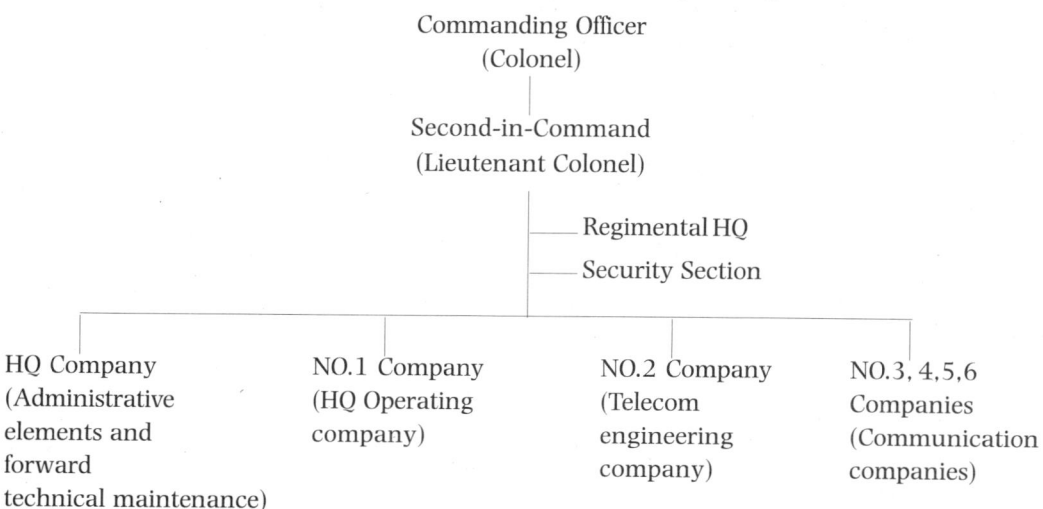

Commanding Officer
(Colonel)

Second-in-Command
(Lieutenant Colonel)

— Regimental HQ
— Security Section

| HQ Company (Administrative elements and forward technical maintenance) | NO.1 Company (HQ Operating company) | NO.2 Company (Telecom engineering company) | NO.3, 4, 5, 6 Companies (Communication companies) |

The main equipments that signal units hold to provide communication to the army are:-

- **Radio Sets:** Low, medium and high power radio sets.
- **Radio Relay:** As a standby to line (Telephone) communication and linked with PLAN AREN/ASCON.
- **Channeling Equipment:** To create a large number of circuits on one channel.
- **Line Equipment:** Field cables and permanent lines for telephone communication.
- **Tele Printers:** Voice frequency equipment.

The Rashtriya Rifles

In the late eighties, it was felt that the army alone cannot effectively deal with the problem of insurgency and militancy raging in the Northeast and J&K and there was a need to raise a tailor-made 'specialist' force trained and equipped for low intensity conflict operations. Thus, in 1990, *Rashtriya Rifles* (RR) – the counter-insurgency force of Indian Army was raised. Initially, the RR was raised for J&K and the Northeast but gradually its all units got deployed in the J&K. The RR units unlike the other army units do not rotate between 'peace' and 'field' locations. The RR units are forever in 'field', combating the insurgents/militants/terrorists. The RR is a 'deputationist' force and receives its manpower on deputation (officers and other rank) from all combat arms, combat support arms and services of the army. The RR organization is based on Counter-Insurgency Force (CIF) HQ, Sector HQ and RR Battalions as shown below:-

Fig. 4.8: Outline Organization of Rashtriya Rifles

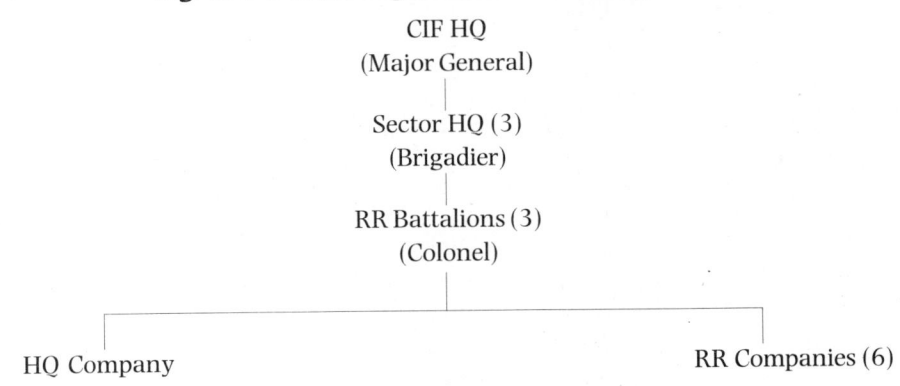

```
              CIF HQ
          (Major General)
               |
           Sector HQ (3)
            (Brigadier)
               |
          RR Battalions (3)
             (Colonel)
               |
       ┌───────┴───────┐
   HQ Company      RR Companies (6)
```

The RR functions under overall operational control of Corps HQ of army. Today, the RR organization comprises over 60 RR Battalions.

The ASC

A soldier must be free from worries regarding supply of food and essential stores during war and peace. The ASC provides this vital support to the army. The old saying "An Army marches on its stomach" is indeed very true.

The ASC, as the name suggests procures stores and carries forward supplies to all units and formations of the army during war and peace. The supplies include rations, fuel, petroleum products, ammunition, medicines and miscellaneous stores required by the army.

Every army formation has special ASC staff to ensure procurement and forward movement of supplies and stores. As the army needs huge amounts of fresh supplies and stores, the ASC enters into big contracts with civilian contractors for fresh or dry rations supplies.

The main responsibilities of ASC personnel in the field are as under :–

- Operating animal transport used in the mountains.
- Operating mechanical transport.
- Carrying ammunition forward to the troops.
- Despatching supplies from the air by parachutes.
- Procurement and supply of fresh, dry rations, fuel and hygiene chemicals.

ASC Battalions carry out multi-farious tasks depending up on the field formation they support. That is why organizations of ASC widely vary. Some sub-units which are found integral to ASC organizations are as under:-

- Animal Transport (Mule) Company: for carriage of artillery or general stores in the mountains.
- Light Truck Platoons: for carriage of stores on hilly roads.
- Heavy Truck Platoon: for carriage of stores in plains and deserts.
- Tank Transporter Platoon: for carriage of battle tanks into the battlefield.
- Supply Platoon: for supplying rations and stores to units.
- Air Despatch Platoon: for air dropping stores from the air.

Organization of a Divisional ASC Battalion in mountains is given at Fig 4.9.

Fig. 4.9: Organization of a Divisional ASC Battalion in Mountains

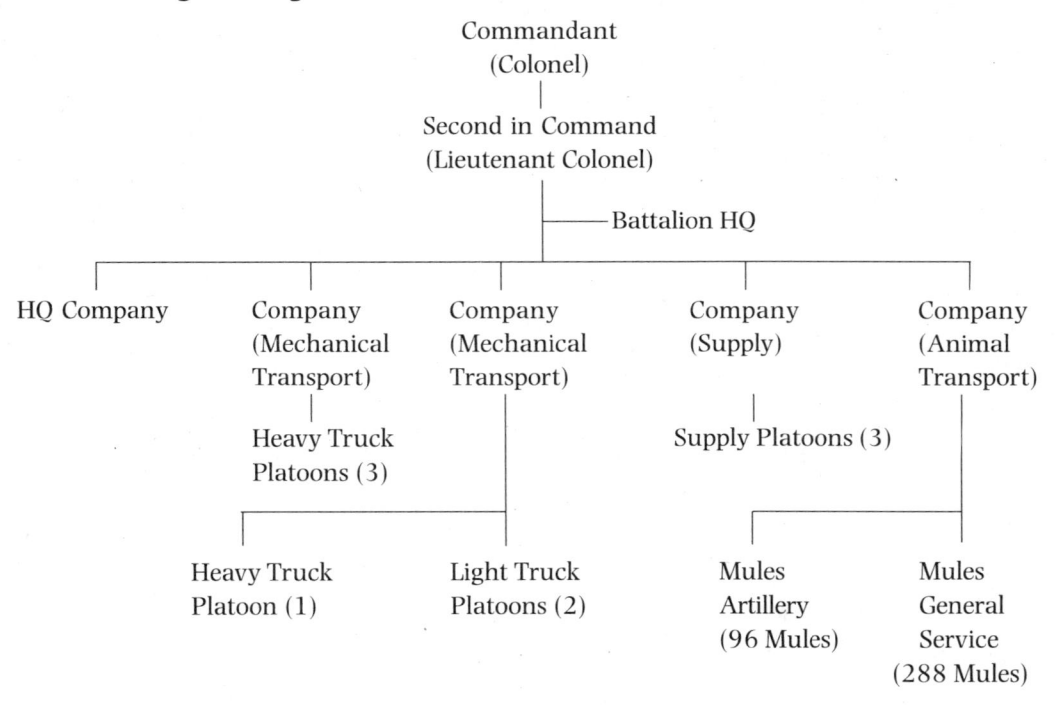

```
                    Commandant
                     (Colonel)
                         |
                 Second in Command
                 (Lieutenant Colonel)
                         |
                    Battalion HQ
   ┌─────────┬──────────┬──────────┬──────────┐
 HQ Company  Company    Company    Company    Company
            (Mechanical (Mechanical (Supply)  (Animal
            Transport)  Transport)            Transport)
                 |          |          |
            Heavy Truck              Supply Platoons (3)
            Platoons (3)
                 |          |                     |
            Heavy Truck  Light Truck  Mules      Mules
            Platoon (1)  Platoons (2) Artillery  General
                                      (96 Mules) Service
                                                 (288 Mules)
```

The AOC

The main task of the AOC is to procure and supply stores, ammunition and clothing for soldiers in the combat zone. These stores include general stores, vehicles, weapons, tanks and artillery guns. The AOC also disposes off unusable or obsolete items through auctions and sales.

There are a large number of ordnance factories in the country manufacturing ammunition, weapons and other important equipment for the Services. The AOC has various depots and store holding units, whose size depends on the battle requirements (see

Fig. 4.10 for organiztion). The AOC staff and units are located right from forward divisions to rear areas. You can recognize an ordnance corps soldier by his landyard and red blue beret. The motto of AOC is *'Shastra se Shakti'*.

The main functions of the AOC can be enumerated as follows:-

- Provisioning of warlike stores and equipment for the army.
- Holding of ammunition, mines, grenades and demolition explosives.
- Holding of technical stores.
- Holding of transport, general stores and clothing for the army.

Fig. 4.10: Organization of Ordnance Unit

```
                    Commandant
                    (Colonel)
                        |
                Second-in-Command
                (Lieutenant Colonel)
                        |
                        |—— HQ
        _____|_____
        |               |                |
    Inventory       Stocking        Administration
    Control         Wing            & Services Wing
                        |
        _____|_____
        |               |                |
    General         Mechanical       Ammunition
    Stores &        Transport &      Technical
    Clothing        Technical        Services
                    Stores
                        |
        _____|_____
        |               |                |
    Conditioning &  Stock           Administration
    Advisory        Movement
```

The EME

The Corps of EME plays a major role in maintaining equipment for war. They repair and maintain weapons, radio sets, radars, vehicles, mechanical and optical instruments of the army. They also manufacture artificial limbs, spare parts and prototype of specialist vehicles. They inspect all such equipment held by the units periodically for their operational fitness.

The EME is also responsible for recovering and evacuating damaged equipment from battle zone to rear areas. They provide technical advice to commanders in the field on all

EME matters. The senior most EME officer i.e. DGEME is a Lieutenant General posted at IHQ of MoD (Army). At command HQ a Major General EME is posted. A Brigadier, DDEME is located at corps HQ EME battalions and field workshops are located in forward areas (see Fig. 4.11 for organization).

In brief the EME is responsible for following :–

- Ensuring operational fitness of vehicles and equipment of the army.
- Technical training.
- Inspection of equipment and advice on equipment maintenance.
- Recovery of vehicles, tanks, guns etc. which are damaged in war of peace.

Fig. 4.11: Organization of an EME Battalion

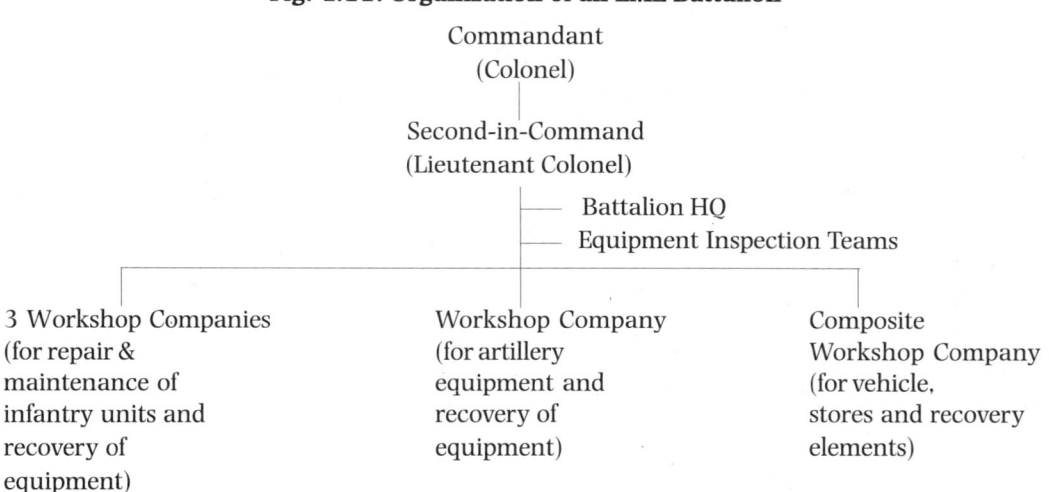

Commandant
(Colonel)
|
Second-in-Command
(Lieutenant Colonel)

— Battalion HQ
— Equipment Inspection Teams

| 3 Workshop Companies (for repair & maintenance of infantry units and recovery of equipment) | Workshop Company (for artillery equipment and recovery of equipment) | Composite Workshop Company (for vehicle, stores and recovery elements) |

The AMC

The East India Company founded Bengal, Madras and Bombay Medical Services in 1764, 1767 and 1779 respectively. It was the beginning of military medical organization of today. Thereafter, four organizations namely, the Indian Medical Service, Indian Medical Department, Indian Military Nursing Service and the Indian Hospital Corps were formally established which provided medical support to the Indian Army. On 3 April 1943, these organizations barring the Indian Military Nursing Service were amalgamated to form the Indian Army Medical Corps. The AMC not only looks after the serving personnel but also their families and the ex-servicemen as well. AMC's roles in providing medical care to the civil population in remote border areas and during the natural calamities is praiseworthy.

The AMC looks after the health of all ranks of the army and the role of AMC includes :

- Maintenance of morale by providing expert medical aid.
- Evacuation of casualties from the front.

Branches of the Army   35

- Conservation of manpower by establishing health services for all ranks.
- Rendering advice to commanders at all level on medical matters.
- Supplying medical stores to various hospitals and units.
- Operating nursing and dental services.

Army runs a Research and Referral Hospital in New Delhi, which is a premier medical institution of the country. Besides above, all command and base hospitals provide modern medical care and treatment to the patients. Medical organization at divisional level is based on field ambulance. Organization of a field ambulance is at Fig. 4.12.

Fig. 4.12: Organization of a Field Ambulance

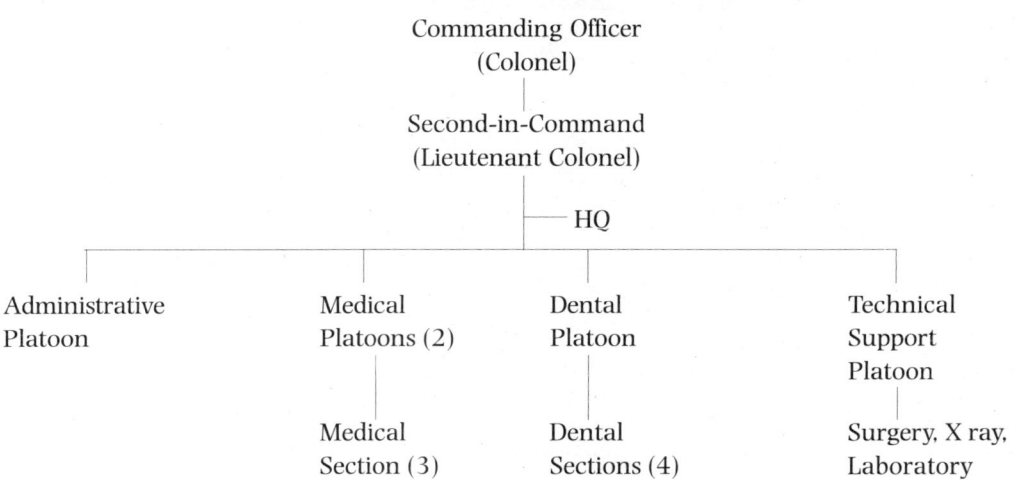

```
            Commanding Officer
               (Colonel)
                   |
            Second-in-Command
            (Lieutenant Colonel)
                   |
                   ├── HQ
   ┌───────────────┼───────────────┬───────────────┐
Administrative   Medical         Dental          Technical
Platoon          Platoons (2)    Platoon         Support
                                                 Platoon
                   |               |               |
                 Medical         Dental          Surgery, X ray,
                 Section (3)     Sections (4)    Laboratory
```

Specialist medical facilities are available even to the forward troops for timely treatment of wounded soldiers. Serious cases are evacuated from the field to rear or base area hospitals by air or road or rail.

Minor Corps/Services

Remount and Veterinary Corps (RVC)

The Indian Army has a corps staffed with qualified veterinary doctors who run field veterinary hospitals and breeding centres. The remount department of this corps is responsible for breeding and supplying horses, mules, camels, cattle and dogs required by the army.

Military Farms

The Military Farms are mostly staffed by a civilian cadre who maintains grass and dairy farms; produces and supplies fodder for the animals of the army. It uses the latest methods of fodder cultivation, establishes dairies for supply of milk and butter for the units deployed in field areas. This department works in close coordination with the RVC for improving the breed of cattle.

The CMP

This is a specialized branch which is responsible for maintaining discipline and to check infringement of rules by the army personnel anywhere in India. Thus, they perform the job of the police within the army. They have a cap badge of their own and wear some special items of dress like 'red beret' and white belts. An ordinary military police jawan can check even senior officers if they fail to conform to the laid down military regulations.

The APS

It is a branch of the Post and Telegraph (P&T) Department which provides its personnel on deputation to army. Such volunteers from the P&T Department undergo basic military training. The APS has established base and field post offices in the remotest field areas for the units and formations serving there. They are without doubt the most efficient organization which provides all postal facilities to the armed forces. The two main Army Post Offices (APOs) are: 56 APO and 99 APO. As army personnel are forbidden to disclose the location of their units to their friends and relatives; their letters are addressed care of these two APOs. Besides providing postal services, the APS also provides facilities like life insurance, money orders, money transfer, saving banks account, saving certificates, philately, newspapers, etc. APS also brings out special commemorative stamps and first day covers for the units and formations which are celebrating their important anniversaries.

The AEC

The AEC is responsible for educating all ranks of the army. AEC personnel are posted in the units and formations where they run classes to prepare other rank for various educational and map reading examinations. They also impart coaching to jawans for passing Army Cadet College (ACC) or Combined Defence Services (CDS) examinations for becoming a commissioned officer. The AEC officers are also posted to cadet training institutes such as National Defence Academy (NDA), Indian Military Academy (IMA) and Officers' Training Academy (OTA), where they teach gentlemen cadets. Besides above the AEC also trains army musicians and clerks.

The Territorial Army

The history of the Territorial Army (TA) dates back to 1920 when separate TA units were raised for the Europeans and Anglo-Indians and Indian Volunteers. In 1948, the TA Act was passed and the TA was formally included in Indian Army on 9 October 1949.

The role of TA is to relieve the army units from mundane peacetime duties during war, render assistance to civil administration during natural calamities and maintain essential services in extraordinary situations such as mass strike by railway, telecom, petroleum, health department employees. TA personnel are called for active service as and when required and this process is known as 'embodiment'.

The TA units are divided in the departmental units such as railways, IOC, ONGC, telecom and general hospital and the non-departmental units like infantry battalion (TA) and ecological battalion (TA). Non-departmental TA units are affiliated to various regiments of the army such as, Infantry TA (PUNJAB).

The ecological TA units have done a commendable services in restoring ecological degradation in Mussoorie Hills and Pithoragarh (Uttrakhand), Bikaner and Jaisalmer (Rajasthan), Samba (J&K), Delhi, Himachal Pradesh and Chambal in Madhya Pradesh. Other non-departmental units have been deployed in counter-insurgency operations in J&K and the Northeast.

The TA is about 40,000 strong force organized in to six TA Group HQs, 42 non-departmental, six ecological and 17 departmental TA battalions.

5
A Glimpse of Life in the Army

Many of us wonder what the Army does in peacetime when there is no war on. Some people believe that they live a life of luxury, drink a lot and generally waste their time in playing golf or card games or hunting. This is far from the truth. As you know our army is deployed all along the Himalayan borders with China, and along the LoC in J&K. Most of these borders are inhospitable, uncongenial in climate, lacking in normal facilities. Even drinking water is not available in some areas. The army formations not deployed on the borders have been busy combating insurgencies in J&K and the Northeast. It is evident that only a small portion of the army gets a chance to stay in a peacetime cantonment, that too for short periods.

This chapter deals with army activities in fields and peace areas, to enable the reader to fully visualize the lifestyle of our solider and officers and their daily activities in peace and field stations.

Life in a Peacetime Location

A military station is called a Cantonment. Here a number of units are billeted in peacetime.

A cantonment is a separate township under a cantonment board which is like a town committee or municipal board. It has some elected civilian members and others nominated by the station HQ. The cantonment board runs all the civic services like a municipal board. Most cantonments have normal *bazaars* and civil population like any small town or locality. The rules and regulations in a cantonment are however strictly enforced. Therefore, you generally find good roads and greater cleanliness in a cantonment as compared to other civil localities.

A number of units are located in a cantonment depending upon the availability of accommodation. These units are generally grouped under a brigade or a sub-area (Static HQ). The station HQ is responsible for general administration, allotment of houses and barracks along with allied facilities.

A unit, i.e. a battalion or a regiment, stays together in what is known as unit lines. These lines generally have a group of living barracks for troops, playground, armoury for weapons and unit office buildings. The JCOs' and NCOs' clubs and Jawans' *langars* (community dining rooms) are also located here along with the unit canteen, recreation room, unit clothing stores, transport park and light vehicle repair sections etc. Barbers, washermen and *safaiwalas* (sweepers), carpenters, blacksmiths etc. posted to a unit also stay here. The family lines of a unit are located nearby where jawans can stay with their families for limited periods.

The officers' messes and living quarters are located slightly away from the unit lines. Married officers live in small bungalows allotted to them in the cantonment area. Bachelors are allotted single rooms near the officers' messes.

There is no restriction in going in and out of a cantonment area for civilians but they cannot enter a unit line without prior permission from the authorities.

A Normal Working Day

In a peacetime cantonment the normal day of a jawan starts before sunrise. Once the Reveille bugle is sounded, jawans 'fall in' (assemble in rank and file) in sports kit. By now every jawan has shaved and washed and is ready for physical training (PT). His platoon commander –a JCO, normally inspects him to make sure that he is properly shaved and well turned out. He inspects his dress to ensure that it is clean and well ironed. Now the jawans are moved 'on the double' (running) or marched off briskly to the unit parade or PT ground. In this assembly the whole unit is together. Here the JCOs and then the officers join the parade. The PT, which is the first parade, involves vigorous exercise and running. After the PT, every one disperses for breakfast and assembles for various other training, parades or tasks after an hour's break. Weapons training, firing, driving training and education classes, as applicable, are carried out till about 12'o clock. At this hour jawans are marched off to clean their weapons and return the weapons and equipment. After this, jawans proceed to the *langars* for lunch. Officers and JCOs now go to attend the office or administrative work as required.

The unit generally has a rest period till the afternoon games, when every one assembles on the sports ground once again and has to play some game or the other, like hockey, football, basketball, practice boxing or swimming. Teams for various competitions also practise at this time. Before the sunset the Retreat bugle is sounded. The flag in the unit's quarter guard is lowered with great reverence in the presence of the duty officer. Night guards also fall in front of the quarter guard where they are inspected and briefed.

By sunset jawans are relatively free and may now wear MUFTI – a specified pattern of civil clothes. They fall in by their sub-units for the 'roll call'. At this parade various orders are passed to them along with the next day's programme. A physical count of all individuals also takes place here. After the roll call Jawans can go to recreation rooms for watching the television or reading the newspaper. Jawans have their dinner early so that they get full rest. After dinner a bugle is sounded ordering 'lighting out' (generally about 10 p.m.). Now every jawan, except those on 'night guard', must go to bed. The JCO and officers' messes are however open till 11 p.m or so. You will notice that every activity of a jawan is regulated according to rules and parade timings.

Unit Institutes

The Unit Quarter Guard

An armed guard is always on the alert in every unit line. This is housed in a special building called the Quarter Guard. The name implies it is a guard for the unit lines or quarters. It usually faces the unit line and has unit arms (rifles, LMG, etc.) deposited in 'Kotes' (armoury). The unit duty officers and JCOs check the alertness of the quarter guard at odd hours during day and night. A bugler which is included in this guard blows various calls at given times announcing various parades or assemblies. Some important bugle calls of a unit are :

- Reveille: At dawn for 'time to leave your beds'.
- Parade Calls: Call for parades during day or night.
- Assembly Calls: Call for unit personnel or certain appointments to assemble together. For *'Sainik Sammelans'* there is a special call.
- Orderly Room Call: For those who would be marched up to a senior for various infringements of rules or for interviews before proceeding on temporary duties or leave.
- Mess or Meal Calls: At given times for meals, these are separate for jawans and officers' mess.
- Fire Alarms: To indicate outbreak of fire or to practise fire fighting.
- Retreat: Sounded at dusk for closing down, back to barracks.
- Last Post/Lights Out: Everyone in bed and lights out.

Every minute of a soldier's life is strictly regulated and these bugle calls summon or prepare jawans for various activities, even rest. A bugle call is a simple but effective signal to commence or terminate activities in a unit line.

Officers' Mess

The officers' mess is like a club with restricted entry for members only. Unmarried officers, who dine here, have to dress up in uniform or mess dress twice a week to have their meals on Dinner Nights. Dinner nights are considered a parade and start at a fixed time when every unit officer dining in the mess has to be present. It is actually a formal dinner with strict rules. For the rest of the week Supper Nights are observed. During these officers can dine in civilian clothes (civies). Formal civilian clothes have to be worn during supper nights. Usually a suit or tie is worn in the mess, depending on the weather. Informal dress is allowed during breakfast and lunch only on holidays and Sundays.

Recreation Room

A special room or barrack is reserved for recreational facilities for jawans within the unit lines. Here, a number of Hindi, English and regional language newspapers and magazines are available, besides indoor games like carrom, table tennis or chess. A TV room may be provided separately. The NCOs from the AEC posted to a unit maintain this facility. Here, they also display important information about the army along with some information on current affairs and health and hygiene. A jawan is allowed to visit the information room at specified times though it is a common room open to all.

Unit School

You may be surprised to know that every unit has a small school where classes are held regularly for jawans and NCOs to educate and prepare them for various examinations. Army education examinations are equivalent to matric or middle class in standard. Various education standards must be attained for promotion from a jawan to an NCO and from an NCO to a JCO. These coaching classes prepare jawans to attain laid down standards.

Unit Canteen

A unit generally has two canteens. One is called a Wet Canteen which is run by a civilian contractor who supplies tea, sweets, snacks etc. at approved rates to the jawans. The other Canteen Services Department or CSD canteen is a general store where goods are sold at lower rates compared to the market. Here, attractive items like electronic goods, motorcycles and cars etc. are also available at lower rates fixed by the CSD. Both these canteen are mobile and move with the units in war and peace. Liquor is also available in the CSD canteen at lower rates but its distribution is strictly controlled and one cannot draw beyond his fixed monthly quota.

Unit Medical Inspection Room (MI Room)

A medical officer from the AMC and a small team with him maintains and runs a small medical clinic in the unit lines. This clinic gives first aid to the sick and injured and is also responsible for inspecting every jawan once a month to ensure that he is fighting fit. When jawans return from leave or any long outing a special medical inspection is carried out to ensure that they have not contracted any disease while on leave in their hometowns. The health and hygiene of the unit is thus looked after regularly. All serious cases are transferred immediately to larger treatment centres or military hospitals. No seriously sick or injured jawan is kept in the unit lines.

Religious Institutes

The commanding officer of a unit is responsible for the religious and the spiritual well-being of his jawans. Depending on the class composition, a unit can have a *mandir, gurudwara,* church or a mosque, or all of these together. In mixed units, rather than having separate religious places, a *sarva dharma sthal* (a common prayer hall) may be provided, where all troops meet for various religious functions. Army life is totally secular. Army jawans are taught to respect all religions and there is nothing unusual to find a Muslim or Christian visiting the unit temple or *gurudwara*. Every officer, JCO and jawan irrespective of his religion, attends and takes active part in the festivals

Siachen: The Frozen Frontier

An Underground Bunker

A Stromeyer Tent

Military Hospital in Siachen

A Crevasse

White out: An Army Post in the Snow

Entrance into an Ice Cave

Casuality Evacuation

A Fibre Glass Hut

Icy Peaks

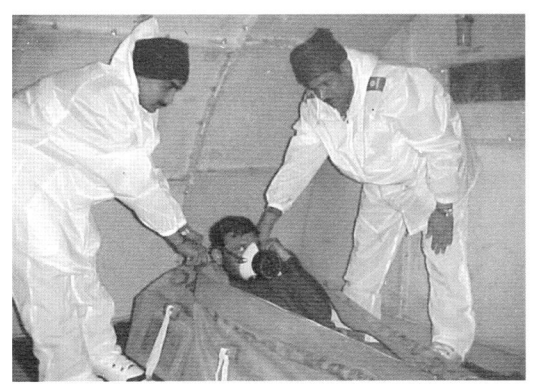

Medical Assistance

Bridge on a Crevasse

Arms and Ammunition in Ice Cave

Living in an Ice Cave

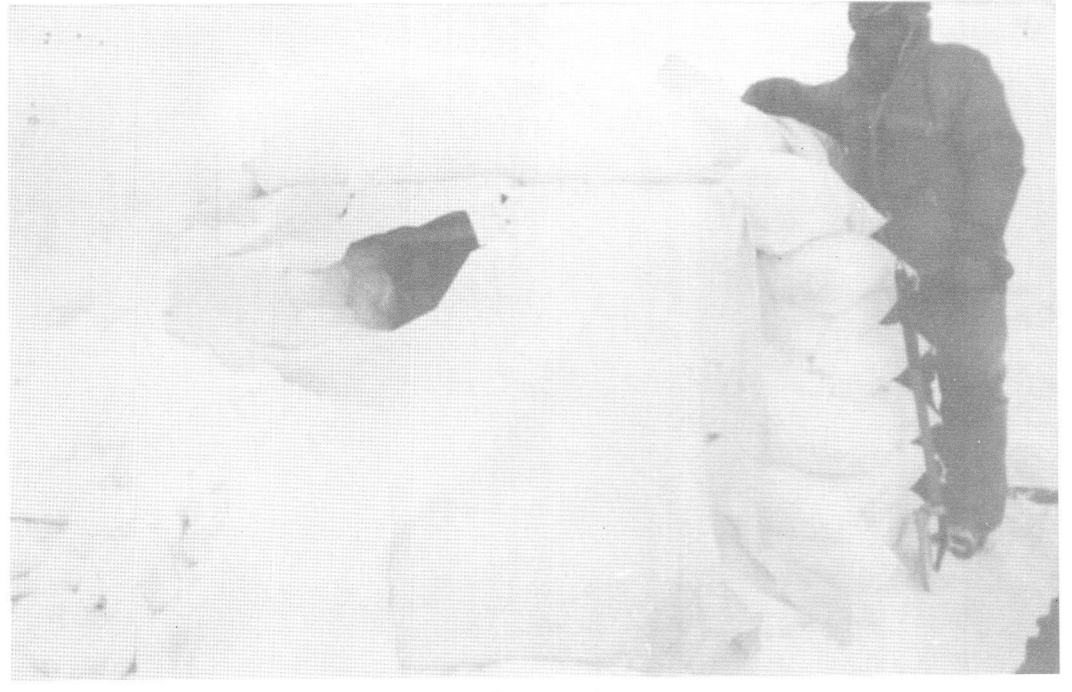

A Fighting Bunker

Pillaring Effect

Habitat in Siachen Glacier

A Solitary Post on the Cliff

A Makeshift Parachute Hut

Climbing the Ice Wall

Pillaring effect on a Helipad

Negotiating a Vertical Crevasse

A Patrol in White out Conditions

All round vigil

The Gorkha charge

Cliff assault

A Contingent of Dogra Regiment

Exploiting the Success

Mud bath as part of Military Training

Toughening Exercise

A Contingent of Dogra Regiment

Crawl like a Snake

Baptised in fire

The Final Rush: Infantry in Assault

Pounding Enemy with TNT

Hauling a dismantled Gun across the mountain

The Bayonet Charge

The Mechanized Infantry in Action

Training in Rapelling

Infantry and Tanks for the Final Assault

An Unit Quarter Guard

Training in Unarmed Combat

Am I smartly dressed?

Fatal Khukri blow

Arm wrestling session in progress

Dhruva: HAL's Advanced Light Helicopter

1965 War: A Graveyard of Patton Tanks

Surrender at Dhaka: 1971 War

Bridge Laying during Operations

The Artillery and the Aviation Corps

The Typhoon: A Smerch Launcher

L 70 Anti-aircraft Gun

Arjun Tank

BM 21 GRAD MBRL

of all religions represented in a unit. A unit *pandit, granthi,* priest or *maulvi* are specially trained, so that they can impart religious teaching with due respect to all religions. These religious teachers maintain unit's religious institutes and conduct various rituals and functions. Every Sunday whole unit gathers to attend religious prayers.

Family Welfare Centre

Every unit maintains a family welfare centre for the jawans' wives. Here, the officers' wives who are generally better educated conduct literacy/educational/vocational classes for the jawans' wives. Family problems and administrative difficulties are also brought to the notice of the senior commander's wife. For example, if there is a water shortage in family lines or a lady doctor is required to attend to the families or a jawan needs to go home due to some pressing family problem, such things may be conveyed to the commanding officer or subedar major through the welfare centre. Computer training, tailoring, embroidery, knitting and various other vocational training is organized here, as some jawans' wives come from remote rural areas and may know little about such things. Health and hygiene and family planning problems are also discussed here. Later important points are passed on to the senior officers of the unit who take appropriate remedial action to keep jawans and their families healthy and happy.

Unit Sainik Sammelan

An unit assembles together for an open session presided over by its commanding officer once a month. All officers, JCOs and jawans are required to attend the *sainik sammelan* in uniform. Jawans have liberty to raise any points or problems regarding administration, training or service conditions for the consideration of the commanding officer. Though, this is considered a parade but there is no bar on raising any points including suggestions for improvement of various systems of the unit. It is an old custom and a good example of democratic functioning within military discipline. An assembly of this kind serves as a safety valve as a jawan can directly approach his commanding officer once a month.

Life in Field Areas

More than half of the Indian Army is deployed on borders. A combat unit generally spends two-three years in a field area and about two years in a peace station in a five- year-cycle. In the border areas troops are deployed in defences in readiness for war. Most of the field areas are in the remote regions without any basic amenities. Troops have to face great hardships in field areas due to harsh weather condition, high altitude and lack of common facilities like living accommodation. The Indian Army has major field stations in the following regions:

- Arunachal Pradesh, Sikkim, Central Himalayas, all bordering Tibet.
- Assam, Nagaland and Manipur, Mizoram (insurgency areas).
- Sugar Sector, in Shimla Hills bordering Tibet.

- Central Sector in Uttarakhand.
- J&K, along international border and LoC, facing Pakistan.
- Eastern Ladakh area bordering with Tibet.
- Siachen in Central Ladakh (J&K) facing Pakistan.
- In J&K, combatting insurgency and terrorism.

In most field areas families cannot join the troops. However, in some soft field areas they may be allowed to stay for short periods.

The majority of army units are deployed on high mountains. Troops live here in bunkers which are dugouts with thick shell-proof roofs. These bunkers are dark and small but provide shelter from enemy fire, strong cold winds, ice and snow. Guards and sentries are ever ready with their weapons on the LoC. They see the enemy daily because in most cases enemy troops are deployed right across the border, within a stone's throw. Defences are on the hill tops and movement up and down is a major problem, even in good weather. To bring down the sick and wounded from these positions to the bases or hospitals is a major problem, since the availability of helicopters and helipads is limited to few areas only. Most of these defences remain cut off from their bases for long spell in winter, or rains. Snow accumulation in the picquets or posts can be up to 20 feet or more in winter at higher altitudes. Only a well-disciplined, dedicated and patriotic force can continue ungrudgingly in such adverse circumstances.

Deployment in *Siachen* Glacier is a special case. Here our troops are fighting on the highest battlefield in the world. Survival at such altitudes in adverse weather conditions is very challenging. Post are maintained by helicopters. Troop movement is done at night to avoid casualties from avalanches. Though the troops in *Siachen* have been provided with best quality clothing, rations and special living shelters but life in glacier is difficult and it takes a great deal of physical and mental robustness to serve there.

A part of the army is deployed on the high passes and plateaus of the Himalayas facing the Chinese in Tibet. There is a very large concentration of troops in the small mountainous state of Sikkim. The famous passes held by the army are Nathu La, Cho La and Jelep La. The life on the passes or the crest line is difficult because of extremely wet climate and frequent electric storms. The landscape is bleak and without vegetation above 11,000 feet. At Nathu La, Chinese troops stare at you from hundred yards or so from their bunkers. A good road connects the pass from Gangtok, the capital of Sikkim, making it easy to reach the pass area.

The life and routine in the field areas can be described only in general terms as conditions differ greatly from region to region. Field areas can be divided into the following categories:-

- Soft Field Areas: Troops are located here in improvised or temporary barracks, mud huts, tents etc. Limited essential facilities are available. Normally electricity is provided in the rear areas and rest and recreation facilities are also provided here.
- Hard Field Areas: The troops live in bunkers or improvised accommodation. Twenty-four hour vigilance is maintained in the border areas due to infiltration by terrorists across the LoC from PoK.

High Altitude Areas

In the Himalayan region heating arrangement for the bunkers are necessary in the winter. This is provided by installing *bhukharis* (heating stoves) which burn coal, wood or kerosene oil. Special clothing is necessary for outdoor work in snowbound areas to avoid frost-bites and other cold weather diseases. Army patrols have to keep moving at night even in bad weather and a man may freeze to death in such conditions without snow clothing.

Soldiers in high altitude areas face problems due to lack of oxygen and uncongenial weather conditions. In Ladakh, (J&K), which is a high altitude desert with an average height of about 11,000 feet above mean sea level, the climate is extremely dry and very cold, vegetation is sparse, and the landscape is harsh and bleak. The whole area remains cut off from the rest of India in the winters which lasts over six months. The only means of communication is by air. Air service is also hazardous and infrequent due to inclement weather conditions. During the winter, troops have to subsist only on tinned rations and precooked foods.

Siachen Glacier

Siachen Glacier is located in the Eastern Karakoram Range of Himalayas. It is the second largest glacier in the world, outside the polar region. Siachen is a 80-km-long icy stretch dotted with peaks ranging between 17,800 – 25,300 feet. The second highest peak in the world, Mount K2 or Godwin Austen is in this region. Temperatures here remain sub-zero throughout the year and plunge to minus 50 degree Celsius in winters. Strong winds and snowstorms are common. Your hand can sustain cold injury in seconds, if you touch an metal surface in winters. High velocity blizzards (snowstorms) and avalanches (huge snowdrifts or slides) take their toll in this 'white hell'. The glacier has many hidden crevasses (deep ravines covered on top by snow and ice) which can become death traps. Even the big snow vehicles which operate here sometimes disappear in these crevasses. A glacier, as you know, is a frozen river of ice which moves very slowly. The rarefied atmosphere and lack of oxygen create great health hazards for our soldiers. Basic human needs can hardly be met. Army has lost more men to inhospitable weather than in enemy action. In such surroundings only the most dedicated and motivated soldiers can survive and keep the enemy at bay.

Routine in Field or High Altitude Areas

Normal life-style comes to a standstill in high altitude areas. Bathing and washing become luxuries. Normal food habits have to be changed as a special diet is needed for survival at higher altitudes. All rations and stores have to be air dropped as there are few surface routes available. Letters are carried by special helicopter couriers to the mountains and dropped at a specified place. Long spells of bad weather keep the skies closed and all direct contact is lost with the rest of the world. Troops have to bear with extreme isolation and privation in such 'white out' conditions.

In Nagaland, Manipur, Assam and J&K, there have been long-drawn insurgencies. The army is deployed in these areas under trying conditions because insurgents and terrorists take shelter in crowded towns or thick jungles. There are regular encounters with the insurgents in which there are fatalities on both sides. Cordon and search operations in jungles, mountains and towns are difficult, which require large strength of troops. In such circumstances there is neither peace nor war.

In the field areas normal training for war is not possible although it is necessary as a unit may be suddenly moved to a desert or the plains during a war. A unit is normally brought back to a peace station for rest, refitting and training every two-three years.

This rotation from field to peace goes on in the life of a soldier. Can you believe that a unit packs and unpacks almost every six month on an average and there are long separations from their families?

6
Traditions and Customs of the Service

Military Etiquette

The code of honour that the Army follows is fostered through various customs and traditions which are legally and morally binding on every officer and soldier. Respect for seniors and juniors even when off duty; courtesy to all women regardless of their status; total truthfulness, dauntless moral and physical courage at all times are some of the norms which have been well established through a code of social conduct laid down by traditions and customs of the service. To be a true soldier one has to learn to be a gentleman first. Here, we will describe some of the customs of service to highlight the code of honour which the army follows on and off parade and the institutions or practices which help in fostering this code of honour.

Officers' Mess

An officers' mess is a place where young officers and new entrants see and learn the basic courtesies and imbibe the noble traditions of the Indian Army. When an officer enters a mess he leaves his belt and baton outside, which symbolises the sword or other weapons carried in war.

The institution of officers' mess was started sometime in the eighteenth century. The customs and traditions of gentlemanly behaviour were fostered and encouraged through this institution in younger officers. To avoid any undue controversies, politics and women are never discussed in an officers' mess. Drinking is allowed but is controlled by the strict bar timings which must be followed. A senior officer who is appointed President of the Mess Committee ensures that mess customs are adhered to and decorum is maintained by the members.

Saluting

A soldier must greet a fellow soldier or show a sign of recognition and respect to a senior. This is necessary to create comradeship and mutual respect among all ranks. This is achieved through saluting or greeting a comrade in arms. A junior salutes first and a senior returns his salute. Saluting dates back to many centuries and is a common feature of all armies of the world. In the old days opening the eye-piece (visor) of a helmet indicated a friendly gesture, as this required taking your hand to your forehead. Later this gesture became a salute. A salute also shows an open palm, indicating symbolically, that no hidden weapon is being carried.

Soldiers, even when not in uniform, are expected to greet each other by some gesture. In a battalion or a regiment this greeting may be *'Jai Hind'* or *'Ram-Ram'* or any other form of greeting followed traditionally. An officer always wishes a lady first regardless of the rank of her husband.

Style of saluting in the Army, Navy and Air Force is also a little different. An army man flashes his full palm parallel to the ground while saluting. Whereas a sailor keeps his palm downwards – facing the ground; perhaps not to show his grease-soiled palm to his seniors. An airman inclines his palm at 45 degrees while saluting. Also the sailors and airmen salute bareheaded whereas a solider only salutes when he is wearing a headgear.

Turnout and Smartness

A soldier is expected to dress smartly according to laid down rules and regulations. He must appear smart and well-groomed on and off parade. Personal cleanliness, neatness of living quarters, even tidiness of vehicles is ensured through well regulated drills and procedures. You will seldom find a military vehicle not properly painted or cleaned. Smartness and cleanliness are a part of discipline and tradition of the armed forces all over the world. Our officers and soldiers staying even in snowbound areas maintain smartness and cleanliness as far as possible.

Drills and Ceremonial Parades

Drill is a part of army life. It instills instant obedience of command and makes a large body of troops act in unison. In the old days elaborate drills were followed on the battlefield in actual combat. Now these drills have been retained for ceremonial purposes. You must have seen soldiers marching in unison on Republic Day or other parades. Their smartness and precise drill movements reflect their dedication and discipline.

The proper way of saluting and marching etc. is also taught to individual and small groups so that good discipline and smartness become a second habit with soldiers.

A soldier learns to take pride in his profession and bears weapons with pride through the discipline inculcated on the parade grounds.

Battle Cry

Infantry regiments have their own distinct 'Battle Cries'. A battle cry is a phrase or a slogan which soldiers shout in unison while attacking an enemy post or defending a post from the enemy attack. It has tremendous inspiring effect on the troops who forget about personal safety and take unbelievable risks in carrying out the mission. History of warfare is replete with examples when a handful of men have fought off determined attacks by enemy despite being outnumbered. Battle cries of infantry regiments are listed in Table 6.1.

Table 6.1: Battle Cries of the Infantry Regiments

Regiment	Battle Cry
The Brigade Of Guards	Bol Pyare, Garud Ka Hun.
The Parachute Regiment*	
The Mechanized Infantry**	
The Punjab Regiment	Jo Bole So Nihal, Sat Sri Akal.
	Jwala Mata Ki Jai.
The Madras Regiment	Veer Madrasi Adi Kolu, Adi Kolu.
The Grenadiers	Sarvada Shaktishali.
The Maratha Light Infantry	Chattrapati Shivaji Maharaj Ki Jai.
The Rajputana Rifles	Raja Ram Chandra Ki Jai.
	Bole Nara Haidiri Ya Ali.
The Rajput Regiment	Bol Bajrang Bali Ki Jai.
The Sikh Regiment	Jo Bole So Nihal, Sat Sri Akal.
The Jat Regiment	Jat Balwan, Jai Bhagwan.
The Sikh Light Infantry	Jo Bole So Nihal, Sat Sri Akal.
The Dogra Regiment	Jwala Mata Ki Jai.
The Garhwal Rifles	Badri Vishal Lal Ki Jai.
The Kumaon Regiment	Kalika Mata Ki Jai.
The Assam Regiment	Rhino Charge.
The Bihar Regiment	Jai Bajrang Bali.
	Birsa Munda Ki Jai.
The Mahar Regiment	Bol Hindustan Ki Jai.
The Jammu And Kashmir Rifles	Durga Mata Ki Jai.
The Ladakh Scouts	Bharat Mata Ki Jai.
The Naga Regiment	Jai Durge Naga.
The Jammu And Kashmir Light Infantry	Bharat Mata Ki Jai.
The Gorkha Brigade	Jai Mahakali, Ayo Gorkhali.

Note:

* The Parachute Regiment believes in carrying out task by stealth, and hence, do not use a battle cry.
** The Mechanized Infantry Regiment has been raised by converting one or two battalions from old infantry regiments and some battalions from the Brigade of Guards. Hence, each battalion uses the battle cry of its parent regiment.

Traditions and Customs of the Service

Battle Honour

A 'battle honour' is an official recognition of a battle in which a unit has participated with credit. The award of a battle honour is a source of pride and inspiration for future generation of soldiers. Battle honours are awarded in the following forms:-

- For a Particular Operation. This entitles a unit to emblazon the name of the battle on its colours, standard or guidon, which are regimental flags held in great reverence. In olden days the colours were kept aloft by a select band of soldiers throughout a battle, and the battle was fought around the colours.

- A Theatre Honour. It is given to a unit when it has performed creditably in a theatre of war. Theatre honours are given exclusively to supporting units.

- An Honour Title. Artillery units are authorised to include an honour title in their official designations. As artillery units do not carry colours, their guns are considered as their flag or colour of honour which must be defended at all cost.

Gallantry Awards

Acts of gallantry and valour in war and peace entitle a soldier to certain awards or medals. These are awarded by the President personally at a special function held at Rashtrapati Bhawan. The details of these awards are given below:

Param Vir Chakra (PVC)

This is the highest decoration for valour awarded – for *'the most conspicuous bravery or some daring or pre-eminent act of valour or self-sacrifice in the presence of the enemy whether on land, at sea or in the air'*.

The decoration is made of bronze and is circular in shape. It has, on the obverse, four replicas of *'Indra's Vajra'*, embossed round the State Emblem in the centre. On the reverse, the words *'Param Vir Chakra'* are embossed both in Hindi and in English with lotus flowers in the middle. The medal is worn on the left breast with a plain purple coloured ribbon. When only the ribbon is worn it has a miniature replica *of* the *'Vajra'* stitched on it.

The award carries a monetary allowance of Rs 1,500 per month and an equal amount per month for each bar.

Maha Vir Chakra (MVC)

This is the second highest decoration and is awarded for *'an act of conspicuous gallantry in the presence of the enemy whether on land, at sea or in the air'*.

It is made of standard silver and is circular in shape. Embossed on the obverse is a five-pointed star with a domed centerpiece bearing the gilded State Emblem in a circle in the centre. On the reverse, the words *'Maha Vir Chakra'* are embossed both in Hindi and in English with two lotus flowers in the middle. The medal is worn on the left breast with a half white and half saffron ribbon with the saffron stripe nearer to the left shoulder.

It carries a monetary allowance of Rs 1,200 per month and an equal amount per month for each bar.

Vir Chakra (VrC)

This is the third in the order of awards and is given for *'an act of gallantry in the presence of the enemy whether on land, at sea or in the air'*.

The medal is made of standard silver and is circular in shape. Embossed on the obverse is a five-pointed star which has an Ashoka Chakra in the centre. Within this chakra is a domed centrepiece bearing the gilded State Emblem. On the reverse, the words *'Vir Chakra'* are embossed in Hindi and English with two lotus flowers in the middle. The Vir Chakra is worn on the left breast with a half blue and half saffron ribbon, the saffron stripe being nearest to the left shoulder.

It carries a monetary allowance of Rs 850 per month and an equal amount per month for each bar.

All members of the armed forces and civilians serving regularly or temporarily under the direction or supervision of any of the services are eligible for any of the three awards.

Ashoka Chakra (AC)

This decoration is awarded for the *'most conspicuous bravery or some daring or pre-eminent act of valour or self-sacrifice on land, at sea or in the air'*.

The medal is made of gilt gold and is circular in shape. Embossed on the obverse is a replica of the Ashoka Chakra surrounded by a wreath of lotuses. Along the edge is a pattern of lotus leaves, flowers and buds. On the reverse the words *'Ashoka Chakra'* are embossed both in Hindi and English with lotus flowers in the intervening space. It is worn on the left breast with a green coloured silk ribbon divided into two equal parts by a saffron vertical line.

It carries a monetary allowance of Rs 1,400 per month and an equal amount per month for each bar.

Kirti Chakra (KC)

This decoration is awarded for *'an act of conspicuous gallantry'*.

It is made of standard silver and is circular in shape. The obverse and reverse are exactly the same as in the case of the AC. On the reverse are embossed the words *'Kirti Chakra'* both in Hindi and English. The Chakra is worn on the left breast with a green coloured silk ribbon and divided into three equal parts by two saffron vertical lines.

It carries a monetary allowance of Rs 1,050 per month and an equal amount per 'month for each bar.

Shaurya Chakra

This decoration is awarded for *'an act of gallantry'*.

It is exactly like the other two medals except that it is made of bronze and the words *'Shaurya Chakra'* are embossed on the reverse. The medal is worn on the left breast with a green coloured ribbon, divided into four equal parts by three saffron vertical lines.

It carries a monetary allowance of Rs 750 per month and an equal amount per month for each bar.

All citizens of India are eligible for the award of the AC, KC and SC.

War Medals

Sarvottam Yudh Seva Medal (SYSM)

The award is made to service personnel for *'distinguished service of the most exceptional order during war/conflict/hostilities'*.

The medal is of gold gilt and is circular in shape and fitted to a plain horizontal bar with standard fittings. On its obverse are the State Emblem and the inscriptions in Hindi and English. On its reverse, it has a five-pointed star. The decoration is worn on the left breast with a gold coloured ribbon with one red vertical stripe in the centre dividing it into two equal parts.

Uttam Yudh Seva Medal (UYSM)

The award is made for *'distinguished service of an exceptional order during war/conflict/hostilities'*.

The medal is of gold gilt and circular in shape its design details are similar to SYSM. The decoration is worn on the left breast with a gold coloured ribbon with two red vertical stripes dividing it into three equal parts.

Yudh Seva Medal (YSM)

The award is made for *'distinguished service of a high order during war/conflict/hostilities'*.

The design details of YSM are similar to SYS and UYSM. The medal is worn on the left breast with a gold coloured ribbon with three red vertical stripes dividing it into four equal parts.

Distinguished Service Medals

Param Vishisht Seva Medal (PVSM)

This medal is awarded in recognition of *'distinguished service of the most exceptional order'*.

The medal is circular in shape and made of gold gilt. It is fitted with a plain horizontal bar with standard fittings. Embossed on the obverse is a five-pointed star, on the reverse it has the State Emblem and the inscription *'Param Vishisht Seva Medal'* in Hindi embossed along the upper rim. The ribbon is golden in colour with one dark blue stripe down the centre.

Ati Vishisht Seva Medal (AVSM)

This medal is awarded for *'distinguished service of an exceptional order'*.

The medal is circular in shape and made of silver. Other design details are similar to PVSM. The ribbon is golden in colour with two dark blue stripes dividing it into three equal parts.

Vishisht Seva Medal (VSM)

This medal is awarded for *'distinguished service of a high order'*.

The medal is circular in shape and made of bronze. Other design details are similar to PVS and AVSM.

The ribbon is golden in colour with three dark blue vertical stripes dividing it into four equal parts.

Sarvottam Jeevan Raksha Padak

This medal is awarded for *'conspicuous courage, under circumstances of very great danger to the life of the rescuer, displayed in an act or a series of acts in saving life from drowning, fire, rescue operations in mines etc'*.

The medal is circular in shape, made of gold and consists of two raised circles, inner and outer. At the top there is a rectangular projection on which are embossed the Sanskrit letters *'Ma Bhai'* and at the bottom is another rectangle embossed with *'Sarvottam Jeevan Raksha'* in Hindi. On the obverse of the medal is embossed in the enter a hand in the *'Abhai Mudra'*. On the reverse in the centre is embossed the State Emblem with the motto *'Satyamev Jayate'* in Hindi in the lower projection. The design of other two medals of this series –Uttam Jeevan Raksha Padak and Jeevan Raksha Padak is similar. The medal is worn suspended from the left breast by a red coloured silk ribbon edged with light blue stripes, and with one green vertical stripe, down the centre.

It carries a cash reward of Rs 2,500 and 50 per cent of the amount for each bar. If the award is posthumous, the cash grant is twice the amount admissible otherwise.

Uttam Jeevan Raksha Padak

This medal is awarded for *'courage and promptitude, under circumstances of great danger to the life of the rescuer, displayed in an act or a series of acts of a human nature in saving life from drowning, fire, rescue operation in mines etc'*.

The medal is worn suspended from the left breast by a red coloured silk ribbon edged with light blue stripes, and with two green vertical stripes down the centre.

It carries a cash reward of Rs 1,000 and 50 per cent of the amount for each bar and double the amount is admissible, if awarded posthumously.

Jeevan Raksha Padak

This medal is awarded for *'courage and promptitude displayed in an act or a series of acts in saving life from drowning, fire, rescue operation in mines etc'*.

The medal is worn suspended from the left breast by a red coloured silk ribbon edged with light blue stripes and with three green vertical stripes in the enter.

It carries a cash reward of Rs 500 and 50 per cent of the amount for each bar and double the amount is admissible, if awarded posthumously.

Sena Medal (SM)

This medal is awarded in recognition of such individual acts of exceptional devotion to duty or courage as have special significance for the army. A bar is given for every subsequent award of the medal. All ranks of the armed forces are eligible for this medal.

The medal is circular in shape, made of standard silver. The mounting is a fixed ring attached to a metal strip ornamented with Ashoka leaves. Embossed on the obverse is a bayonet, pointing upwards and on the reverse is an armed sentry and the inscription *'Sena Medal'* in Hindi along the upper rim.

The ribbon of the medal is red with a thin silver grey stripe down the enter.

Nau Sena Medal (NM)

This medal is awarded in recognition of such individual acts of exceptional devotion to duty or courage as have special significance for the navy. A bar is given for every subsequent award of the medal. All ranks of the armed forces are eligible for this medal.

The medal is pentangular in shape with curved sides made of standard silver. The mounting is a fixed ring attached to a metal strip ornamented with Ashoka leaves. Embossed on its obverse is the naval crest and on the reverse a trident within a circle of rope and the inscription *'Nau Sena Medal'* in Hindi along the upper rim.

The ribbon of the medal is Navy blue in colour with a thin silver grey stripe down the centre.

Vayusena Medal (VM)

This medal is awarded in recognition of such individual acts of exceptional devotion to duty or courage as have special significance for the air force. A bar is given for every subsequent award of the medal. All ranks of the armed forces are eligible for this medal.

The medal is a four-pointed star made of standard silver. The mounting is a fixed ring attached to a metal strip ornamented with Ashoka leaves. Embossed on its obverse is the State Emblem in the centre encircled by a wreath of leaves. On its reverse is a representation of a Himalayan Eagle with the inscription *'VayuSena Medal'* in Hindi.

The ribbon is in alternative stripes of saffron and silver grey, each running diagonally from right to left.

SM, NS and VM (for gallantry) awardees are entitled to a monetary allowance of Rs 250 per month and an equal amount for each bar to the medal.

Parakram Padak (Wound Medal)

The medal is awarded to the personnel who has sustained injuries as a result of direct enemy action in any type of operations or counter-insurgency operations since 15 August 1947.

The medal is circular in shape, made of cupro-nickel, and fitted to a ring. It has embossed on its obverse the State Emblem with its motto and the inscriptions *'Parakram Padak'*.

7
Recruitment in the Army

Recruiting Organization

An Assistant Director General who holds the rank of a Major General heads the army recruiting organization at IHQ of MoD (Army). He deals with the recruitment of jawans and selection of the officers. Based on the manpower demand projected to the recruitment organization by the army, recruitment quota for the various regions of the country is worked out and the recruitment-cum-selection process is set in to motion.

Officers' Selection System

The officers' selection system has been adopted from the US and British systems evolved after the First and Second World Wars. In 1942, the British Army developed the psychological tests and group testing techniques which are used in India today. Research based on World War experience, led to the conclusion that there should be 15 basic qualities in a person to enable him to lead his men successfully in battle. These qualities are:

- Effective Intelligence. Ability to achieve practical results.
- Reasoning Ability. Rational thinking under stress.
- Organizing Ability.
- Power of Expression.
- General Awareness. Inquisitiveness and desire to acquire knowledge about his environment and surroundings.
- Social Adaptability. Adaptability and adjustment within the social environment.
- Co-operation. Willing co-operation within a group.
- Sense of Responsibility. A sense of responsibility to willingly discharge obligations.

- Determination. Ability to achieve results despite obstacles and setbacks.
- Courage. Both moral and physical, ability to take calculated risks willingly.
- Stamina. Ability to withstand mental and physical stress.
- Initiative. Ability to go ahead and originate purposeful action.
- Self Confidence. Confidence to face adverse situations and the ability to assess one's own abilities.
- Decisiveness. Ability to take timely and resolute action.
- Liveliness. To remain buoyant and cheerful in adversity and to create a cheerful atmosphere around him.
- Group Influence. Ability to exert purposeful influence on a group to encourage each individual of the group to do his best.

Selection Organization

The army has three selection centres for officers. They are located in Allahabad, Bhopal and Bangalore.

Each selection centre has a number of Services Selection Boards (SSBs). The selection centre is headed by a Major General who is also the President of one of the SSBs. The other presidents are Brigadiers. Each board has two interviewing officers i.e. the President and Deputy President, one or two Group Testing Officers (GTOs) and one to two psychologists.

Tests at SSBs

On arrival candidates face a screening interview and only successful individuals are considered for further tests. Each candidate is assessed independently by three members of the SSB –the interviewing officer, the GTO and the psychologist. Each member applies a different technique to assess each candidate. They only compare notes at the end. Thus, an unbiased and comprehensive picture of each candidate emerges.

Psychological Tests

These are held for the candidates who clear the screening interview to test their aptitude and 'Officer's Intelligence Rating'. All psychological tests are conducted against time.

Thematic Appreciation Test (TAT)

A candidate is shown a picture or a sketch and he is expected to write a story on the theme in just three minutes.

Word Associate Test (WAT)

A series of words are shown to the candidates who have to write their spontaneous reaction to each word against the time.

Situation Reaction Test

A candidate has to react to a certain stress situation in a given time frame by writing down his course of action.

GTO Tests

After the psychological tests candidates are divided into small groups and are tested in the following ways for their leadership ability and group behaviour:

- A Group Discussion - on any topical subject.
- Extempore Lectures - for three minutes, on a given subject.
- Progressive Group Tasks - to solve a given problem as a group.
- Obstacles - to negotiate about 10 obstacles and participate in a group obstacle race.
- Group Planning - a group is given a simple problem or stress situation for which a solution is to be worked out.
- Command Task - to assess leadership qualities in candidates.

Interview

A 30 to 40 minute interview is arranged with the President or the Deputy President of the board for each candidate separately to judge the individual.

Medical Examination

All successful candidates are tested for medical fitness by the medical boards located within the selection centre.

Final Selection

Based on the results of the UPSC written examination (where applicable) and the interview, a final merit list is prepared; depending on the available vacancies, order of merit and medical fitness successful candidates are detailed to join various training establishments for example NDA, IMA, OTA etc.

Women's Special Entry Scheme

Traditionally women served in the armed forces as doctors and nurses. In 1992, entry of women as regular officers in aviation, logistics, law, engineering and executive cadres was permitted. Thousands of spirited young women responded to this historic opportunity.

Women except in the non-medical cadre, serve as Short Service Commissioned (SSC) officers and can serve in the armed forces for a period ranging from 5/10/14 years. They can reach up to a rank of lieutenant colonel/commander/wing commander in the armed forces. On release women officers receive gratuity and are not entitled to pension. Women in the medical branch can serve both as Permanent Commissioned (PC) or SSC officers as doctors and nurses. Enrolment of women in below officers' rank in the armed forces has not yet started.

Eligible women can serve as officers in the following branches of the armed forces: -

- Army: Engineers, signals, AAD, intelligence, ASC, AOC, EME, AEC, and JAG branch.
- Navy: All branches (except as submariners and divers).
- Air Force: Flying (transport aircraft and helicopters), technical and administration branches.

Lady Officer Cadets (Army) undergo a six-month pre-commission training at OTA, Chennai.

Table 7.1: Type of Entries: Officers' Cadre

Entry	Course Commence-ment (each year)	Age (at the time of joining)	Educational Qualification	Mode of Selection	Applying Procedure
NDA Entry	Jan and July	16 ½–19 yrs	12th class of 10+2 system of education or equivalent.	NDA Exam by UPSC and SSB interview.	Apply in response to advertisement during Mar & Oct.
Direct Entry	Jan and July	19-24 yrs	Degree or equivalent at the time of joining the course.	CDS Exam by UPSC and SSB interview.	Apply in response to advertisement during Apr & Oct.
Engineering Graduates	Jan and Jul	20-27 yrs	Engineering degree in notified discipline.	Direct SSB interview.	Apply to ADG Recruiting (TGC Entry) Army HQ in response to advertisement during Apr and Oct.
University Entry Scheme	July	19-25 yrs (Final year) 18-24 yrs (Pre-Final Year)	Final and pre-final year students of Engineering Degree course.	Campus interview and SSB interview.	Apply in response to advertisement in May.
10+2 Technical Entry Scheme	Apr and Oct & Nov	16 ½ -19 ½ yrs	10+2 PCM (70% aggregate to apply)	Direct SSB interview.	Apply in response to advertisement in Jan & Jul every year.
Short Service Commission (Non-Technical)	April and Oct & Nov	19-25 yrs	Degree or equivalent at the time of joining the course.	CDSE conducted by UPSC and SSB interview.	Apply in response to advertisement during Apr & Oct.

Recruitment in the Army 59

Short Service Commission (Technical)	Apr and Oct	20-27 yrs	Engineering degree in notified discipline.	Direct SSB interview.	Apply in response to advertisement during Apr & Oct.
Short Service Commission (NCC Special Entry Scheme)	Apr and Oct	19-25 yrs	Graduate with 50% aggregate marks, two years service in NCC Senior Div (Army) with minimum 'B' Grade in 'C' Certificate Exam.	Direct SSB interview.	Apply in response to advertisement in Jun & Dec through NCC Directorate.
Women Special Entry Scheme (Officers) Technical/ Non-Technical/ Specialist	Apr and Oct	Technical/Non Technical 19-25 yrs Specialist 21-27 yrs	B.E/B. Tech/B.Sc./B.A/ B.Com/BBA/BCA. Post Graduate.	Direct SSB interview.	Apply in response to advertisement in Feb/ Mar.
JAG	Oct	21-27 yrs	Graduate with LLB/LLM with 50% marks. Registered with Bar Council of India.	Direct SSB interview.	Apply in response to advertisement in Feb/ Mar.

Recruitment of Other Rank

Recruitment of other rank is controlled by Additional Director General Recruiting at IHQ of MoD (Army). Recruitment is based on annual requirement of troops by various arms and services and is conducted through a network of 13 Recruiting Zones, 58 Branch Recruiting Offices (BROs), 47 Regimental Training Centres and an Independent Recruiting Office at New Delhi. Recruitment of Indian and Nepali Gorkhas is looked after by the Gorkha Recruiting Depots.

Recruitment is done through 'open rally' system to ensure transparency and easy access for all candidates. It is merit-based where the candidates have to fulfill stringent physical, written and medical standards.

Certain dispensations in these standards are given to the domiciles of remote areas, wards of serving soldiers and ex-servicemen and the candidates belonging to some other categories.

Selected candidates are despatched to various training centres, where they undergo recruit training which may last for six months or more. The minimum educational qualification required for recruitment in army as a soldier (General Duty) is presently Matric or its equivalent. Certain categories of entry and the eligibility criteria are given in Table 7.2.

Table 7.2: Categories of Entry and the Eligibility Criteria

Category	Educational Qualification	Age
Soldier General Duty	SSLC/Matric.	16-21 yrs
Soldier Technical	SSLC/Matric (Maths & English) 45% aggregate marks in Class Xth.	16-23 yrs
Soldier Clerk/Store Keeper Technical	SSLC/Matric (Maths, English & Science) 45% aggregate marks in Class Xth.	16-23 yrs
Soldier Nursing Assistant	SSLC/Matric (Maths, English & Biology) 45% aggregate marks in Class Xth.	16-23 yrs
Soldier Tradesman • General Duties • Specified Duties	 Non Matric Non Matric	 16-20 yrs 16-25 yrs
Havildar Education • Group 'X' • Group 'Y'	 Post Graduate/Trained Graduate B.A/B.Sc. (Matric with English & Maths).	 20-25 yrs 16-25 yrs
JCO Religious Teacher	Graduate in any discipline. In addition, qualification in his own religious denomination.	27-34 yrs
JCO (Catering)	10+2 with science and one year cookery diploma/certificate from a recognise Food Craft Institute.	21-27 yrs
Surveyor Automated Cartographer	B.A/B.Sc. with Maths having passed Matric & (10+2) with Maths & Science.	20-25 yrs

Note: Dispensation in education qualification for enrollment as Soldier (GD) is permissible to some selected States/Region/Class and Communities.

Physical Fitness Tests

To determine the physical fitness of the candidates, the following tests carrying 100 marks are held: -

- One-Mile Run.
- Pull Ups.
- Balance.
- Nine-Feet Ditch.

Written Examination

Common Entrance Examination (CEE) is conducted on all last Sunday of the month. The CEE has two papers as under: -

- Paper I – Compulsory for all soldier categories. It comprise of questions on IQ, numerical ability, general knowledge and current affairs. Duration of paper is 60 minutes. Maximum marks are 100 and a candidate has to obtain 32 marks to pass.
- Paper II – It is for the candidates who want to enroll themselves as soldier (technical/clerks/store keeper/nursing assistants). Paper II is in addition to Paper I that such candidates have to qualify. The duration of the paper is 30 minutes; maximum marks are 50 and pass marks are 16.

Pay and Allowances

Officers

Pay scales of officers and stipend of gentleman/ women cadet are as under:-

Table 7.3: Pay Scales of Officers

Rank	Start	Yearly Increment	RankPay	Maximum
Gentleman Cadet	-	-	-	Rs 8,000
Lieutenant	Rs 8,250	Rs 300	-	Rs 10,050
Captain	Rs 9,600	Rs 300	Rs 400	Rs 11,400
Major	Rs 11,600	Rs 325	Rs 1,200	Rs 14,850
Lieutenant Colonel	Rs 13,500	Rs 400	Rs 1,600	Rs 17,100
Colonel	Rs 15,100	Rs 450	Rs 2,000	Rs 17,350
Brigadier	Rs 16,700	Rs 450	Rs 2,400	Rs 18,050
Major General	Rs 18,400	Rs 500	-	Rs 22,400
Lieutenant General	Rs 22,400	Rs 525	-	Rs 24,500
Vice Chief of Army Staff and Army Commanders			Rs 26,000 Fixed
Chief of Army Staff			Rs 30,000 Fixed

PBOR Pay scales of the PBOR are as under:-

Table 7.4: Pay Scales of the PBOR

Rank	Start	Yearly Increment	Maximum
Sepoy	Rs 3,250	Rs 70	Rs 4300
Naik	Rs 3,425	Rs 85	Rs 4700
Havildar	Rs 3,600	Rs 100	Rs 5100
Naib Subedar	Rs 5,620	Rs 140	Rs 8140
Subedar	Rs 6,600	Rs 170	Rs 9320
Subedar Major	Rs 6,750	Rs 200	Rs 9550

Fair and Assured Promotion

- From Lieutenant to Lieutenant Colonel on time scale.
- From Lieutenant Colonel to higher ranks on selection basis.
- Financial increments will continue till the age of retirement even if superseded.
- A Jawan can become a commissioned officer through ACC or Regimental Commission Officer entry scheme.

Group Insurance

- Insurance cover of Rs 7.5 Lac at a premium of Rs 250 per month for Jawans and JCOs. Officers are insured for Rs 15 Lac at a premium of Rs 1,500 per month.
- Post-retirement extended insurance of Rs 4 Lac and 2 Lac for officers and other rank respectively, on a nominal premium for 25 years or 75 years of age, whichever is earlier.

Other Benefits

- Free rations.
- Furnished accommodation and allied facilities at concessional rates.
- Free medical facilities for self and family.
- Conveyance allowance.
- Canteen facilities.
- Group housing schemes.
- Soft loans for purchase of car/scooter and for house-building.

- Resettlement courses before retirement.
- Study leave.
- 60 days annual leave.
- 30/20 days casual leave.
- Leave travel concession.
- Concession in rail and air travel.

8
A Brief History of the Wars and Conflict after Independence

First Indo-Pak War, 1947-48

The Background

When British rule came to an abrupt end in August 1947, the subcontinent faced the trauma of the partition accompanied by bloodshed and chaos. In these chaotic conditions the British Indian Army, the Navy and the Air Force were ordered to be divided on communal lines. At the time of partition the ratio of British and Indian units was roughly 1:2 and all forces in India were under the overall command of the C-in-C, India.

The officer cadre was largely British. Therefore, at the time of partition, officers of Indian and Pakistan armies had little experience in higher command or higher direction of war. The division of the army on communal lines had split units, sub-units, weapons and ammunition depots and even hospitals. The Partition Council set up in June 1947 was entrusted with the responsibility of dividing the Indian forces. The Armed Forces Reconstitution Committee functioned under Field Marshal Auchinleck, who was then C-in-C in India. The terms of reference for this committee were that the Indian Army would cease to exist on 15 August 1947 and India and Pakistan will reconstitute the assets in their own territories.

The Raider's Attack, October 1947

Even before the Indian and Pakistan armies could settle down, the Pakistani leaders chose to sponsor an invasion of J&K through a tribal force assembled under retired army officers. The Maharaja of J&K who was still wavering on the status of his state finally decided to seek India's help.

To begin with, a propaganda war was started against the Maharaja, followed by a series of raids on the borders of the princely state. When the Maharaja refused to yield, a full-blooded invasion followed. On 22 October 1947, hordes of tribesmen organized into units and armed with machine guns, mortars and other weapons attacked J&K.

The broad plan of this attack at the beginning of the 1947-48 Indo-Pak War can be described as follows:-

- Local raids in Jammu and Poonch areas in September-October 1947.

- Attack on Mirpur-Kotli (Western areas of Jammu province) in October-November 1947.

- Annexation of Gilgit and Skardu and raids towards Leh from August-November 1947.

- Attacks on the Kashmir Valley, Gurez, Tithwal with the objective of capturing Srinagar in October 1947. This operation was named *Operation Gulmarg*.

- Major attacks in Jammu province from Poonch to Mirpur in October 1947.

The main force of raiders in the Kashmir Valley came via Muzaffrabad. The J&K State Forces units located here could offer little resistance as their Poonchi elements joined the raiders. Domel was their next objective. It fell to the raiders on 23 October 1947. In the Battle of Uri a small garrison under Brigadier Rajinder Singh of the state forces managed to blow up the Uri Bridge and thus delayed the advance of the raiders towards Baramulla and Srinagar. At this stage there was nothing which could stop the marauders from overrunning Srinagar, but they indulged in loot, rape and murder enroute which antagonized the local people and they resisted.

The Maharaja appealed for armed assistance from India on 24 October 1947. The then Defence Committee under Lord Mountbatten considered his request and agreed to assist the Maharaja provided J&K formally acceded to India. Our political leaders had argued that without a formal accession being signed troops could not be entered. This condition was conveyed to the Maharaja who acceded to India on 26 October. And thus, to save J&K from the invaders, 'Operation JAK' was launched by the Indian Army. Arrangements were made to despatch some available army units in Delhi by air to Srinagar. On 27 October at 08:30 AM, an infantry company of 1 SIKH and a composite company of Royal Indian Artillery led by Lieutenant Colonel D.R. Rai, Commanding Officer 1 SIKH landed at Srinagar. Army HQ was trying hard to induct an infantry brigade by air in Srinagar and another in Jammu, by road.

The situation was very critical; raiders had reached Baramulla and were held up by two platoons of state forces garrisoned there. Lieutenant Colonel Rai decided to reinforce the beleaguered troops and his men linked up with them by noon, the same day. On 28 October, 1 SIKH did their gallant best but could not stop the raiders at Baramulla and Pattan towns, as the enemy attacked and bypassed their hastily dug defences to reach the outskirts of Srinagar. Lieutenant Colonel Rai was killed in action at Baramulla. He was awarded MVC posthumously.

On 1 November 1947, HQ 161 Infantry Brigade, 1 SIKH, 1 (PARA) KUMAON, a company of 4 KUMAON and some minor units were entrenched from Pattan to Srinagar trying to check the onslaught. On 3 November, company of 4 KUMAON under Major

Somnath Sharma at the airfield, was attacked by about 700 raiders. The Kumaonis fought bravely and held ground; Major Somnath Sharma was killed in action and was awarded the first PVC of independent India, posthumously. Those were very trying times for the Indian Army and the people of J&K.

Situation in Jammu sector was more critical but could not be helped due to paucity of resources. Garrisons of state forces at Poonch, Mirpur and Kotli were besieged and attacked repeatedly by the enemy. Despite shortage of ammunition and supplies and mounting casualties the forces held on. The air force air-dropped ammunition and supplies and strafed enemy concentration which brought some relief to the troops. 50 Parachute Brigade responsible for Jammu sector was outstretched on road Pathankot –Jammu – Banihal – Anantnag , keeping the line of communication open. However, gravity of situation forced army to commit troops in this sector. Troops captured Nowshehra, Jhangar, Kotli, Rajauri. Mirpur could not be captured while Kotli was evacuated being untenable.

The raiders were soon driven out of the valley and pushed into a corner in Mirpur-Kotli and Poonch. Now regular Pakistan Army units were inducted to confront the Indian Army in Uri, Tithwal and other sectors of Kashmir, and Jhangar and Poonch sectors of Jammu. In Kargil (Ladakh) sector General Thimayya employed the tanks of 7 CAVALRY all the way up the treacherous slopes of the Zojila Pass. It was a remarkable feat indeed, as tanks can seldom operate on such heights. The enemy ran away abandoning his strong positions on the mountains of Kargil sector.

However, Indian leadership was content with a few tactical victories, had the war carried on with same verve and tempo the Indian Army would have recaptured all those areas of J&K which till today remain in Pakistani occupation.

The Sino-Indian War, 1962

India's boundary with the China-Tibet region stretches from northwest Kashmir to the trijunction of Indian, Burmese (Myanmar) and Chinese territories. China claims a large part of our territory in Arunachal Pradesh, Uttrakhand-Tibet border and Aksai Chin in Ladakh. China considers these borders disputed and in the 1950s had objected to Indian police posts being located in these border areas.

In 1962, after a period of tension the Chinese reacted violently and pushed back a post of Assam Rifles at Khenzamene (in Arunachal Pradesh) from its position. In October 1962, another serious clash took place in western Arunachal Pradesh over Dhola post near the Thag La ridge. The Chinese inflicted heavy casualties on an Indian Brigade positioned in this area. This brigade was not equipped to fight at such heights and was positioned in a valley which was overlooked by the Chinese troops. The Indian Army at this stage was in a state of neglect and not equipped for a war in the mountains.

In Ladakh the Chinese attacked some Indian posts on 19/20 October. These were overrun due to superior Chinese strength despite gallant resistance offered by the Indian troops.

In November 1962, the Chinese continued their advance towards Tawang and Walong sectors in the Eastern theatre, and captured Tawang and Sela. In Ladakh, Chushul was built into a strong position. However, the Chinese succeeded in breaking through this position after suffering heavy casualties.

It is evident from the above actions that the Indian Army was sent to fight in high mountains without proper training, planning or experience. However, our troops fought bravely against heavy odds regardless of casualties and hardships. On the midnight of 20 November 1962 the Chinese announced a ceasefire and the border war came to an end.

This operation proved that the Indian Army needed more strength, modern weapons and equipments; and sustained training to fight both in the mountains and plains, or else the Nation's sovereignty would be in jeopardy.

The Second Indo-Pak War, 1965

Nehru's death in 1964 had created political uncertainty in the country and an impression in Pakistan that India was no longer politically or militarily strong. In Pakistan, Field Marshal Ayub Khan was well entrenched in power and liberal American arms aid and assistance had provided him with the latest aircrafts and battle tanks. By 1965, the Pakistan Army had been trained and poised itself to go on an offensive in Kashmir. It appeared that Pakistan's aim was to keep the war confined to J&K, but the leadership lacked the courage to attack openly. A secret plan of armed infiltration was therefore adopted. The invasion was carried out in three stages as under:-

- A limited offensive was launched in the Kutch region in May 1965 to test the political waters and to draw India's forces away from Punjab –the main battle front.

- Armed infiltration in J&K was launched with a view to seize power and declare independence of J&K. The idea was to tell the world that it was a local uprising. A revolutionary council was formed to appeal for military assistance from various countries including Pakistan.

- In Jammu, a major offensive was to be launched to capture Chhamb and Akhnur Bridge, soon after the uprising in Srinagar had taken place.

The main miscalculation on Pakistan's part was to believe that the Kashmiris would help the infiltrators and rise against the established government in J&K. The other miscalculation was to presume that India will not counterattack in Punjab due to her political and military weakness.

Battle in the Rann of Kutch

Rann is a remote salt plain of coastal Gujarat which remains flooded with shallow salt waters for nearly six months in a year. Only a few small islands of dry land or *'bets'* remain above the water line. This area provided the opportunity for Pakistan to tryout various new weapons supplied to them by the US and also to draw the Indian Army away from Punjab and J&K. India however resisted the temptation of deploying her strike forces or other reserves from Punjab into this area. A few battles were fought here in which Pakistani tanks were used. A ceasefire was arranged in May 1965.

Operation Gibralter: Armed Infiltration in J&K, August 1965

The Operation HQ for Operation Gibralter was set up in Murree under Major General Akhtar Hussain Malik. He had approximately 30,000 men under his command, divided into eight to ten groups, named after famous Muslim generals. The force was trained to infiltrate in nominated areas and overthrow the existing regime with the help of Kashmiri collaborators.

This force was launched in the first week of August 1965, divided into various task forces as under:-

- Tariq Force — Approximately six company strong force which was launched into Kargil area.
- Qasim Force — Its three columns were infiltrated into Gurez.
- Khalid Force — It was a large force supported by about 400 Mujahideens which was employed in Tithwal Sector.
- K. Force — It was employed in Uri Sector.
- Salahuddin Force — It was launched in to Gulmarg, Srinagar and Mandi (in Jammu Divison).
- Nusrat Force — It infiltrated in to Rajauri – Mendhar sector.
- Ghaznavi Force — It infiltrated in to Poonch – Rajauri sector.
- Babar Force — It infiltrated in to Naushera – Chhamb sector.

It was planned that the Salahuddin force along with some other groups would concentrate in Srinagar by 8 August 1965 and mix up with the devotees assembling for the festival of the Sufi Saint Pir Dastgir, a much revered saint in J&K. An armed revolt or a coup would be staged followed by a declaration of liberation by a Revolutionary Council, after seizing the radio station, Srinagar airfield etc. The revolutionary council was to proclaim on the air that it was the sole legitimate government of J&K and was also to seek help and recognition from all countries.

The infiltrators were however detected before they could carry out the intended coup. The information came from the Kashmiri Muslims themselves, who did not respond to this call of liberation. Pakistan at this stage had little mass support in the Valley and that is why this ingenious Pakistani plan failed.

The Indian counteraction against the various advance bases for Pakistani infiltration cut off the infiltrating columns. Now these columns were on the run, hunted by the Army and the local police alike. Pakistan at this stage started a full-fledged war by attacking Chhamb *(Operation Grand Slam)*. After limited success, *Operation Grand Slam* also fizzled out and Pakistan had to go on the defensive, the Indian forces went on the offensive in Lahore Sector and reached the outskirts of Lahore. This war taught Pakistan quite a few lessons. They now realized that they could not match the Indian Army in an open war and that all Indian people, Hindus, Muslims, Sikhs and Christians stood like a rock against Pakistan.

The Third Indo-Pak War, 1971

By 1970 Pakistan had created a terrible mess for itself in East Pakistan. East Pakistan, which was greatly exploited by the West wing, was restive and wanted greater autonomy. Sheikh Mujib-ur-Rehman, the most popular Bengali leader, was put behind bars and was even tried for treason. This angered the Eastern wing greatly.

In the 1970 general elections Sheikh Mujib-ur-Rehman's Awami League won hands down and emerged as the majority party of entire Pakistan. Now a plan was hatched to undo the election results by other means. A crackdown was ordered and all Bengali paramilitary and police forces were disarmed. A full-scale revolt followed this action in East Pakistan and demands for an independent Bangladesh were now made openly. By the middle of April 1971, outlying rural areas were out of Pakistan's control. This was the beginning of the struggle for Bangladesh in brief and the main cause of the third Indo-Pak war in December 1971. India was interested in helping East Pakistan gaining independence as millions of refugees from East Pakistan were pouring into India and great atrocities were being committed against the people.

Course of Operations, October-December 1971

Border clashes started in October-November 1971 and India instructed her forces to enter East Pakistan in self-defence in November 1971.

During the preceding weeks the Indian Army had concentrated in full strength against East Pakistan and was ready to launch a major offensive. However, on 3 December 1971 Pakistan precipitated the issue by launching pre-emptive air strikes against Indian airfields in Punjab, Kashmir, Rajasthan and Uttar Pradesh.

The Indian Army now launched an offensive into East Pakistan from three directions. 2 Corps operated from the Southwest in Jessore-Jhenoda Sectors, 33 Corps launched an offensive from Northwest in Rajshahi-Dinajpur-Rampur area, while 4 Corps attacked from the East in Sylhet-Akhaura-Comilla-Chanpur Sectors. 101 (Commnication Zone) Area launched operations in the central sector from Kamalpur. As the race for Dacca commenced in right earnest, the Pakistan Army found it was in no position to offer any great resistance. Dacca was captured by 11 December; and the war was over by 16 December 1971.

The Indian Air Force totally eliminated the Pakistan Air Force over East Pakistan by 5 or 6 December 1971 and the Navy fully blockaded all ports and routes of withdrawal and reinforcement for the Pakistan Army. Now the Pakistan Army faced a total defeat and surrendered en masse.

Pakistan seemed to flounder at every step while the Indian leadership, both political and military, stood firm and resolute.

In the West both India and Pakistan used a holding strategy. Pakistan however launched a major offensive into Chhamb area in J&K but was unable to gain ground.

Thus the two-nation theory proved wrong. It was the cultural divide between West and East Pakistanis, although they both were Muslims, which divided Pakistan. It was proved conclusively in 1971 that it is language, culture and social factors which unite a country not religion or a forced political arrangement.

The Proxy War

In 1984 Pakistan had gained considerable expertise in launching covert operations due to her role in Afghanistan. Training of Kashmiris, and supply of suitable weapons to start a proxy war in J&K was now easy for them. They created conditions for 'sponsoring terrorism' through a virulent anti-India campaign. Religious fundamentalism was also encouraged in a big way over a period of time. Later indoctrination and training of selected Kashmiri dissidents was organized in Pakistan to raise militant cadres.

Gradually political unrest was fomented by Pakistani agents and the loyalties of local police and government servants were subverted systematically. Specially trained groups organized 'anti-government', and 'anti-Indian' agitations and engineered incidents to provoke the authorities to take strong action against the locals. Alienation of the local population from India was the main aim of Pakistan in this phase.

The next phase of 'sponsored terrorism' was planned and inspired from across the borders by Pakistan. This phase opened with bomb blasts, kidnappings, assassinations and arson, punctuated by violent demonstrations. Due to India's rising military capability sponsored terrorism and insurgency was a far safer method of reviving the Kashmir issue than fighting a war. It was a low-cost, long-term option to internationalize the J&K issue, while Pakistan watched from a safe distance. It was without doubt a well-planned low-intensity war launched with the political and strategic objectives of snatching Kashmir from India.

Pakistani designs have not succeeded because the Indian Army stands firm on the LoC and is combating insurgents effectively all over J&K. The Indian Army is well prepared to deal with Pakistan in case it dares start a war. We as citizens must watch the situation and be mentally prepared to give full support to the war effort – if war is thrust upon us by Pakistan.

Appendix

OUTLINE ORGANIZATION OF INTEGRATED HQ OF MoD (ARMY)
CHIEF OF ARMY STAFF

VICE CHIEF OF ARMY STAFF
- DG of Military Operations
- DG of Military Intelligence
- DG of Operational Logistics
- ★ ADG of Operational Logistics

DEPUTY CHIEF OF ARMY STAFF (A)
- DG of Signals
- DG of Info Systems
- DG of Military Training
- ★ ADG Staff Duties

DEPUTY CHIEF OF ARMY STAFF (B)
- DG of Mechanized Forces
- DG of Artillery
- DG of Army Air Defence
- DG of Infantry
- DG of Rashtriya Rifles
- ★ ADG of Financial Planning
- ★ ADG of Weapon & Equipment
- ★ ADG of Perspective Planning
- ★ ADG of Army Aviation
- ★ ADG of Territorial Army
- • DDG Defence Security Corps

ADJUTANT GENERAL
- DG of Manpower & Personnel Services
- ★ ADG of Manpower Policy & Planning
- ★ ADG of Personnel & Services
- ★ ADG of Recruiting
- DG of Discipline Ceremonial & Welfare
- Provost Marshal
- Judge Advocate General
- DG of Medical Services
- DG of Dental Services
- Army Group Insurance Directorate

QUARTER MASTER GENERAL
- DG of Supply & Transport
- ★ ADG of Remount Veterinary Corps
- ★ ADG of Army Postal Service
- • Deputy Director General of Military Farms
- • Deputy Director General Pioneers

MASTER GENERAL OF ORDNANCE
- DG of Ordnance Services
- DG of Electronics & Mechanical Engineers

MILITARY SECRETAY

ENGINEER – IN – CHIEF
- DG of Works

Indian Navy

by
Vice Admiral (Retd) GM Hiranandani, PVSM, AVSM, NM, PhD

Vice Admiral GM Hiranandani joined the Navy in 1949. After initial training with the British Navy from 1949 to 1953, he specialized there in gunnery and missiles in 1957 and at the British Naval Staff and Tactical Colleges in 1965.

From 1969 onwards he was associated with the Navy's Russian acquisitions.

During the 1971 War, he was the Fleet Operation Officer Western Fleet. The initial idea for fragile missile boats to be towed by Fleet ships and released like falcons evolved from his practical experiments at sea and culminated in the successful attack on 8 December.

At sea, he served in a battleship, an aircraft carrier, in cruisers, destroyers, frigates, and a minesweeper. He commanded the Cadet Training Ship in 1970 and commissioned the first Russian missile destroyer in 1980.

He was Director Combat Policy and Tactics (1974-77), Chief of Staff Western Naval Command (1981-82), Deputy Chief of the Naval Staff (1983-84), Commander in Chief Southern Naval Command (1985-87) and Vice Chief of the Naval Staff (1988-89).

Admiral Hiranandani was awarded the NM (Gallantry) in the 1971 Indo-Pakistan War, the AVSM in 1979 for his services as Director Combat Policy and Tactics and the PVSM in 1986 for re-vitalising the Navy's training institutions.

After retiring in 1989, he was appointed to the Union of India's Public Service Commission where he found time to acquire a doctorate for his thesis on *The Manning of Future Hi-Tech Military Systems in India - The Political and Economic Challenge.*

On retiring from the UPSC as its officiating Chairman in 1995, Naval Headquarters asked him to write the ongoing official history of the Indian Navy. *Transition to Triumph* covering the period 1965 to 1975 was published in 1999. *Transition to Eminence* covering the period 1976 to 1990 is published in 2004. The next volume covering the period 1990 to 2000 will be published in 2009.

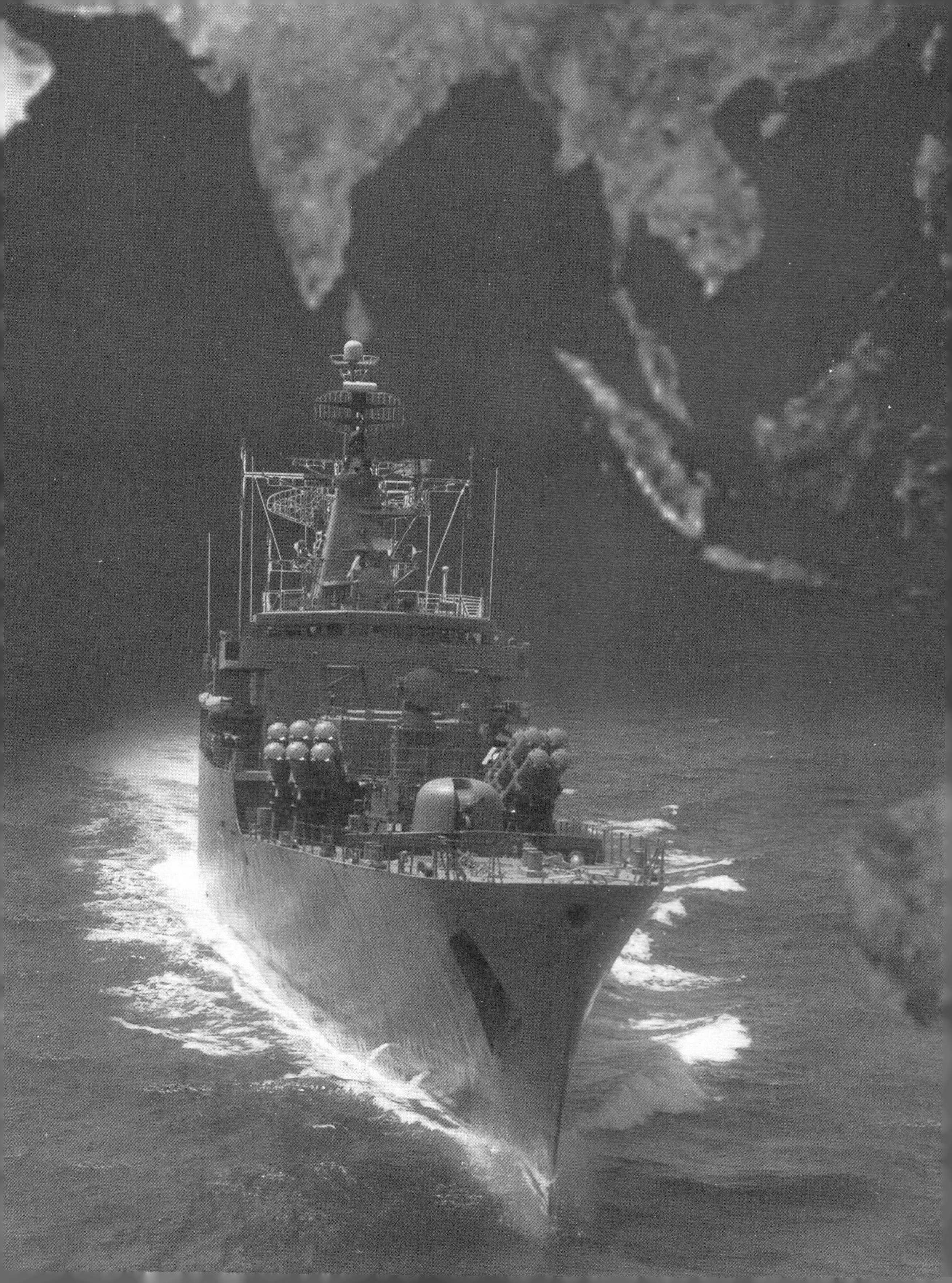

9
INDIA'S MARITIME BACKGROUND

In the Millennia Prior to the Europeans

India's maritime history dates back several thousand years. The world's earliest archaeologically 'dated' tidal dock is at Lothal located at the head of the Gulf of Cambay in Ahmedabad District. It dates back to the Saraswati-Sindhu civilization of over 5000 years ago when the Rann of Kachch was the delta of the mighty River Saraswati.

Kautilya's Arthashastra of the 4th century B.C. describes in detail the Admiralty department in the Mauryan Empire's maritime organization.

From the fifth century AD onwards, the Vijayanagaram kingdom of south India and the Kalinga kingdom of east India extended by sea their maritime and commercial presence to Malaya, Sumatra and Western Java. The Chola dynasty maintained ships for the protection of their seaborne trade. After the decline of the Cholas, the Arabs became pre-eminent in the maritime trade network of the northern Indian Ocean

In the west, Indian trade with the countries in the Mediterranean Sea flowed along two well-established maritime routes – one through the Red Sea to Cairo and Alexandria, and the other through the Persian Gulf and up through Basra and Baghdad to the coast of Lebanon.

The carrying trade across the Arabian Sea to ports in the Red Sea and the Persian Gulf was mainly in the hands of Arab ship owners and Arab navigators. The Arabs, however, were neither instruments of any national policy nor had they the support of any organized government. Their seamanship linked Africa and Persia with Malaya and Indonesia.

The eastern reach of the maritime network extended to the ports of South East Asia and the South China Sea. Shipping was largely in the hands of Gujarati Muslim merchants, plying between Cambay and Malacca. Chinese vessels plied between southern China and Malaya, while Malay and Javanese craft plied in Indonesian waters.

This pattern supported India's overseas trade. Coastal shipping was mainly Muslim, and the shore based merchants feeding the shipping lines were mainly Hindu.

European Contests for Naval Dominance of the West Coast

In 1500, the principal states in India and its west coast were:

- The Muslim Kingdoms of Delhi, Gujarat, Berar, Bidar, Ahmednagar and Bijapur, and
- The Hindu Kingdoms of Vijayanagar, Kannanur, Calicut and Cochin.

Both the Zamorin of Calicut and the Raja of Cochin maintained squadrons of armed ships to counter predators of their coastal trade.

Portuguese cannon-fitted merchant ships arrived on Kerala's Malabar Coast in 1498 to procure pepper. Despite the opposition of the Zamorin's squadron, they were able to control the trade of the Malabar Coast.

The Muslim rulers of the countries at both ends of the western maritime network decided on combined action to counter the Portuguese:

- The rulers of Arabia and Egypt were aggrieved at being deprived of the duties they levied on Indian goods passing up the Red Sea and across Egypt on their way to Alexandria.
- The Muslim kingdoms of Gujarat and Bijapur realized that having dominated the Malabar ports, it was only a matter of time before the Portuguese attempted the conquest of the northern ports. Both kingdoms negotiated with the Sultan of Egypt for joint action against the Portuguese.

The Sultan responded swiftly. His squadron of ships was re-equipped at Suez and reached Aden in 1507.

In 1508, the Portuguese squadron sailed north and was anchored off Chaul when the Egyptian squadron arrived and defeated the Portuguese.

Despite occasional defeats, Portuguese shipborne cannon-power overcame opponents in contests for dominance over the spice and textile trade. From their headquarters at Goa, the Portuguese ruled the North Indian Ocean for almost a century before their maritime supremacy was challenged.

The Dutch and the English entered the Indian Ocean from 1600 onwards. The French came later. For the next two hundred years, armed merchant ships of their East Indian Companies and the squadrons of their respective navies fought each other for control at sea.

European Contests for Naval Dominance of the East Coast

In 1611, the English established their first trading post for cotton textiles at Masulipatam on the Coromandel Coast in southeast India. The Dutch, knowing that the Portuguese had no forts in the islands of Java or Sumatra, went directly to the main source of spices, the Spice Islands -

the Celebes and the Moluccas - and secondarily to India's Malabar Coast for pepper and cardamom and to Ceylon[1] for cardamom and cinnamon. The Dutch succeeded in setting up trading posts on the Coromandel Coast between Madras and Ceylon and at the head of the Bay of Bengal and by the 1660s had steadily replaced Portuguese rule.

The Maratha Navy in the 17th and 18th Centuries

Very early in his campaigns to challenge Mughal power, Shivaji realized the importance of protecting the coastal flank of his land operations. His ships patrolled the west coast defying Portuguese, Dutch, English and Mughal ships.

The Portuguese, headquartered in Goa, took note of the growing power of Shivaji's warships and signed a treaty of friendship with him. The Viceroy undertook to supply him with cannons at a fair price in return for a promise that he would not molest Portuguese ships.

Within fifty years of the English arrival in Surat in 1612, Shivaji attacked Surat from landward in 1664 and again in 1670 with his ships patrolling the sea off Surat.

At the time of his coronation in 1674, Shivaji had 57 major ships of war (excluding smaller craft) with a total fighting strength of over 5,000 men. By the time he died in 1680, Shivaji had a fleet of two hundred fighting ships of various sizes.

In the 1690s, there was a marked increase in piracy. European, Arab and local pirates began to attack and loot Arabian Sea commerce. Arrangements were made between Mughal emperor Aurangzeb and the English, French and Dutch companies trading on India's west coast for the allocation of distinct areas in which their companies' ships were to cruise against the pirates. The Dutch were allocated the Red Sea, the French were allocated the Persian Gulf and the English were allocated the west coast of India.

Shivaji's ablest naval commander, Kanhoji Angre, who rose to be Admiral of the Maratha fleet, countered the English ships. By the early years of the eighteenth century, he established himself as a virtually independent ruler, with his capital at Gheria (now known as Vijaydurg). Kanhoji's ships dominated the entire west coast. All English attempts to capture Gheria from landward and from seaward suffered losses. The English failure to conquer Gheria increased Kanhoji's power and prestige and no trading vessels dared to pass down the coast without an escort of European ships-of-war. In their encounters at sea, English, Dutch and Portuguese ships were unable to decisively overcome Maratha ships.

After Kanhoji died in 1730, his sons maintained the power of the Angre fleet for a further 25 years. After their death, Kanhoji's grandson refused, as his father and grandfather had done, to be subservient to the Maratha Peshwas ruling in Poona. In 1755, the Peshwa sought the help of the East India Company to subjugate the Angres to the rule of Poona. Over the next year, the Peshwa's Maratha troops and Maratha ships joined with English troops and ships of the East India Company and the English Navy to destroy, one by one, the coastal forts under whose cover Angre ships had operated unchallenged for over a century. The end result was English supremacy over the west coast of India.

It is an irony of history that to this day many believe that Indian rulers neglected being strong at sea. It needs to be more widely known that, as happened repeatedly in India, Indians conspired with Europeans to destroy fellow Indians. It was a Maratha Peshwa who sought the help of the English to defeat a fellow Maratha Angre clan whose ships had held sway over the west coast of India for a hundred years against the ships of the Portuguese, the English and the Dutch.

The Anglo-French Contests on the East Coast 1740 to 1815

The geopolitical scene during this period was:

- In north India, the Mughal Empire was in decline. In western India, the Marathas were dominant. In peninsular India, there was competition between the Marathas, the Mughals and the local rulers for regional political primacy.

- In Europe, there were recurrent wars between England and France. These wars were mirrored in India by military campaigns on land The English decided to contest France's Indian Ocean trade. Both sides depended on naval power for success. Clashes took place between English and French ships off India's east coast and in the Bay of Bengal. Seeing Indian rulers fighting each other, the French and English supported rival sides. Indians and Europeans alike looked to their own interests and such gains that might come their way in the confused fighting.

- In the European East India Companies, the greed of employees had started defrauding profits. This led gradually to the taking over of each Company by its Government and the conversion of the territory over which it exercised trade monopoly into a colony. The colony gradually became the source of raw materials for the factories being spawned in Europe's 18th century Industrial Revolution. In turn, the colony became a cosseted market for the products of its colonial ruler's factories. The responsibility for the security of distant colonies passed from each Company's armed merchant ships to each nation's Navy. Mutually expedient political and naval alliances between the European colonising powers safeguarded their maritime trade from disproportionate depletion.

The French moved first into the Bay of Bengal. An improvised fleet from Mauritius relieved the English siege of Pondicherry, blockaded Madras by sea, defeated English ships in two naval actions and drove them up to Calcutta. The French captured Madras in September 1746 but failed to take the neighbouring English fort of St. David which had become a second centre of English power in south India. In 1747-48, aided by the presence of an English fleet, Fort St David withstood a French assault. In the treaty that ended the war, France returned Madras to the English. Similar see-saw contests continued for the next sixty years.

The principal factor for the French lack of success was the English command of the sea. The French could get no Indian allies for lack of money and no money for lack of supply from France.

Until the end of the 18th century, Portugal, Holland, France and England continued to engage in naval encounters in their respective regions to retain local control of the sea routes that linked their overseas colonies to the parent country. England emerged victorious from this struggle.

British Supremacy in the Indian Ocean after 1815 until 1947

In 1805, the English fleet's victory over the combined French and Spanish fleets at the Battle of Trafalgar made England the world's sole superpower. England became Britain. By 1850, India became the hub and the centre-piece of British power in Asia.

To cope with threats to India from landward, Britain crafted Afghanistan and Tibet into 'buffer' states between Tsarist Russia and Manchu China.

India's first revolt for independence in 1857 compelled Britain to formally take over the governance of India and disestablish its East India Company.

Britain's Navy assumed strategic responsibility for the Indian Ocean. It developed naval bases in the North Indian Ocean from where its warships could control the sea lanes and refuel (initially with coal and later with oil), replenish fresh water and provisions, carry out essential maintenance and be dry-docked without having to return all the way to Britain:

Britain's base in:	Controlled the sea lane:
Simonstown (South Africa)	- around the Cape of Good Hope.
Aden	- to and from the Red Sea and the Suez Canal.
Bahrain	- through the Persian Gulf.
Trincomalee (Ceylon)	- across the North Indian Ocean.
Singapore	- at the southern entrance to the Strait of Malacca.

Until the 1914-18 World War, the core of British naval strategy was to prevent rival powers from establishing a naval base in the Indian Ocean. Without access to a friendly naval base, no hostile warship could operate in this huge Ocean for any length of time. In that war, even though the German cruiser Emden successfully bombarded Madras, sank a number of merchant ships and paralysed shipping in the north Indian Ocean for some months, it was eventually cornered and sunk.

In the next World War, Japan occupied India's Andaman and Nicobar Islands in December 1941 and Japanese aircraft bombed Visakhapatnam. Japanese air power, both shore based and aircraft carrier based, inflicted heavy losses on British warships off Singapore, Colombo and Trincomalee. This forced Britain's Eastern Fleet to withdraw to Madagascar off the east coast of Africa and virtually vacate the North Indian Ocean until it could be reinforced in 1944.

The cost of the 1939-45 World War left Britain economically exhausted. The naval predominance that it had in the previous century passed to the United States of America. After this World War, the European colonies in Asia and Africa became independent. Two superpowers, the United States of America and the Soviet Union, shaped new conglomerations under their headship to contest for global dominance. On attaining independence in 1947, India chose not to align with either of these opposing military groupings.

In 1964, Britain's persistent economic difficulties led to its decision to withdraw from its bases "East of Suez." In 1965, before granting independence to Mauritius, Britain leased the island of Diego Garcia to the United States.[2] The US Navy's assumption of strategic responsibility for the Indian Ocean impelled the Soviet Union to deploy its warships to the Indian Ocean from 1967 onwards. Since the Soviet Union did not have any naval base in the region, its warships carried out maintenance at selected anchorages.

10
THE NAVY'S DEVELOPMENT AFTER INDEPENDENCE IN 1947

When India attained Independence from Britain in 1947, she had no overseas territorial interests. The role of the Navy was straightforward - to defend India from seaward aggression.

Independent India's overriding priority was to remove economic and social backwardness. Her foreign policy was one of friendship with all, with particular empathy towards countries that were attaining independence after colonial rule. Territorial border disputes with neighbouring countries that were a legacy of de-colonization were to be resolved bilaterally or in the forum of the British Commonwealth or in the United Nations.

The Acquisition of Ships from Britain

Even though the budget allocations to the Navy after Independence in 1947 were not high, a modest force was gradually built up. India had chosen to remain a member of the British Commonwealth. As part of the "Commonwealth's defence against the Soviet Union", Britain provided warships to India, as it did to the other members of the Commonwealth. Between 1947 and 1961, a reconditioned aircraft carrier, two reconditioned cruisers, six reconditioned destroyers, three new anti-aircraft frigates, five new anti-submarine frigates and six new minesweepers were acquired from Britain.

After China's Intrusion in 1962

The Chinese intrusion in the northern and north-eastern land borders in 1962 inflicted serious and humiliating military reverses. It led to a comprehensive review of national security to determine the pressing requirements of the Army, Air Force and Navy based on the premise of continuing hostility from both Pakistan and China.

To enable the Army to concentrate its attention on the land borders with Pakistan and China, the Navy took over the coastal defence batteries and the responsibility for coastal defence. The

Army also handed over to the Navy the garrisoning and defence of the Andaman and Nicobar (A & N) Islands; this would help to cope with Indonesia's naval build up that had commenced in 1958 with assistance from the Soviet Union.

The 1963 review recommended that in addition to the Fleet in the Arabian Sea, the Navy should have a second Fleet in the Bay of Bengal, along with refit, repair, maintenance and logistic support facilities. Approval was accorded for the acquisition of additional ships, submarines and aircraft. These requirements were projected to the United Stares, the Soviet Union and Britain. Only the Soviet Union was willing and able to meet the Navy's requirements.

The Leander Frigate Project

In accordance with India's resolve to become self reliant for 'core' defence requirements like naval ships and submarines, an agreement was concluded in 1964 for Mazagon Docks to collaborate with British shipbuilders to build three Leander class frigates. The first frigate was to be built in Mumbai in step with its latest counterpart being built in Britain for the British Navy. This would ensure that the personnel deputed from India would acquire hands-on training and facilitate step-by-step transfer of the latest shipbuilding technology.

The Changeover to Russian Naval Acquisitions

In 1965, a succession of events precipitated the decision to acquire the ships and submarines that the Soviet Union had offered in 1964, the acceptance of which had been deferred:

- In April, Pakistan intruded into Indian territory in Kachch.[3]

- In May, Britain informed India that due to its financial difficulties, and having extended credit for the Leander Frigate Project, it could not extend additional credit for building a submarine in Britain.

- In June, Indonesian naval and air intrusions increased in the Nicobar Islands.[4] The Navy recommended an immediate increase in naval presence in the Bay of Bengal to deter such intrusions.

- Britain's inability to extend credit to build a submarine (and its earlier expressed inability to meet the Navy's requirements for ships) and the need for increased naval presence in the Andaman and Nicobar (A & N) islands resulted in the decision to accept the offer of ships and submarines that the Soviet Union had made in September 1964.

In September 1965, an agreement was concluded for the acquisition from Russia of four submarines, a submarine depot ship, five submarine chasers, two landing ships and five patrol boats, all for deployment in the Bay of Bengal and the A & N Islands.

The 1965 War

The Navy did not play any significant role in the 1965 War.

After the Chinese attack in 1962, the Army had handed over the garrisoning and defence of the A & N islands to the Navy. Between 1962 and 1965, close relations had developed between Indonesia and Pakistan. Pursuant to Indonesia's intrusions in the islands in 1964, the Navy maintained a presence there with whatever ships were available.

Pakistan's actions in 1965 became the pattern for its intrusions into India in subsequent years.

The April intrusion in Kachch had ended in a ceasefire. On 5 August 1965, Pakistan launched its Operation Gibraltar. Sixty companies of Pakistani personnel masquerading as freedom fighters, armed with modern weapons and explosives, infiltrated across the cease-fire line over a 700-kilometer front from Kargil to Chamb. Their task was to blow up bridges and disrupt movement, to raid supply dumps, to kill VIP's and to cause arson. The Indians as well as the local Kashmiris were taken by surprise. On 5 August itself, some infiltrators were apprehended. They described the whole plan in a broadcast on All India Radio on 8 August 1965. On hearing this broadcast, Pakistan realized that their secret plan was now open knowledge.

On 9 August, as per its pre arranged plan, Pakistan announced a rebellion in Kashmir Within days, it became clear to the world that this was a propaganda hoax. By 11 August, the Pakistan Army realized that Operation Gibraltar had flopped irretrievably. From 15 August onwards, the Pakistan Army stepped up its violation of the cease fire line on the Srinagar-Kargil-Leh road. Indian troops swiftly occupied critical heights like Haji Pir across the cease fire line and destroyed infiltrator hideouts.

When Pakistan Army HQ found that the tide was turning against them, pressure mounted to retrieve the situation by launching Operation Grand Slam to capture Akhnoor and Amritsar. However, this operation would require the Pakistan Army to move across the international border between India and Pakistan, with all its attendant implications for all-out war. Nevertheless, on 1 September, a column of seventy tanks and two brigades of troops crossed the border and drove towards Akhnoor Bridge to cut off India's supply line from the Punjab to Kashmir. The Pakistan Army achieved initial surprise at Chamb.

When Pakistan's intrusions had started in August, all the operational ships of the Indian Fleet were in the Bay of Bengal. The Fleet suggested returning to Bombay, but was told that it was Government policy to avoid escalating the situation.

When the Pakistan Army crossed the international border on 1 September, the Fleet was recalled to Bombay. Ships headed for Bombay at best speed. They arrived a week later.

Meanwhile, intense air battles took place over Chamb during the next few days. By 5 September, the IAF halted the Pakistani columns before they could reach the Akhnoor Bridge.

On the morning of 6 December, the Indian Army retaliated. It crossed the international border at Wagah and headed for Lahore. As anticipated, the Indian thrust towards Lahore compelled Pakistan to pull back its troops from Kashmir to defend Lahore.

On the afternoon of 7 September, Pakistan Naval HQ directed a task group, comprising its cruiser, five destroyers and a frigate, to bombard the IAF installation near the coastal town of Dwarka the same night. The task group arrived off Dwarka at midnight. Dwarka was blacked out and could only be identified on radar. After a four-minute bombardment, the task group withdrew at full speed. The bombardment caused no physical damage either to the air force installation or to the temple at Dwarka..

However the attack outraged India and humiliated the Navy. There were questions in Parliament as to where the Navy was and what it was doing. The fact was that the ships of the Fleet were just arriving in Mumbai after two months in the Bay of Bengal and were replenishing before sailing for patrol.

Until the ceasefire on 23 September, no contact occurred with any units of the Pakistan Navy. Throughout the Fleet's patrol off the Kachch coast, the policy not to escalate action at sea remained in force.

The ostensible target for the bombardment was the Indian Air Force homing beacon installed on the coast near Dwarka. This provided the fig leaf for the Pakistan Naval Headquarters to symbolically show that it could carry out a hit-and-run raid in retaliation against the Indian Army's crossing the international border on the morning of 6 December in its thrust towards Lahore. The outrage of the Indian public enthused Pakistan to such an extent that to this day it celebrates the day as Pakistan's Defence Day.

The Arrival of the Russian Acquisitions

From 1968 onwards, the Russian ships and submarines that had been contracted for in 1965, started arriving in India. The 1960s technology in these Russian ships was more advanced than the 1950s technology that had entered service between 1958 and 1961 in the new British frigates. On the other hand, these Russian vessels and their machinery and equipment had been designed for the Soviet Navy – for colder temperatures, for colder and less corrosive seas, for Russian dietary requirements, for Russian naval norms of fresh water consumption/capacity, etc.

Almost as soon as the ships and submarines commissioned, the Indian side started suggesting modifications. Interaction between the Navies and with the designers and shipyards in the Soviet Union enabled modifications to be incorporated to the extent possible before delivery. This positive interaction led the Navy to place orders in end 1971 for five more submarine chasers and four more submarines.

The Acquisition of British Anti-submarine Helicopters

In 1964, the US had loaned the Pakistan Navy its first submarine, the Ghazi. After the 1965 War, the Pakistan Navy's programme for acquiring French Daphne class submarines with longer-range homing torpedoes made it clear that it intended to concentrate its offensive potential in submarines and deploy its surface flotilla defensively.

At this time, the US Navy was developing anti submarine helicopters equipped with 'dunking' sonar that could be lowered into the sea while hovering and also armed with an air dropped, anti submarine homing torpedo. This combination overcame the hazard that surface ships faced of being torpedoed when combating a submarine. Firstly, being airborne, the helicopter could not be hit by a submarine torpedo. Secondly, by having a sonar device, whose depth under the surface could be raised and lowered to obtain maximum detection range, the helicopter could overcome adverse hydrology and deprive the submarine of its ability to evade detection by lurking below the temperature layers of the sea. Britain was developing equivalent Seaking helicopters for its Navy.

In 1969, approval was accorded for the Navy to acquire from Britain six Seakings and their homing torpedoes. In 1970, an order was placed for their delivery in 1971. The Seakings arrived a few months before the Indo Pakistan war broke out in December 1971.

The Acquisition of Russian Anti-ship Missiles

After the Pakistan Navy's bombardment of Dwarka in the 1965 War, the Navy had been deliberating measures for the defence of the Kachch coast against Pakistani hit-and-run raids.

In the early 1960s, the Soviet Union had supplied small, fast, thin-skinned boats armed with surface-to-surface missiles (SSMs) to the Indonesian and Egyptian Navies. These boats had also been offered to the Indian Delegation that had visited Russia in 1964, but their acquisition had been accorded lesser priority because their effectiveness had yet to be proved in war.

In the 1967 Arab-Israel war, anti-ship missiles fired from an Egyptian missile boat deployed for harbour defence, summarily sank, within minutes, an approaching Israeli frigate at a range well beyond the latter's guns. This incident heralded the eclipse of gun battles between warships and the transition to swift missile engagements beyond visual range.

In 1968, approval was accorded to acquire missile boats from Russia, primarily to deter Pakistani ships from bombarding the Kachch coast. In 1969, an agreement was concluded with Russia for the supply of missile boats.

By 1971, four submarines, a submarine depot ship, a submarine rescue vessel, two landing ships, five submarine chasers, five patrol boats had arrived from Russia and were based in Visakhapatnam. Though they had been acquired for the Bay of Bengal and the A & N Islands, they had started exercising in the Arabian Sea as well. The eight missile boats were based in Bombay.

To support these Russian acquisitions, work had commenced in

- Visakhapatnam on the construction of a new Dockyard, of submarine support facilities, of torpedo preparation facilities and of training facilities.
- Bombay for the missile preparation facilities.

The 1971 War

During the months preceding the outbreak of war in December 1971, an innovative concept was evolved, and rehearsed, of Fleet ships towing the tiny, limited range but fast and powerful, missile boats into the Arabian Sea from where they could be detached, under escort, to carry out a missile attack and to be taken back in tow after the attack.

Operations in the Arabian Sea

The Pakistan Air Force attacked Indian airfields on 3 December. The Navy's first missile boat attack on Karachi was launched on night 4/5 December from the south along the coast - it sank a Pakistani destroyer and a coastal minesweeper. The Pakistan Navy Flotilla prudently withdrew into Karachi harbour.

The Western Fleet launched the next attack from the southwest on night 8/9th December – the missile boat attack on Karachi was to be accompanied by the gun bombardment of towns on the Makran coast to divert attention from the missile boat group. The bombardment group, under the cruiser Mysore, called off the bombardment after apprehending a Pakistani merchant ship after it had distracted attention towards the Mysore group by transmitting an SOS to Karachi. The missile boat attack achieved surprise. Fortuitously, one missile set Karachi's fuel storage [5] tanks on fire and another hit the Pakistan Navy's tanker, the Dacca, at the anchorage.

The two missile attacks, within days of each other, resulted in international shipping seeking from the Government of India in New Delhi assurance for safe passage out of Karachi. The Western Fleet had achieved dominance of the sea approaches to Karachi.

Anticipating that the Pakistan Navy would deploy its latest French submarines off Bombay and the Kachch coast, the Navy's shore stations had been plotting the positions of a Pakistani submarine's transmissions.

On 8 December, two Indian naval frigates, Khukri and Kirpan, were sailed from Bombay to 'flush' this submarine away from the Kachch coast where ships were assembling for the third missile boat attack on ships off Karachi.

On the evening of 9 December, the Pakistani submarine Hangor successfully torpedoed and sank the Khukri. A sustained anti-submarine operation over the next four days was unable to prevent the Hangor's return to Karachi.

On the evening of 10 December, an Alize aircraft was sent to probe suspicious activity near the Indo-Pakistan naval border off Jakhau. It ended in a fatal chance encounter. The Alize fell prey to a Sidewinder missile fired by a homeward-bound Pakistani fighter aircraft.

Operations in the Bay of Bengal

In the Bay of Bengal, there was no threat from enemy surface warships. At the very beginning of the war, the submarine threat ceased to exist after the US-loaned, Pakistan submarine, Ghazi, exploded at the entrance to Visakhapatnam harbour whilst on a mine-laying mission. There was no air threat after the IAF attacks grounded all Pakistan Air Force aircraft in East Pakistan.

Ships of the Eastern Fleet enforced contraband control and cut off supplies to Pakistan's troops in East Pakistan. Naval aircraft operating from the aircraft carrier Vikrant immobilized Pakistani merchant ships and cratered airstrips which Pakistani forces might use to escape capture. An amphibious landing at Cox's Bazaar cut off the road escape route into Burma.

Pakistan's forces in the east laid down their arms on the 16 December, after a short, sharp campaign of thirteen days and the new nation of Bangladesh came into being.

In the west, the war ended on 17 December when Pakistan accepted India's offer of a ceasefire.

Lessons of the 1971 War

The Navy learnt invaluable lessons in this war. Two conclusions shaped the Navy's planning for its future warships.

The first conclusion was that large-calibre gun battles between warships were no longer likely. Anti-ship missiles would dominate future surface warfare. Small calibre guns and decoys would be essential for defence against incoming missiles. This led to the decision that future ships should be equipped with SSMs, high rate of fire small calibre guns and anti missile decoys.

To start with, a squadron of eight longer-range missile boats was acquired from Russia. The next step was to make wider use of the Russian missiles. A complete Russian missile boat system was lifted out of a boat and fitted on board a British frigate. Another system was lifted out and reinstalled as a missile coast battery to defend Mumbai.

From 1976 onwards, all new ships like the Russian 800-ton ocean-going rocket boats, the Russian 5,000 ton Rajput class destroyers, the Indian Godavari class frigates, the Indian Khukri class corvettes, and their successors, were equipped with missiles, rapid fire guns and active/passive means of anti-missile electronic warfare. In due course, the new improved Seaking helicopters and the new Sea Harrier carrier-borne aircraft were also equipped with anti ship missiles.

The second conclusion was that defence against a modern submarine required a three dimensional anti-submarine capability:

- In the air – Maritime Reconnaissance Anti-Submarine Warfare (MRASW) aircraft and better anti-submarine helicopters with better torpedoes.
- In ships – longer range sonars, longer range anti-submarine weapons and better prediction of hydrological conditions to assist detection.
- Under the sea –Hunter-Killer (SSK) submarines

Indo-Russian Interaction in Indigenous Warship Design

As soon as ships and submarines started arriving from Russia from 1967 onwards, it became evident that they had been designed for operating in a cold and dry climate and in cold, low salinity seas. They had not been designed to operate in the hot, humid climate and warm, saline, highly corrosive seas typical of Indian waters. As the Navy gained experience of operating Russian vessels in tropical conditions, it identified the essential alterations and additions required to 'tropicalise' the Russian designs.

Each vessel was covered by a twelve-month guarantee period during which the Russian 'guarantee specialists', deputed to India by the respective 'Original Equipment Manufacturers' (OEM) factories, rectified shortcomings and replenished spare parts consumed. The feed back by these specialists to their respective factories in Russia reinforced the Navy's projections to the Russian side of essential improvements. As a result, each successor series of Russian acquisitions gradually became better than their predecessors.

The contracts for the supply of ships, submarines and aircraft catered also for their associated infrastructure. These encompassed facilities for the maintenance, repair and refit of equipment, the storage, maintenance and preparation of weapons, the training of crews in schools fitted with identical equipment and simulators on which the crews could practise operating procedures and tactics.

The Navy's successful operations during the 1971 Indo-Pakistan War led to two positive developments:

- Approval was accorded for the Navy to acquire Russian MRASW aircraft, Russian rocket boats and Russian destroyers having Russian anti submarine helicopters.
- The Russian side responded positively to the Navy's requests for better equipment in future Russian acquisitions and for the installation of Russian weapons in Indian-built destroyers, frigates and corvettes interfaced with European and indigenous equipment.

This expanding scope of cooperation in warship building required that agreements be signed at the right time, to ensure that equipment reached the warship building yards - Mazagon Docks in Bombay, Garden Reach in Calcutta and Goa Shipyard - at the right time to avoid delays in their construction schedules. A Joint Indo-Russian Group on Shipbuilding was set up in 1987 to smooth the way and clear problems in the licensed production of missile boats and the design assistance for the fitment of Russian weapon systems in indigenous warships.

The Acquisition and Indigenous Construction of German SSK Submarines

The Navy's quest for the indigenous construction of submarines had started in the 1970s. In 1981, after ten years of evaluations and negotiations, contracts were signed for two submarines to be built in Germany followed by two to be built in Mumbai using equipment packages received from Germany. The contract had an option clause for two more submarines.

As had been done in the case of the Leander Frigate Project, personnel were deputed to learn all aspects of submarine design, construction, overseeing, factory acceptance and sea trials. To facilitate transfer of technology, personnel from the Navy and from Mazagon Docks were deputed to Germany whilst the first two submarines were being constructed. These two submarines arrived in 1987.

The 3rd and 4th submarines being built in Mazagon Docks took longer to complete than had been anticipated -welding technology had to be readjusted for Mumbai's hot and humid climate. These two submarines were commissioned in 1992 and 1994.

The performance of the four German submarines fully met the Navy's operational requirements.

Negotiations for the 5th and 6th submarines had to be discontinued in 1987 because of a sharp fall in the value of the rupee versus the deutsche mark from the mid-1980s onwards. This made the German equipment packages very expensive. The option for the fifth and sixth submarines was not exercised.

In the 1990s, evaluations and negotiations commenced on the resumption of submarine construction. These concluded in 2005 when approval was accorded for the construction by Mazagon Docks in Mumbai of six French design submarines capable of firing anti-ship missiles whilst submerged.

11
CONTEMPORARY NAVAL WARFARE

The preceding narrative of the Navy's development since 1947 has discussed how the lessons of war led to improvements in ship design to cope with advances in technology. The ensuing narrative discusses the prevailing concepts of naval warfare and the roles of the navy's ships, submarines and aircraft.

Surface Ships

The mass of a navy is comprised of surface ships. These are designed for specific roles:

- Aircraft carriers (also known as Air Defence Ships) form the core of a Fleet or Carrier Task Force – they are huge, well armed, floating airfields far out at sea from which carrier-borne aircraft can repeatedly take off and land instantly. Their role is discussed later.

- Destroyers are larger than frigates which are larger than corvettes, all of which have the endurance to operate far from the coast and withstand very rough seas. Destroyers and frigates are equipped for the anti-ship, anti-aircraft and anti-submarine roles. Corvettes, being smaller, are equipped for either anti-ship or anti-submarine roles – they are less costly and affordable in larger numbers.

- Offshore Patrol Vessels (OPVs) also have the endurance to operate far from the coast and withstand very rough seas but they are lightly armed because their role is 'patrol' and not 'combat'. Being less costly, they are affordable in larger numbers.

- Fleet tankers refuel ships far out at sea and also provide them with fresh water and provisions to enable them to stay at sea instead of having to return to harbour.

- Landing Ships are designed to transport troops and their vehicles and land them on beaches in places where there are no jetties. These are being superseded by larger ships whose heavy-weight-lifting helicopters will quickly air lift men and material directly to where they are required inland rather than go via the beach.

Aircraft Carrier INS VIRAAT

Guided Missile Destroyer INS RANVIJAY

Indigenous Project 16 Guided Missile Frigate INS GANGA

Hunter-Killer Submarine INS SHISHUMAR

Indigenous Leander Class Frigate INS UDAYGIRI

Indigenous Project 16 A Guided Missile Frigate INS BRAHMAPUTRA

Guided Missile Destroyer INS RANVIR

Anti-ship missile fired by INS BRAHMAPUTRA

Western Fleet ships in line abreast on both sides of the Fleet tanker

Indigenous Sail Training Ship INS TARANGINI

Indigenous Guided Missile Destroyer MYSORE following VIRAAT

On board the first guided missile destroyer INS RAJPUT after her arrival from Russia in 1980. Sitting left to right: Mr Rajiv Gandhi (later Prime Minister of India), Commanding Officer Captain (later Vice Admiral) G M Hiranandani explaining the ship's fire power, and Mr Shivraj Patil (then Minister of State for Defence and presently Home Minister of India)

Aerial view of the new Naval Base under construction at Karwar on the west coast of India

Vertical / Short Take & Land (VSTOL) naval fighter, the Sea Harrier

Indigenous Guided Missile Destroyer INS DELHI

Guided Missile Stealth Frigate INS TALWAR

Amphibious Landing Platform Dock INS JALASHWA

Naval Operation Cactus that forestalled the coup in the Maldive Islands in November 1988. Merchant ship, hijacked by the fleeing leaders of the coup, being "persuaded" by small calibre naval gunfire to stop and surrender the Maldivian VIPs taken as hostage.

Eastern Fleet ships exercising in the Bay of Bengal with indigenous Fleet Tanker INS ADITYA

Sea Cadet Corps Sail Training Ship VARUNA

Indigenous DHRUV (Advanced Light Helicopter-ALH) landing on Indigenous Guided Missile Frigate INS GANGA

Missile armed ships of the Western Fleet - destroyer (right), frigate (centre) and corvette (left) berthed alongside in Mumbai

Indigenous Cadet Training Ship INS TIR

Sea Harrier doing a Short-Take-Off from VIRAAT's ski-jump. Dual role (anti-submarine and anti-ship) Seaking helicopters parked on the right of the ski jump with rotor blades folded.

Landing Ship INS GULDAR capable of beaching five main battle tanks during amphibious operations

Marine Commandos (MARCOS) exercising infiltration from seaward

Stamp commemorating the Indian Navy's International Fleet Review 2001

Stamp commemorating India's 5000-year-old Maritime Heritage

Combat Information Centre

Western Fleet ships replenishing at sea

Floating Dock FDN 1 in Port Blair.

Marine Commandos exercising slithering down to a ship's deck from a hovering commando-carrying Seaking helicopter

Western Fleet in Line Ahead formation

Western Fleet steaming-past the flagship VIRAAT

Indigenous CHETAK helicopter on the flight deck of a ship

Seaking helicopters in formation

- Coastal defence is provided by missile boats and minesweepers. Coastal patrols are carried out by seaward defence boats (SDBs) and fast attack crafts (FACs).
- Survey ships carry out hydrographic surveys for updating charts, training ships train cadets and a variety of vessels fulfil specific functions.

Innovation in Warship Design and Indigenous Research & Development

'Hybridisation' had began in 1976, when the entire SSM system and close-range gun system of a 200-ton Russian missile boat was disconnected and re-installed in a 15-year old British anti-submarine frigate along with the latest Italian electronic warfare systems, thereby giving the Fleet an ocean-going, missile warfare capable frigate.

From the 1980s onwards, new ships entered service with their new sonars, radars, electronic warfare systems, missiles, torpedoes propulsion and power generation systems. The Navy was fortunate to acquire such a wide variety of technologically modern equipment.

The Navy's gifted young officers grasped the opportunity to improvise in warship design by successfully integrating and installing Russian, European and indigenous systems and equipment in Indian-built hulls.

An entire Russian anti-ship and anti-aircraft missile system and gun system, identical to the newly acquired 800-ton Russian rocket boats [6], along with indigenous and European equipment, was installed in a hull design evolved from the preceding Leander class frigates. Three Godavari class frigates entered service in the 1980s.

Once the intricacies had been mastered of interfacing electrical and electronic equipment, regardless of their origin, voltage and frequency, there was no looking back.

Appreciative of the success of Indian innovation, the Russians offered their latest weapon systems for the series of ships that followed - the 1,500 ton missile corvettes of the Khukri class, the 4000-ton missile frigates of the Brahmaputra class and the 6,500 ton missile destroyers of the Delhi class.

To replace the earlier missile boats, licensed production commenced in India of 400-ton gas-turbined missile boats.

Side by side with these innovations in warship design, the Naval R&D laboratories developed sensors, weapons and systems better suited to India's tropical climate conditions and with maximum indigenous content.

The outstanding naval R&D project of the 1980s was the APSOH sonar, specially designed for hot and humid tropical conditions and proved at sea in Indian waters for a full year during extensive trials. Its derivatives continue to be fitted in the Navy's latest ships, twenty years after it was first developed. Less spectacular, but equally important R&D developments for the Navy were the ongoing development, and improvement, of the sensors, weapons systems and munitions already in service.

Innovation in surface warship design continues to flourish in all the new types of warships being built in India's warship building yards.

India's Warship Building Yards

The 5,000-year-old Malabar teak beams found in the ruins of Ur in Babylon at the head of the Persian Gulf testify to the antiquity of Indian shipbuilding.

The English East India Company set up its first trading post at Surat in 1613. Ships displacing 800 to 1,000 tons built of Malabar teak at Daman, were found to be superior to their English-built counterparts, both in design and durability. In 1661, the English East India Company moved its headquarters from Surat to Bombay. The Bombay Dock, still in use today in the Naval Dockyard, was completed in July 1735. In 1735, at the invitation of the Company, the talented young Parsi shipbuilder, Lovji Nusserwanji Wadia, moved from Surat to Bombay to start building ships.[7]

The Bombay Dock in the Naval Dockyard could not cope with the increasing demand for Indian-built ships. A new dock at Mazagon was completed in 1774. Ships started being built there in 1801. Mazagon's first dry dock was built in 1839 and the second in 1865.

Between 1735 and 1884, a succession of master shipbuilders of the Parsi Wadia family built, in Mazagon and in the Bombay Dockyard, more than 300 ships for the Company, for the British Navy and for private owners.

The oldest Bombay-built wooden warship still afloat today, HMS *Trincomalee,* was launched in Mazagon in 1814 and fitted out in the Bombay Dockyard between 1814 and 1817; it carried 46 guns and displaced 1,065 tons.[8]

In the second half of the 19th century, several developments took place.

- Two major British shipping companies, Peninsular and Orient (P & O) and British India Steam Navigation Company (BISN) established a monopoly of all sea-borne passenger traffic and sea-mail delivery 'East of Suez'. In 1860, the P & O acquired Mazagon Docks at Bombay to build, maintain and repair its ships operating in the Arabian Sea and westward and southwest ward of India. BISN acquired the Garden Reach Workshops in Calcutta to repair and maintain its ships operating in the Bay of Bengal and eastward and south-eastward of India.

- The Suez Canal opened in 1869 and seaborne traffic multiplied.

- Steel hulls replaced wooden hulls. Steam-driven ships replaced sail driven ships. Mazagon Docks' famed skills of building wooden warships were no longer relevant in building steel-hulled, steam-driven warships. Mazagon Docks switched to develop ship repair skills. In every British war east of Suez, ships of both these companies were converted in their dockyards at Bombay and Calcutta to ferry thousands of Indian troops to and from the battle zones.

Post-Independence Acquisition of Mazagon Docks Limited (MDL) and Garden Reach Workshops - GRW (later renamed Garden Reach Shipbuilders and Engineers-GRSE)

In 1957, V. K. Krishna Menon became India's Defence Minister. He was an unwavering pioneer of self-reliance in defence particularly for core requirements of warships, tanks and aircraft. The choice for building warships lay between MDL and GRW. He appointed a committee to look into MDL's capabilities for building frigate-sized warships in the context of the pending offer of the P&O Group to sell MDL to the Government of India. After negotiations, both MDL and GRW were purchased in a package deal. In the years since then:

- MDL has built, and continues to build, the Navy's missile armed destroyers, frigates, corvettes and submarines.
- GRW, renamed as GRSE, has built frigates and missile-armed corvettes, a fleet replenishment tanker and fleet tugs, survey ships and fast attack craft. It is building the Navy's offshore patrol vessels, landing ships and fast attack craft.

Goa Shipyard Limited (GSL)

In the end 1940s, the Portuguese had established a small yard to repair the barges that carried iron ore down the rivers to ships at anchor for export to Japan. After Goa was liberated from Portuguese rule in 1961, the yard was entrusted to MDL Mumbai on lease.

When the lease agreement with MDL ended in 1967, the yard became an autonomous subsidiary of MDL and renamed itself as Goa Shipyard Ltd (GSL). Under this subsidiary arrangement, MDL provided GSL with technical know-how for shipbuilding and ship repair, assistance in securing orders and purchase of materials, and transferring, at book value, machinery from MDL's yard at Mumbai.

GSL expanded the existing workshops, set up new workshops and built new slipways and berths. Between 1980 and 1987, GSL built minor war vessels like Landing Craft, Torpedo Recovery Vessels, survey craft and Seaward Defence Boats.

From 1990 onwards, GSL has built offshore patrol vessels, survey ships, missile craft, extra fast attack craft and a sail training ship

Augmenting India's Warship Building Capacity

The Navy's experience has shown that the rate at which its warships retire from operational service is, and will remain, higher that the rate at which their indigenous built replacements can enter service. Short and long term measures are in hand to increase warship-building capacity:

- In Mumbai, MDL is acquiring an additional 'Wet Basin'.
- In Kolkata, GRSE have taken over Rajabagan Shipyard and Hooghly Dock & Port Engineers is being revived.

- In Goa, GS is setting up a new building dock and a ship-lift system.
- In Vizag, Hindustan Shipyard is being revived.
- Private sector organizations like ABG Shipyard and Bharati Shipyard are engaged in capacity-enhancement. ABG Shipyard has commenced mobilising funds for its 'green-field' project in Surat.

Submarines & Anti-submarine Warfare

Submarines are potent weapon platforms. Their traditional tasks have been to attack enemy warships and enemy submarines. In recent years, submarines have successfully attacked land targets at long ranges with precision guided missiles fired when submerged.

Submarines are designed to minimise the chances of their being detected and to withstand anti submarine attacks. They are equipped with accurate and lethal weapons both for attack and for self defence.

Stealth and Snorting

The modern, diesel-electric propelled 'hunter-killer' (SSK) submarine is very stealthy, provided the utmost care has been taken to minimize its self noise.[9] Carefully handled, she can be as quiet as the grave. At low speeds, the soft hum of her electric propulsion power unit is almost undiscernable. Unlike a nuclear propelled submarine, she has no reactor requiring the support of numerous mechanical subsystems, all of which are potential noise-makers.

When dived, the submarine is propelled by a set of huge electric batteries. Depending on how much battery power is used up (the higher the speed, the quicker the battery runs down), the batteries have to be recharged regularly by diesel generators. Just as a car's diesel engine needs an intake of air, so does the diesel engine of a submarine's diesel generator.

Batteries can be recharged either by being on the surface to suck in air (more vulnerable) or by remaining at periscope depth and sucking in air through a tube called a 'snort' (less vulnerable). When a diesel-electric submarine comes to periscope depth and raises her snort mast to suck in the air required to run her diesel generators to recharge her batteries, the process is known as 'snorting'.[10]

Even though a submarine hull is not visible whilst snorting, the acoustic noise of its diesel engines can be heard by another submarine if in the vicinity. Its periscope and snort masts that stick out just above the water can be detected on ship and aircraft radar. The ions in the diesel exhaust can be 'sniffed' by detectors fitted in MRASW aircraft. There is little a submarine can do about these limitations, except to stop recharging and 'crash dive' every time it detects the radar emissions of an approaching anti-submarine aircraft / helicopter or its passive sonar hears the noise of approaching ships.[11]

Submarine Tactics

During war, a submarine patrolling in adversary waters comes up near the surface only when she has to recharge her batteries. Even then, she will only do so at night, and for the shortest possible time, so as to minimize the chance of being detected and "localised" for attack.[12]

For successful attack, a submarine relies on concealment and surprise rather than concentration of force. A submarine attack is usually more successful because it detects the ship earlier and can deliver a high weapon-density attack before being detected - this ability provides surprise.

To avoid mutual interference, submarines operate singly. When more than one submarine is deployed in the same adversary region, each submarine is given a specific demarcated area in which to operate.[13]

A submarine stalks its prey just like a cat stalks a mouse. The crux of submarine tactics is to sink the adversary ship, get away from the scene and survive the anti submarine counter attack that is sure to follow.

Should anti submarine forces succeed in 'localising' a submarine, it either fights like a cornered beast or goes silent and tries to slip away.

Anti-submarine Tactics

Sound Propagation under the Sea

Sound is virtually the only form of energy that propagates usefully underwater, where electromagnetic waves, including light, are rapidly attenuated.

The temperature of the sea becomes cooler as depth increases. This change in temperature affects the velocity (and hence the path) of the sound waves transmitted by a sonar. Temperature layers in the sea refract sound waves much the same way that a prism refracts light.[14] As a result, a shadow zone is created which is not insonified. Under these conditions, by operating in this shadow zone, a submarine **can, without** being detected, move close to its target to within torpedo firing range

The way to **detect** a submarine lurking in a shadow zone or below a temperature layer is to position the **sonar,** or the SSK submarine, in the same shadow zone or below the same temperature layer. This is achieved on board ships by lowering a large towed sonar dome (called Variable Depth Sonar - VDS) to the required depth whilst maintaining speed. Anti submarine helicopters lower their small sonar dome (called "dunking sonar") whilst hovering. MRASW aircraft achieve this by dropping sonobuoys.

In anti-submarine tactics, MRASW aircraft, ASW helicopters, sonar-fitted warships and 'hunter-killer' submarines are the predators and submarines the prey.

The crux of anti submarine tactics is to compel a submarine by repeated and intense attacks to remain dived and thereby exhaust its batteries, reduce its mobility to evade attack and hit it with weapons to force it to surface and surrender.

MRASW Aircraft

When a submarine is sighted on surface or it makes a wireless transmission that betrays its presence by giving Direction Finding (D/F) equipment an approximate position of the transmission, a MRASW aircraft speeds to that position.

The objective of an MRASW aircraft is to obtain an initial position of a submarine. For example, an indication on its detector of the "magnetic anomaly" created by the submarine's steel hull or a "sniff" of diesel exhaust ions from a submarine recharging its batteries or a disappearing radar contact suggestive of a submarine having crash dived to evade detection. As soon as the MRASW aircraft obtains an initial position, it drops a number of sonobuoys to "localise" the contact and if possible to attack it with its air dropped homing torpedoes. The MRASW aircraft, therefore, is in the first line of submarine location, detection and attack.

Modern conventional submarines (and their batteries) are designed to minimize the need to snort to a few hours every few days. This time is too short for an MRASW aircraft to get an accurate enough localisation. On the one hand, an MRASW aircraft may choose not to use its radar to detect the submarine's snort mast sticking out of the water because to do so would reveal its presence to the submarine. On the other hand, continuous patrols by MRASW aircraft operating their radar can constrain a submarine's freedom to recharge its batteries by causing it to crash dive to evade being "localised".

In rough weather and poor sonar conditions, localization by an MRASW aircraft could be as poor as an area of several hundred square miles, almost like looking for a needle in a haystack.

However as soon as a submarine has been localized and accurately tracked, the aircraft attacks it with its own weapons. Additional MRASW aircraft can help to maintain pressure on the submarine to remain dived.

Anti-submarine Ships and their ASW Helicopters

As soon as the MRASW aircraft localizes a contact, ships designed for anti-submarine warfare and having anti-submarine helicopters on board proceed to the area where the MRASW aircraft's sonobuoy patterns have been laid.

Anti-submarine helicopters can search a given area quicker and, being airborne, they cannot be hit by submarine fired torpedoes. After ascertaining the progress on localization from the MRASW aircraft, they either lay their own sonobuoys to localize the contact or use their dunking sonar to search. If the sonar search is passive, their sonars listen for tell tale noise of submarine presence.

If the sonar search is active and a submarine is present, the sonar receives an acoustic echo back from the submarine hull and the submarine can be tracked by sonar transmissions. As soon as the submarine's position and movements are accurately determined, helicopters release their anti submarine homing torpedoes. Helicopter attacks continue until the submarine is hit and sinks or she surfaces and surrenders because her batteries have exhausted.

A submarine knows when it has been detected on sonar - it can hear the sonar transmissions. It knows it will come under attack. It will try to evade helicopters. When cornered, it may choose to attack the ship because a ship can be instantly sunk by submarine-fired torpedoes.

The role of the anti-submarine ship is to stand-off outside the range of the submarine's torpedoes and keep on re-fuelling and re-arming the helicopters until the submarine nears exhaustion. She then moves in to fire intensive barrages of anti submarine rockets and homing torpedoes.

Submarine Search and Kill (SSK) Submarines

The advantage of having submarines to search and kill enemy submarines is that both share the same undersea environment to detect and track each other, without being limited by shadow zones and temperature layers. Using active sonar would immediately betray presence. Detection by passive sonar requires high skills in picking up even the faintest noise emanating from the adversary SSK. It is for this reason that, during SSK design and construction, great importance is given to making machinery silent and minimizing noise levels.

SSKs are deployed in areas where there is likelihood of encountering only adversary submarines and there is no possibility whatsoever of own anti submarine forces mistaking own SSK for an adversary SSK. The contest is between two dived SSKs.

Once the adversary SSK has been detected and tracked and the fire control problem solved, wire guided torpedoes are fired in a way that the adversary SSK would not have time to fire its own wire guided torpedoes in self defence. In effect, this means getting as close as possible to the adversary before firing - but in so doing, it also means that the adversary SSK may hear you and fire its own torpedoes before you fired yours. The direction from which the retaliatory torpedoes would come is usually predictable - straight down the direction that the incoming torpedo's homing head starts its active sonar transmissions. At this moment, decoys can be released to seduce the incoming torpedo away.

Submarine warfare and anti submarine warfare are driven by constantly evolving frontier technologies. With long years of peace interspersed by sharp short-duration wars, success depends on:

- Continuous, intensive training of highly motivated and experienced personnel.
- Sustaining the highest standards of material readiness of the platforms (ships, submarines, aircraft and helicopters) and their sensors (sonars, radars and EW) and their weapons (torpedoes, rockets and depth bombs).

The Navy's Submarine Arm

The eight Russian submarines that were inducted in the 1960s and 1970s, were replaced by more modern Russian submarines in the 1980s and 1990s. These are being modernized and given the capability to fire missiles when submerged.

The four SSK submarines of German design that entered service in the 1980s and 1990s will be augmented from 2012 onwards by a new design of French submarines that will be capable of firing anti ship missiles whilst submerged.

These submarines will be built at Mazagon Docks in Mumbai.

The Role of the Navy's Air Arm

The unique characteristics of a Fleet at sea are its mobility and its capability for carrying out a variety of missions. There is however a tactical problem that has to be solved.

Even when a Fleet is operating outside the range of the adversary's shore-based strike aircraft, there will always be the threat from the adversary's long range Maritime Reconnaissance "MR" aircraft whose anti ship missiles can damage surface ships. There is therefore the need for own carrier-borne aircraft to shoot down the adversary MR aircraft as quickly as possible after it is detected and before it releases its missiles at our ships. Only aircraft carriers can provide this capability.

The setting is straightforward. The adversary's MR aircraft has to determine, on its radar, the direction and distance from which to fire its missiles. To do so, it has to expose itself to detection by the target ship's radar and other electronic detection systems. Starting from the time that an MR aircraft is detected, a carrier-borne aircraft, either already airborne on patrol or ready on deck for immediate take off, is required to shoot down the MR aircraft before it releases its missiles or, if the missiles have already been released, to overtake the slower MR aircraft and shoot it down thereby reducing the number of MR aircraft that the adversary can deploy against our Fleet.

Carrier-borne aircraft are designed to be very versatile:

- For the "air defence" role they have radar to detect and track adversary aircraft and air-to-air missiles (AAMs) to shoot them down.
- For the "anti-ship attack" role, they can be armed with anti-ship missiles.
- For the "ground attack" role, they can be armed with precision guided weapons and bombs.
- For the electronic warfare role, they can be fitted with the appropriate pods.

The Navy acquired its first aircraft carrier, the Vikrant, second-hand from Britain in 1961. It acquired its second aircraft carrier, the Viraat, second-hand from Britain in 1987. Vikrant was decommissioned in 1997. It will be grouted in the seabed in Bombay Harbour as a museum. Viraat is still in service.

In 2004, approval was accorded for the acquisition of the aircraft carrier Gorshkov, second-hand from Russia, along with its MIG-29 aircraft specially adapted for carrier-borne take off and landing. In an extensive, four-and-a-half year refit, the Gorshkov would be extensively refitted and nearly 80 per cent of its equipment replaced with modern equivalents. Expected to commission as INS Vikramaditya in 2009, she would serve the Navy for over two decades, during which period the indigenous Air Defence Ship (ADS) would enter service.

In 2000, approval was accorded for the construction of the indigenous ADS in Kochi Shipyard. Construction of the ADS commenced in 2004. It is expected to commission by 2012.

12
NAVAL OPERATIONS AFTER 1971

Operations in Support of the Indian Peace-Keeping Force (IPKF) in Sri Lanka

Operations started with the induction in naval ships of the troops of the IPKF on 29 July 1987. The de-induction started in August 1989 and by October 1999, the bulk of the IPKF had withdrawn. The operation terminated on 24 March 1990, when the final contingent of the IPKF sailed out of Trincomalee on board ships of the Eastern Fleet. When the last elements withdrew, there still had been no solution of the political problem.

These operations fulfilled the strategic objectives that had been indicated by Prime Minister Rajiv Gandhi in his letter to President Jayawardene when the Indo-Sri Lankan Accord had been signed in July 1987.

From the Navy's point of view, the objective was met that for the strategic security of India's southern seaboard "Trincomalee or any other ports in Sri Lanka will not be made available for military use by any country in a manner prejudicial to India's interests".

As soon as the last contingent of the IPKF was de-inducted from Sri Lanka in March 1990, ships and aircraft of India's Navy and Coast Guard were deployed to patrol the Palk Strait to curb the smuggling of arms and ammunition, poaching, illegal immigration and activities of Sri Lankan Tamil militants. This patrolling continues round the clock.

Operations in Support of the Maldivian Government in 1988

Whilst operations in Sri Lanka were in full swing, a crisis erupted in Male, the capital of the Maldive Islands. On the night of 2/3 November 1988, between 300 and 500 armed, Tamil/Sinhala speaking mercenaries landed in Male harbour by boats from a mother ship and captured key locations in an attempted coup. The President went into hiding and, in the early hours of 3 November, sought India's help and immediate intervention.

During the next 24 hours, the nearest naval ships were diverted to Male at maximum speed and naval reconnaissance aircraft established surveillance over the Maldive Islands. On the night of 3/4 November, IAF aircraft landed troops on Male's airport on Hulule Island.

On learning that these troops were headed for Male, the mercenaries hijacked a merchant vessel named 'Progress Light' and, taking Maldivian VIP hostages with them, set course for Colombo. In Male, law and order was restored as soon as Indian troops arrived there on the morning of the 4th November.

The frigate Godavari was diverted towards Colombo to embark, by helicopter, the team of negotiators that had been flown from Male to Colombo.

During the night of 3rd / 4th, naval reconnaissance aircraft shadowed all moving contacts. At first light on the morning of the 4th, the aircraft confirmed detection of the Progress Light and homed the frigate Betwa as soon as it reached on the night of 4th / 5th. Godavari, who had by then embarked the negotiators from Colombo, arrived by midday on the 5th November.

Negotiations for the release of the hostages made no progress. The mercenary leader insisted that the Progress Light would proceed only to Colombo and demanded intervention by an international team. The Sri Lankan Government intimated that the rebel ship would not be allowed to enter Sri Lankan waters. The Maldivian Government desired that the Progress Light should not be allowed to proceed to Colombo.

Throughout the 5th, the negotiators were unable to dissuade Progress Light from steaming towards Colombo. On the 6th morning, when Progress Light was 60 miles from Colombo, pressure commenced with small arms fire, followed by air-dropped depth charges ahead of the ship, followed by a gun broadside across the bows. When, despite a final warning, Progress Light still refused to stop, a broadside was fired on the forward cargo section. The ship stopped immediately.

Naval commandos boarded the ship and rescued the hostages. Godavari's helicopter evacuated the injured hostages to the Military Hospital at Trivandrum. Progress Light, already listing and flooding, capsized on the 7th morning, 56 miles southwest of Colombo. The mercenaries were handed over to the authorities at Male.

Patrols along the Gujarat and Maharashtra Coasts

Consequent to the bomb blasts in Mumbai in March 1993, patrols were instituted to prevent terrorists from landing arms, explosives and contraband. Joint patrols by the Navy and the Coast Guard continue to this day

Deployments in Support of the United Nations Humanitarian Operations in Somalia September 1993 to December 1994

Somalia is located on the Horn of Africa at the western end of the Arabian Sea. Civil war erupted there in 1993. The United Nations called for assistance to control the situation, provide humanitarian aid and transport UN personnel, relief and medical supplies. In response to this call, a naval task group was despatched to Somalia. It remained on station off the Somalian port of Mogadishu for the next ten months.

Anti-militant Operations in the Andaman Islands

The proximity of the Andaman Islands to countries on the eastern rim of the Bay of Bengal has fostered gun-running and arms smuggling by militant, dissident and secessionist groups of the region.

Small vessels smuggle arms / explosives and infiltrators to the northern Andaman Islands for onward transmission to militant groups in the states of northeast India

Based on intelligence inputs, the Navy and Coast Guard conduct joint operations to interdict this infiltration and gun running activity

Deployment of the Fleet in the North Arabian Sea during the Kargil War 1999

In February 1999, Pakistani troops masquerading as freedom-fighters, crossed the Line of Control in the Kargil area of Kashmir. They established themselves on the heights overlooking Kargil to disrupt traffic on the National Highway carrying supplies from Srinagar to Leh, The intrusions were detected in May.

The Army and the Air Force commenced intense artillery and air attacks to destroy the intruder's hide-outs.

The Navy sailed the Western Fleet from its base in Mumbai to the North Arabian Sea to establish surveillance and ensure that there was no surprise from seaward. In early June, units of the Eastern Fleet joined the Western Fleet.

In the ensuing weeks, as military and air operations continued in Kargil, the Fleet alternated between "offensive" and "offensive defence" deployments. To exert psychological pressure, ships patrolled off the Makran Coast along which Pakistan's oil supplies come from the Persian Gulf. Aware of this vulnerability, the Pakistan Navy avoided any naval misadventure.

The intensive firepower of Indian artillery, the precision strikes by Air Force aircraft and the determination of troops in adverse weather steadily evicted the intruders from post after post. Facing defeat, Pakistan withdrew its troops behind the LoC. Operations ended on 16 July 1999.

Deployment of the Fleet in the North Arabian Sea in 2002 after Terrorists' attack on Indian Parliament in December 2001

In October 2001, terrorists attacked the Jammu and Kashmir Legislative Assembly in Srinagar. On 13 December 2001, terrorists carried out a partially successful attack on the Indian Parliament in Delhi whilst it was in session. The nation was outraged. The Indian Armed Forced mobilized for war. This was the first full scale mobilization after the 1971 war with Pakistan.

The Army completed its mobilization in the first week of January 2002 and the army and the air force were ready for operations in Punjab and Rajasthan. The Western and Eastern Fleets had assembled in the North Arabian Sea.

Before war could erupt, diplomatic intervention by the United States and European governments led to the Pakistani President's broadcasting an assurance on 12 January that Pakistan would not permit any terrorist activity from its soil. Offensive preparations were stopped but India's Armed Forces remained deployed.

On 14 May 2002, terrorists struck the family quarters of the Indian Army garrison near Jammu. By this time, the Pakistan Armed Forces had mobilized. It was assessed that large scale offensive action by India would lead to a stalemate. Despite the high tension, war did not erupt.

India's Armed Forces remained deployed until 16 October 2002 when the Government ordered demobilisation.

Assistance Rendered by the Navy in Peacetime

Integral to the Navy's day to day operations and training are the myriad facets of the assistance that the Navy provides in peacetime at sea and in the island territories. Together with the Army and the Air Force, the Navy assists in disaster relief operations, particularly in the calamitous cyclones that devastate the coastal areas every year.

The Indian Ocean Tsunami of December 2004

Seabed tectonic plate movement off the north-western tip of the Indonesian island of Sumatra at midnight of the 25/26 of December generated the largest regional oceanic wave in living memory. In a few hours, it devastated the coastlines of countries on the rim of, and in the vicinity of, the Bay of Bengal.

As soon as the tsunami[15] hit the A & N Islands and the east coast of India, naval divers were rushed to the affected areas. Within 36 hours, naval ships and aircraft were on their way with rescue teams and relief materials to afflicted Indian territories and coastal areas, as well as to Sri Lanka and Maldives in response to their appeal for urgent assistance.

Within days, it became the largest rescue, relief and rehabilitation operation ever undertaken by the Navy. Naval ships and aircraft delivered over 910 tons of relief materials, including 450 tons of provisions and 20 tons of medicines in addition to drinking water, blankets, sheets, durries, tents and portable generating sets, together with portable engineering support tools and material. Teams of army engineers embarked in ships to help restore electricity and water supplies. During the relief operation:

- 32 ships, 21 helicopters, 8 Dornier and Islander aircraft and over 5,500 personnel had been deployed. The Navy spent a total of 775 ship days.

- Hundreds of personnel from the naval establishments at Visakhapatnam, Arakkonam,

Chennai, Tirunelveli, Ramnad and Kochi assisted the tsunami-affected coastal areas of Andhra Pradesh, Tamil Nadu, Pondicherry, Kerala, the A & N Islands and the neighbouring countries of Sri Lanka, the Maldive Islands and Indonesia.

- Three survey ships were converted into 46-bed hospital ships - INS Nirupak operated off Banda Aceh in Indonesia, INS Jamuna in Trincomalee in Sri Lanka and INS Nirdeshak in the A & N islands. Scores of medical teams were deployed on the east coast, the A & N islands and in the neighbouring countries.

- Three ships operated in the Maldive Islands. The first arrived in Male on 28 December, the second on 29 and the third on 30th. To restore water supply in the affected islands, naval rescue and relief teams pumped out seawater from flooded wells and restored electricity by repairing water-logged portable generating sets.

By the first week of January:

- In Sri Lanka, three ships in Trincomalee and two ships in Galle had set up medical camps and relief kitchens. They commenced supporting rehabilitation activity and providing technical assistance. Naval divers cleared the harbour of sunken boats, trawlers and debris. Naval Hydrographers prepared and handed over fresh hydrographic surveys of both harbours to facilitate safe navigation.

- In Indonesia, two ships were deployed off the west coast of Sumatra with relief supplies, medicines and medical stores.

Evacuation of Civilians from Lebanon

In July 2006, Israel reacted vehemently to the rocket attacks on Israeli settlements by Lebanon's Hezbollah. Israel declared the city of Beirut and its seaward approaches and southern Lebanon as a war zone and carried out unrelenting air attacks. A large number of civilian Indian citizens and their families sought swift and safe exit out of the war zone.

A four-ship flotilla of the Western Fleet was in the vicinity, paying goodwill visits to ports in the Mediterranean and Red Seas. After obtaining assurance from Israel of safe passage into and out of Beirut Harbour, these four ships carried out non-stop shuttle trips between Beirut and Larnaca in Cyprus from where the evacuees proceeded by Air India to destinations in India. When the operation terminated, 2,280 persons, mostly Indian, had been evacuated. This total included nationals of Nepal, Sri Lanka and Lebanon. India was the only country whose evacuation operation extended beyond its own nationals.

Operation Sukoon was the largest post-independence civilian-evacuation operation undertaken by the Navy.

13
THE FORESEEABLE FUTURE

In earlier centuries, the European East Indian Companies needed oriental aromatics, textiles and spices. They made extensive investments and contested for dominance of Indian seas. Today, global interest centres on the oil and gas resources of the Persian Gulf. American and European oil companies have made extensive investments in the Persian Gulf where the US Navy is the predominant naval power.

Over the years, the US has developed the island of Diego Garcia, 1,000 miles south of India, into a large base for its naval and air forces deployed in the Indian Ocean. Diego Garcia will remain indispensable for the US's Indian Ocean operations.

MARITIME CHOKE POINTS

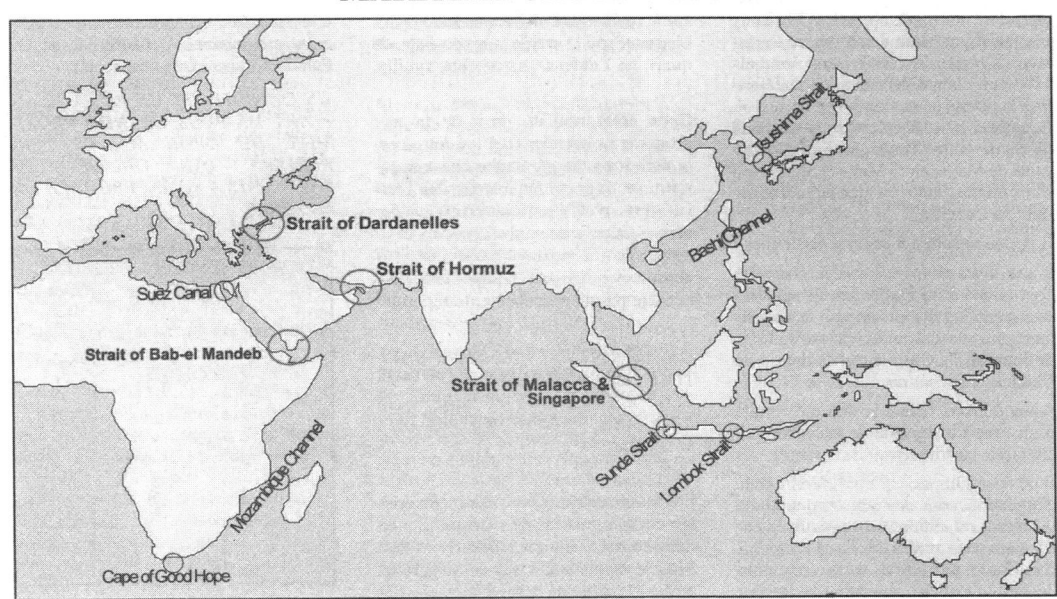

India, China and Japan, whose economies are critically dependant on the uninterrupted flow of oil and gas, have a strong interest in ensuring that the sea lanes through which their oil comes do not fall under the sway of entities potentially hostile to their well-being.

There is basis for serious unease, particularly where international straits are located. The Strait of Hormuz, the Strait of Bab el Mandeb, the Strait of Malacca, and the Mozambique Channel are zones where the seaways narrow to an extent that makes it easy for militant and terrorist entities to dislocate the flow of tankers carrying petroleum products and ships carrying high value cargo. The safety of the sea lanes compels the deployment of naval forces in these regions.

The US, Japan and Europe expect India's Navy to share responsibility for the security of these sea lines of communication

China's Navy too is concerned about the security of its oil and gas supplies coming by sea. China has financed the development of Pakistan's ports in the North Arabian Sea and China's Navy will have access to these ports.

The primary area of Indian maritime interest ranges from the Persian Gulf in the north to Antarctica in the south and from the Cape of Good Hope and the east coast of Africa in the west to the Strait of Malacca and the aechipelagos of Malaysia and Indonesia in the east.

India's geo-strategic significance is evident from the above map. India encounters Russia and China in the north, the Persian Gulf in the west and Southeast Asia in the east. In the North Indian Ocean extending from the coast of Africa to the coast of Malaysia, India is the largest, stable, respected, multi-ethnic democracy. It does not have any overseas territorial interests. It has a modern and efficient Army, Navy and Air Force. It is accepted as a rising economic power having the potential, and the responsibility, for a regional role in the years ahead.

Today, bilateral agreements foresee cooperation in protecting the sea lines of communication. Navies of the United States, Russia, France, Britain, Southeast Asian and Indian Ocean countries look forward, just much as the Indian Navy does, to holding joint exercises and building bridges of friendship.

The Navy's foreseeable role is clear:

- To deter aggression from seaward, should aggression occur, to deliver a punishing response?
- To be a catalyst for peace, harmony and tranquillity in the Indian Ocean Region by extending friendship and co-operation to maritime nations on the rim of the Indian Ocean.

14
THE INDIAN NAVY TODAY

The Indian Navy is a three dimensional force operating above the sea, on the sea and below the surface of the sea.

Command and Control

The Chief of the Naval Staff (CNS) exercises operational and administrative control of the Navy from the Integrated Headquarters of the Ministry of Defence (Navy) located in New Delhi. He is assisted by the Vice Chief of the Naval Staff (VCNS) and three other Principal Staff Officers - the Deputy Chief of the Naval Staff (DCNS), the Chief of Personnel (COP) and the Chief of Material (COM).

The Navy has three commands, each under the control of a Flag Officer Commanding-in-Chief:-

- The Western Naval Command (HQ in Mumbai).
- The Eastern Naval Command (HQ in Visakhapatnam).
- The Southern Naval Command (HQ in Kochi).

The Western and the Eastern Naval Commands are operational commands and exercise control over operations in the Arabian Sea and the Bay of Bengal, respectively. The Southern Command is designated as the Training Command.

The spearheads of the Navy are its fleets - the Western Fleet based at Mumbai and the Eastern Fleet based at Visakhapatnam. Besides, a flotilla each is based at Mumbai, Visakhapatnam and Port Blair (in the A & N Islands) to provide local naval defence in its respective region. Ships are based also at other ports along the east and west coasts and in the island territories They help to maintain a naval presence,.

Naval Officers-in-Charge (NOICs) under each command are responsible for the local naval defence of the ports under their jurisdiction.

The defence of the A & N Islands is the joint responsibility of all three Services and is coordinated by HQ, A & N Command, located at Port Blair. This is India's first Unified Command and is headed by a C-in-C from the three services in rotation.

The local naval defence of the Lakshadweep group of islands in the Arabian Sea is the responsibility of the NOIC, Lakshadweep.

The Flag Officer Naval Aviation (FONA) based at Goa, oversees all matters pertaining to the Navy's Air Arm.

The Flag Officer Submarines (FOSM) is also the Assistant Chief of the Naval Staff (Submarines) based in Naval Headquarters, New Delhi. He oversees all submarine aspects.

Base Support

To maintain, repair and refit ships and submarines, the Navy has two major dockyards located at Mumbai and Visakhapatnam. The new third major Dockyard at Karwar, supported by its Base Depot, INS Kadamba, will be the second Dockyard on the west coast; when fully developed, it will have the capacity to berth and sustain most of the ships on the western seaboard.

Smaller "Ship Repair Yards" at Kochi and Port Blair are equipped to support the ships based at these ports and to assist visiting ships.

Major aircraft maintenance and repair organizations exist at Kochi and Goa.

Logistic support is provided by a network of Weapon Equipment Depots (WEDs), Naval Armament Depots (NADs) and Naval Store Depots (NSDs), which are located on the east and west coasts. Base support facilities are manned largely by civilian personnel.

Training

The Southern Naval Command headquartered in Kochi administers several naval training establishments:

- **INS Mandovi** located in the estuary of the River Mandovi at Goa is the temporary Naval Academy. All officer candidates (other than NDA entry) undergo initial naval training which varies from six months to 3 years. The new Naval Academy nearing completion at Ezhimala on the coast of Kerala near Kannur (Cannanore) is supported by its Base Depot, **INS Zamorin,**

- **INS Chilka** located on the shore of Orissa's Chilka Lake is the initial training establishment for sailors. After recruitment, all sailors undergo basic naval training here for six months before they branch off into various trades for specialist training.

- **INS Venduruthy** located on the Ernakulam Channel in Kochi is the parent establishment housing the professional and specialist training schools for the Executive/Seaman branch. Specialist schools impart training to officers and sailors in anti-submarine warfare, navigation and direction, communications and electronic warfare, seamanship, maritime warfare & tactics, underwater diving, leadership etc.

- **INS Dronacharya,** located on Kochi's sea shore for firing practices, imparts basic and advanced specialist training to officers and sailors in Missile and Gunnery Warfare.
- **INS Garuda,** located alongside INS Venduruthy on Willingdon Island in Kochi, houses the School for Naval Airmen (SFNA) and the Naval Institute of Aeronautical Technology (NIAT) which impart basic and advanced specialist training to officers and sailors of the Air Arm in the respective specialisations.
- **INS Satavahana** located at Visakhapatnam imparts basic and advanced specialist training to officers and sailors of the Submarine Arm. The Escape Training School (ETS) for submariners functions under INS Satavahana.
- **INS Shivaji** located on a lake at Lonavla between Mumbai and Pune imparts basic and advanced marine engineering training to officers, artificers and sailors, where Officers undergo B Tech level training at the Naval College of Engineering.
- **INS Valsura** located near the coast at Jamnagar (Gujarat) imparts basic and specialist electrical and electronic training to officers, artificers and sailors of the Electrical branch.
- **INS Hamla** located on the coast at Marve near Mumbai imparts training to officers and sailors of the Logistic cadre. Officers graduate in the Long Logistics Management Course. Sailors undergo courses related to catering, stores management and computers.
- **INS Kunjali** located in south Mumbai imparts training to officers and sailors of the Provost (i.e. Naval Police) branch.
- **Other Centres.** Training is a continuous process on board ships and submarines and also in the air squadrons based in INS Hansa in Goa, INS Rajali in Arakonam (near Chennai), INS Utkrosh in Port Blair and Naval Air Station Kunjali in Mumbai.

15
Career Opportunities

Executive Branch

In the Navy, the path to Command is through the Executive Branch. Only sea- going officers of the Executive Branch can exercise command of ships, submarines and aircraft. Seaman officers of the Executive Branch can specialize in one of the following:

- Aviation
- Submarines
- Gunnery & Missiles
- Anti-submarine Warfare
- Navigation and Direction
- Communications
- Hydrography
- Diving

Officers who have specialized in Logistics, Naval Armament Inspection, Law and Air Traffic Control also form part of the Executive Branch.

Engineering Branch

The Navy's ships, submarines and aircraft are fitted with propulsion systems and machinery of the latest technology. Engineer officers are responsible for keeping their machinery systems serviceable. Opportunities exist for them to work in shore jobs in naval dockyards and indigenous production units. An Engineer officer's career is interspersed with technical courses up to post-graduate level in India and abroad to keep abreast of developments in engineering technology.

Naval Architects specialize in warship construction. They are involved with the design, construction, quality control repair and new construction work of warships and submarines. With the increased tempo of indigenous construction of ships and submarines, the Naval Architect cadre provides excellent opportunities for keeping abreast of international developments in ship building technology. The Navy has the largest pool in India of trained Naval Architects.

Electrical Branch

A warship is a mini floating city with its integral power generation and distribution system. In addition, complex missile systems, underwater weapons, fire control systems, radars, sonars, radio communication and electronic warfare equipment are a significant segment of a warship's equipment. Most of this equipment is either computer-based or computer-aided and incorporates the latest technology in electronic engineering. Electrical officers are responsible for keeping all this equipment working at peak efficiency. As in the case of Engineer officers, excellent opportunities exist for post-graduate courses in India and abroad.

Officers of the Engineering and Electrical Branches can also volunteer to serve in the Naval Air Arm and the Submarine Arm.

Education Branch

Education officers impart scientific and methodical instructions, including theoretical aspects of technical subjects, to all Branches of the Navy and also in general education. Additionally, an Education officer can specialize in Oceanography and Meteorology and also in some of the specializations of the Executive Branch.

16
Officers' Entry

Branch/ Type of Entry	Unmarried Men/Women	Age limit (Years)	Educational Qualifications
Executive Branch			
Permanent Commission			
• Cadet Entry (NDA) (Through UPSC)	Men	16 ½ - 19	10 + 2 or equivalent with Physics & Maths.
• Cadet Entry (10+ 2) Naval Academy (Through UPSC)	Men	16 ½ - 19	10 + 2 or equivalent with Physics & Maths.
• Graduate Special Entry Naval Academy (written examination conducted through UPSC)	Men	19 - 22	B. Sc. (Physics & Maths) or BE.
• NCC Special Entry Naval Academy	Men	19 - 24	B. Sc. (Physics & Maths) or BE with Naval Wing Senior Div NCC 'C' Certificate.
• Direct Entry Naval Armament Inspection Cadre	Men	19 ½ - 25	Degree in Electronics/Elect / Mech. Engg or Post Graduate Degree in Electronics or Physics.
• Direct Entry Law Cadre	Men	22 – 27	A degree in Law qualifying for enrolment as an advocate under the Advocates Act 1961 with minimum 55% marks.

Short Service Commission			
• Law Cadre	Men & Women	22-27	A degree in law qualifying for enrolment as an advocate under the Advocates Act 1961 with minimum 55% marks.
• Logistics Cadre	Men & Women	19 ½ - 25	BA (Economics), B. Com, B. Sc. (IT), CA/ICWA, Catering Technology, BCA or MCA, BE/B Tech in Mechanical, Marine, Electrical, Marine, Electronics, civil Computer, IT, Architecture with minimum 60% marks in aggregate.
• Air Traffic Control	Men & Women	19 ½ - 25	A first class science graduate with Physics & Maths or M.Sc. with Physics or Maths securing minimum 55% marks.
• Hydro Cadre	Men	19 ½ -25	A graduate with minimum 55% marks with Physics & Maths in 10+2 level. Graduate with Physics and Chemistry In 10+2 level holding Naval Wing Senior Division 'C' Certificate or BE/B Tech with minimum 55% marks in any discipline.
• Executive (General Services)	Men	19½ -25	Same as Hydro Cadre.
Education Branch			
Permanent Commission	Men	21-25	A Master's Degree in one of the following with at least 50% marks: - (a) Physics (with Maths in B.Sc.) or (b) Maths (with Physics in B. Sc.) or Engineering Degree in Elect/Electr/Computer Science/IT with minimum 60% marks.
Short Service Commission	Men & Women	21-25	- do-

Officers' Entry

Branch/ Type of Entry	Unmarried Men/Women	Age Limit (Years)	Educational Qualifications
Engineering Branch (Marine Engineers)			
Permanent Commission			
• Cadet Entry (NDA)	Men	16 ½ - 19	10 +2 or equivalent with Physics & Maths.
• Cadet Entry (10 + 2) (Tech)	Men	16 ½ - 19	10+2 or equivalent with Physics, Chemistry & Maths with (minimum 75% marks in aggregate of PCM), minimum 50% marks in English either in 10th or 12th class).
Short Service Commission			
• Direct Entry (Tech Branch)	Men	19 ½ - 25	A degree in Marine/Mech / Aeronautical/ Control/ Metallurgical/Production Engineering with minimum 55% marks.
• Direct Entry (Submarine Cadre)	Men	19 ½ - 25	BE (Mechanical) with minimum 55% marks.
• University Entry Scheme (UES)	Men	19 - 24	A degree in course mentioned at (c) above with minimum 60% marks up to VI th semester.
Engineering Branch (Naval Architects)			
Permanent Commission			
• Cadet Entry (10 + 2) (Tech)	Men	16 ½ - 19	10+2 or equivalent with Physics, Chemistry & Maths with (minimum 75% marks in aggregate of PCM, minimum 50% marks in English either in 10th or 12th class).
Short Service Commission			
• Direct Entry (Naval	Men/Women	21 - 25	BE in Mechanical / Metallurgy/ Architecture Civil/ Aeronautical/Naval Architecture with minimum 60 % marks.

• Special Naval Architect Entry Scheme (SNAES)	Men/Women	21-25	BE in Naval Architect with minimum 60% marks.
Electrical Branch			
Permanent Commission			
• Cadet Entry (NDA)	Men	16 ½ - 19	10 +2 or equivalent with Physics & Maths.
• Cadet Entry (10 + 2) (Tech)	Men	16 ½ - 19	10+2 or equivalent with Physics, Chemistry & Maths with (minimum 75% marks in aggregate of PCM, minimum 50% marks in English either in 10th or 12th class).
Short Service Commission			
• Direct Entry (Technical Branch)	Men	19 ½ - 25	Degree in Elect/Electronics/ Avionics / Instrumentation & Control/ Telecommunication Engg with minimum 55% marks.
• Direct Entry (Submarine Cadre)	Men	19 ½ - 25	Degree in Elect/Electronics/ Telecommunication/Control Engg with minimum 55% marks.
• University Entry	Men	19 - 24	A degree in courses mentioned Scheme (UES) at (c) above with minimum 60% marks up to VIth semester.

Terms and Conditions

1. Women are eligible to apply for Short Service Commission in Air Traffic Control, Law and Logistic Cadres, Education Branch and Naval Architecture cadre.

2. The duration of a Short Service Commission is 10 years, extendable to 14 years.

3. The training of officers selected through the above entries normally commences in the month of Jan & Jul every year. Advertisements calling for applications from eligible candidates are published in *Employment News* and important newspapers in Apr/May and Sep to Nov. The selection procedure includes UPSC written examination (for NDA, 10+2 (Ex) and Graduate Special Entry), Interview at a Services Selection Board and Medical Examination in Apr/May and Sep to Nov.

4. All BE/B Tech courses should be AICTE approved, Other degrees should be from a recognised university.

5. University Entry Scheme (UES) is applicable for final year students only (VIIth semester).

6. The above information is broad guidelines and is subject to change as per the induction requirement of the Indian Navy.

7. Further information can also be obtained from JDMPR (R&R), Integrated Headquarters of Ministry of Defence (Navy), Sena Bhavan, New Delhi – 110 011. Phone : 011- 23010151/ 23010097, Fax (011)23011282. Website: www.nausena-bharti.nic.in

Sailors' Entry

Artificers

Artificers are the top layer of the Navy's technical sailor expertise. They are given extensive training, are better paid and given more responsible technical responsibility. They operate and maintain the Navy's complex systems and equipment. Engineering artificers operate and maintain steam powered machinery, diesel engines and gas turbines. Electrical artificers maintain guided missiles, automatically controlled weapons, radars, sonars, computers, radio and electronic systems.

The Navy trains its own artificers. The Naval Artificer Apprenticeship Diploma is recognized by the Ministry of Human Resource Development.

Seaman Branch

This is the largest branch of the Navy's sailors. Seamen duties include operating weapons and weapon systems, radars and sonars and shipboard seamanship. Every Seaman specializes in one of the following disciplines:-

- Gunnery - Missiles
- Anti-submarine Warfare
- Navigation
- Communications
- Diving
- Survey.

Engineering Branch

Warships, submarines and naval aircraft are fitted with technologically advanced engineering machinery. Engineering branch sailors operate and keep machinery serviceable. The efficiency of machinery depends on their judgement and skill.

Electrical Branch

Warships, submarines and naval aircraft are fitted with their own power generation and distribution systems. Electrical branch sailors are responsible for the upkeep and maintenance of all electrical, electronic and weapon equipment.

Logistics Cadre

Sailors of this cadre provide logistic support in one of the following disciplines:-.

- Writer
- Stores Assistant
- Steward
- Cook
- Topass.

Medical Branch

Medical branch sailors are trained to look after the sick and the injured. Their specializations include Physiotherapy, Advanced Nursing, Radiography, Laboratory Assistant, Operation Room Technician, Dental Operating Room Assistant, Blood Transfusion etc.

Sailors for the Submarine Arm and the flight crew of the Naval Air Arm

Sailors for these two arms are selected from their parent branches subject to (i) their volunteering, (ii) clearing the aptitude test and (iii) fulfilling medical standards.

Naval Recruitment Centres

Arakonam	Jalandhar	Lonavla (Maharashtra)
Ambala	Jammu	Mumbai
Chennai	Jamnagar	Ranchi
Chilka(Orissa)	Jodhpur	Srinagar
Coimbatore	Kohima	Shillong
Dehradun	Kochi	Shimla
Delhi	Kanpur	Tirunelveli

Guwahati	Kolkata	Vasco-da-Gama (Goa)
Gwalior	Leh	Visakhapatnam

Note:

i) The above centres are not permanent and are subject to change due to administrative reasons.

ii) For Lakshadweep group of islands, Naval Officer-in-Charge, Lakshadweep (NOIC) (L) at Kochi should be contacted.

List of Recruiting Offices

Recruitment details can be obtained by contacting/writing to the nearest Zonal Recruiting Officer/Branch Recruiting Office/Airmen Selection Centre/Zila Sainik Board/any of the Naval Recruiting Establishments as below:-

The Recruiting Officer
INS Hamla
Marve Malad
Mumbai – 400064
Tele: 022-8822570 Ext. 268

The Recruiting Officer
INS Chilka
PO. Chilka
Dist: Khurba (Orissa)
Pin: 572037
Tele: 06756-27370

The Recruiting Officer
INS Agrani
Red Fields, Coimbatore
Pin: 641081
Tele: 0422-315531 Ext. 907

The Recruiting Officer
INS Shivaji
Lonavla
Pune-410402
Tele: 0211-84861-67
Ext. 2300

The Recruiting Officer
INS Circars,
Naval Base
Visakhapatnam-530014
Tele: 089-592227

The Recruiting Officer
INS Venduruthy
Naval Base
Kochi-682004
Tele: 0484-662847

The Recruiting Officer
INS Valsura
Jamnagar
Gujarat-361150
Tele: 0288-550264-65
Ext. 2481

The Recruiting Officer
INS Netaji Subhash
Hastings, Kolkata-700022
Tele: 033-2420430 Ext. 492
Tele: 747365 Ext. 126

The Recruiting Officer
National Hydrographic Office
107-A, Rajpur Road
Dehradun, UA-248001

The Recruiting Officer
INS Gomantak
Vasco-da-Gama
Goa-403802
Tele: 0834-513950 Ext. 2702

The Recruiting Officer
INS Jarawa
C/o Navy Office
Port Blair – 744102
Tele: 03192-32012 Ext. 2225

The Recruiting Officer
INS Angre
C/o Fleet Mail Office
Mumbai – 400001
Tele: 022-2661702/2660862

The Recruiting Officer	The Recruiting Officer	The Recruiting Officer
INS India	INS Adyar	Govt. of Jammu & Kashmir
Dalhousie Road	C/o Navy Office	Civil Secretariat
New Delhi – 110011	Chennai – 600009	Srinagar, J&K
Tele: 011-23010610	044-5360531 Ext. 222	Tele:0194-536798

Notes:

1. Dutch ships first visited Ceylon in 1602 and found the local king eager to enlist Dutch help against the Portuguese. In 1610 and 1612, when the Sinhalese again sought help, the Dutch signed treaties. In 1638 and 1639, the Dutch captured Batticaloa and Trincomalee respectively. In 1642, the Dutch and the Portuguese signed a 10-year truce treaty, followed by a 1644 treaty for sharing the cinnamon producing areas. In 1656, a Dutch fleet blockaded and captured Ceylon, except for the Portuguese strongholds of Mannar and Jaffna in the north of Ceylon that were supported by their Indian strongholds of Nagapattinam and Tuticorin. In 1657, the Dutch evicted the Portuguese from Tuticorin and in 1658 from Mannar, Jaffna and Nagapattinam.
2. Located in the middle of the Indian Ocean, Diego Garcia's huge protected anchorage gave it the potential of a ship, submarine and air base. The island's sparse plantation labour was relocated to Mauritius and thereby removed all possibility of political agitation.
3. Prima facie, the intrusion was to resolve a border claim. Subsequent revelations in Pakistani memoirs revealed that it was a rehearsal for a more aggressive operation planned for taking over Kashmir in August-September of that year.
4. Aceh, the northern tip of Indonesia's island of Sumatra and which was struck by the tsunami in December 2004 is separated from Indira Point, the southern tip of India's Great Nicobar island, by a mere 90 miles.
5. A fuel tank at the Keamari tank farm at Karachi was first set on fire by Indian Air Force Hunter aircraft gunfire on the morning of 4th December. This fire must have been brought under control because no fire was visible on the horizon when the missile boats arrived off Karachi at midnight 4th/5th December –In the second missile boat attack on the night of 8th/9th December, the missile that hit a fuel tank caused a huge conflagration that depleted the fuel reserves at Keamari
6. Known in Western naval parlance as "Nanuchkas".
7. This shipyard was the forbear of today's Naval Dockyard at Bombay that celebrated its 250 th Anniversary in 1985. In 1750, it had Asia's first contemporary dry dock. Its predecessor – the dock at Lothal, located at the northern tip of the Gulf of Cambay - was built circa 3000 BC.
8. 'Trincomalee' was constructed by Indian craftsmen using Indian materials under the direction of Jamsetjee Bomanjee Wadia. When she arrived in England in 1819, the Napoleonic Wars had ended. She spent the next 25 years in reserve and became obsolescent. In the 1840s, she was converted into a corvette – 24 large cannons replaced her 44 smaller cannons. For the next 12 years, she sailed the oceans of the world in anti slavery patrols, fishery protection, disaster relief, coastal surveys and Arctic exploration. By the late 1850s, sailing warships had become obsolete. In 1857, she was converted into an afloat training ship for reserve sailors. (Her Bombay-built sister, the 84-gun battleship Ganges, was converted into an afloat training ship for serving sailors.) In the mid 1890s, she was acquired by a philanthropic ship preserver and renamed Foudroyant. In the 1990s, she underwent an extensive restoration. In 2002, she was renamed Trincomalee and was opened to the public as the last classic frigate of the sailing era. (Source: *Trincomalee: the last of Nelson's Frigates* by Andrew Lambert, Chatham Publishing House,2002)

9. Self noise is a critical parameter in submarine design and construction. It has to be rigorously monitored and minimized throughout a submarine's operational service. The ocean offers natural visual and electro-magnetic camouflage. By reducing the noise generated by the submarine at or below the natural noise of the sea, the submarine can effectively conceal itself in the ocean.
10. The "snort" is a waterproof hollow tube that can be raised and lowered when at periscope depth, through which air can be sucked in for the diesel engines. Prior to the invention of the "snort", submarines had to be on the surface to recharge their batteries and when batteries were low, became very vulnerable to ramming, sudden attack, etc. In effect, the snort enables the submarine to recharge batteries with her hull below the surface and only the top of the snort being visible.
11. The great advantage of a nuclear propelled submarine is that it does not need to come to the surface to recharge batteries because it does not need propulsion batteries. The nuclear reactor heats water to generate steam that runs steam turbines that drive the propeller. Its mobility and endurance when dived has none of the limitations of a diesel-electric propelled submarine.
12. Since recharging batteries exposes the diesel-electrical submarine to detection, or in other words to be "indiscreet", the parameter "indiscretion rate" (how often a submarine is compelled to be indiscreet) is regarded as vital as 'self noise' in submarine design and in the technology of submarine batteries.
13. For a short period in 1942-43, during the 1939-1945 World War, German U-boats operated successfully as *'wolf packs'* against convoys in the Atlantic Ocean. This was possible because submarines generally operated on the surface and dived only for the attack.
14. Every sea area is subject to its unique diurnal and season effects and also prevalent and changing currents. The combination of these effects causes different temperature patterns at different depths.
15. A tsunami is a seismically-generated ocean wave triggered by a very high intensity under-sea earthquake. Prior to the recent 25th December 2004 tsunami, reportedly the last tsunami to hit the Indian Ocean was on 26th January 1941.

Indian Air Force

by

Air Marshal (Retd) BK Pandey, PVSM, AVSM, VM

Air Marshal BK Pandey was trained as a transport aircraft pilot in the IAF. He has 5,500 hours of flying experience and has been a qualified flying instructor who has flown a variety of piston-engined, jet-engined and transport aircrafts. He did Higher Air Command Course, Senior Defence Management Course, Air Staff Course and National Security Course (National Defence College) during his illustrious service.

During 1989-92, he served in a diplomatic assignment at the Embassy of India, Kabul in war-torn Afghanistan. He was instrumental in setting up the only English Medium School in Kabul.

Air Marshal was actively involved in IPKF operations in Sri Lanka (1987-88). He held the appointment of Director, Systems Applications at Air HQ, dealing with the development of space programmes and later commanded Air Force Station, Agra. He also held the appointment of Director Operations, Transport and Helicopters. He was Deputy Commandant of the National Defence Academy, Pune. He was also deputed to the Cabinet Secretariat, New Delhi.

Air Marshal was Air Officer Commanding-in-Chief, Training Command at Bangalore.

Air Marshal Pandey is M. Sc. (Defence & Strategic Studies) from Madras University and fellow of the Aeronautical Society of India.

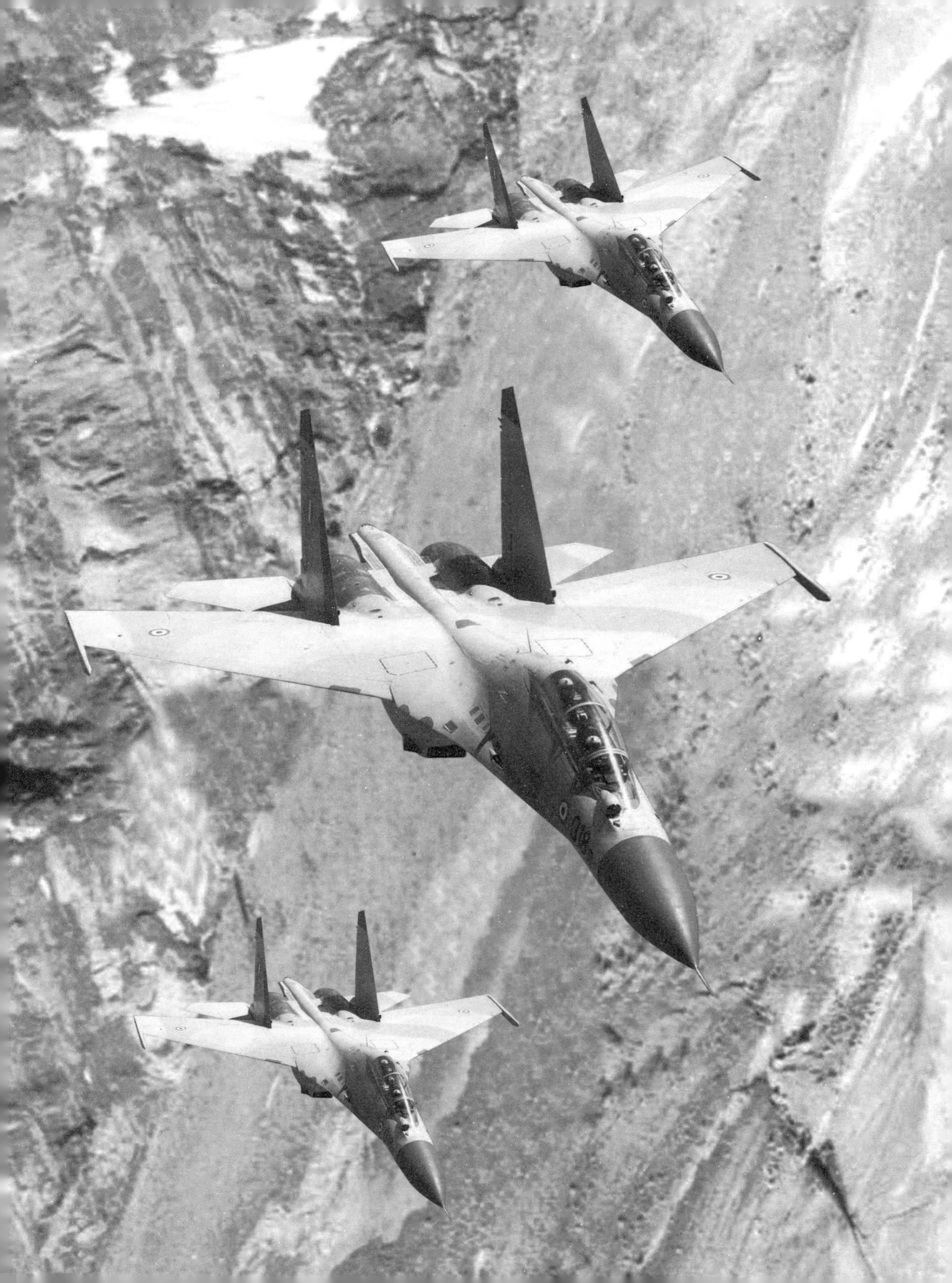

17
THE HISTORY OF THE INDIAN AIR FORCE

Foundation

The IAF is the youngest amongst the three armed services of India. Formally established on 8 October 1932, 'A' Flight of No. 1 Squadron was raised on 1 April 1933 at Drigh Road, Karachi. The flight had four Wapiti II-A bi-planes designed for reconnaissance and attacking ground targets from the air and not for aerial combat with other aircraft. The flight was manned by six British trained Indian officers and 19 airmen. Soon after its formation, 'A' Flight was deployed in operations against the rebel tribesmen in North Waziristan (now in Pakistan) where it had the very first opportunity to gain operational experience. By 1938, No. 1 Squadron had three flights with 16 officers and 662 airmen and was relocated at Ambala.

Burma Campaign

In 1942, during World War II, in an effort by the British forces to check the Japanese advance, No. 1 Squadron under the command of Squadron Leader K.K. Majumdar, affectionately known as 'Jumbo', was reequipped with Lysanders and moved to the East and deployed in Burma (now Myanmar). Following the defeat of the British forces in Burma, No. 1 Squadron was pulled out and sent back to its parent base. However, the squadron now under the command of Squadron Leader Arjan Singh, returned to the eastern front to participate in the allied counter-attack in Burma two years later. This time it was equipped with the latest fighter aircraft, the Hurricane, and rendered an excellent account of themselves. Other squadrons that contributed to the success of the Burma Campaign were No. 7 Squadron led by Squadron Leader P.C. Lal who later became the Chief of Air Staff as Air Chief Marshal, and No. 6 Squadron under Squadron Leader Mehar Singh, another flier known for his bold and daring escapades later in J&K. Jumbo Majumdar who died in 1946 in an accident, was twice decorated with (DFC). Arjan Singh was also awarded the DFC in addition to a host of others who were honoured with some award or the other. The IAF lost 50 pilots in Burma alone. As an acknowledgement of their contribution to the success of the campaign in Burma, the prefix 'Royal' was conferred by the British Government on the IAF, which was now known as the Royal Indian Air Force (RIAF). Through the war years, new squadrons were raised and by 1945, the strength of the RIAF had gone up to nine squadrons with 1,600 officers and 27,000 airmen.

Pangs of Partition

With World War II coming to an end, the RIAF was downsized considerably in respect of manpower. At the time of partition, the available assets were divided between the two newly emerged independent nations with India retaining seven out of the 10 squadrons and roughly 80 per cent of the manpower. The remaining three squadrons formed the nucleus of the newly created Royal Pakistan Air Force (RPAF). Barely two months after partition, the RIAF went into action to foil an attempt by invading forces from across the western borders of J&K State to capture the airfield at Srinagar. The operations against the invaders continued till the ceasefire in January 1949. However, logistic air support to the Indian troops deployed in the border areas continues till today.

Transition to the Jet Age

In the year 1950, India became a Republic and the prefix 'Royal' was dropped. Air Marshal Subroto Mukherjee, a founder member of No 1 Squadron, was the first Indian officer to assume charge of the IAF on 1 April 1954 as C-in-C and CAS. The first major expansion and re-equipment plan was undertaken in the period 1953 to 1960 during which the combat fleet of the IAF moved in to the jet age with the induction of the latest jet fighter and bomber aircraft such as the French Ouragan, renamed *Toofani* and Mystere IVA as also the British Gnat, Hunter and Canberra. The transport fleet was revitalized with the procurement of the American Fairchild Packet C 119 G and the Illyushin (IL) 14 Russian transport aircraft to augment the fleet of DC 3, Dakotas. Mi 4 helicopters were also acquired from the USSR.

Decade of the Sixties

The decade of the sixties began with the trauma of Sino-Indian Conflict in which the IAF did not get a chance to test its mettle, its employment being limited to logistic support and casualty evacuation. However, the conflict served to accelerate the process of expansion. The IAF received the Otter and Caribou transport aircraft from Canada, the MiG 21, SU 7 second generation jet fighter aircraft and AN 12 transport aircraft, and SA 2 SAMs for high altitude area air defence, all from the Soviet Union. The Alouette III helicopters were acquired from France and these were later manufactured under licence by HAL and renamed as *Chetak*. The HF 24 *Marut*, the first and only indigenously designed and built ground attack aircraft, though somewhat under-powered, entered operational service. The first major air war with Pakistan was fought in 1965, primarily on the western front in which the newly inducted Gnat, Mystere, Hunter, *Marut* and Canberra aircraft played a major role. After the war, plans were drawn up to progressively build up the strength of the IAF to 45 Squadrons by the early Seventies with the manpower strength of around 100,000. By 1968, the IAF had 26 combat squadrons and 12 transport squadrons inclusive of aircraft for the MR role.

Liberation of Bangladesh

The decade of the Seventies began with the second major air war with Pakistan in December 1971. Operating on both the western and eastern fronts, the IAF had the opportunity for the comprehensive employment of all the elements. Apart from the intense aerial combat, raids on enemy airfields and attack on important ground targets by combat squadrons on both fronts, a brigade-size para force was dropped by the transport fleet behind enemy lines at Tangail in Bangladesh to hasten the collapse of the resistance by Pakistani forces. The helicopter fleet was employed to enable ground forces to leapfrog across the numerous water obstacles in the eastern parts of Bangladesh. While the IAF maintained an edge over the PAF in operations undertaken in support of ground forces on the western front, the IAF had established total command of the air on the eastern front. The Pakistani regime in Bangladesh capitulated following a precision strike by a MiG 21 on the Government House, while a high level meeting was in progress to review the situation that had become quite precarious after two weeks of fighting.

Post-1971: Emergence of a Regional Power

Plans for a comprehensive Air Defence Ground Environment Scheme (ADGES) was drawn up in the mid-Seventies to provide a gap-free detection capability at low, medium and high altitudes along the entire length of hostile borders. The ADGES was managed by a well-knit command, control and communication structure to provide swift response to intrusion in to Indian airspace. Flying training was reorganized with the commissioning of Air Force Academy at Dundigal, 40 km north of Secunderabad. Induction of a new piston-engined trainer the HPT 32, *Deepak* and a jet trainer the HJT 16, *Kiran*, both designed and produced within the country by HAL. The combat fleet was strengthened further with the induction of the Anglo-French Jaguar in 1978 and the MiG 21 Bis multi-role aircraft, both to be licence manufactured in India by HAL. The Mi 8 helicopter was inducted to strengthen the rotary-wing fleet. The Air Force lost the MR role as it was handed over to the Navy along with existing resources of role-oriented Super Constellation aircraft.

Apart from witnessing the historic first and the only foray in to space by a young IAF officer Squadron Leader Rakesh Sharma, the Eighties were characterized by another round of re-equipment and expansion. The long range strike fleet was augmented by the MiG 27 and the French multi-role Mirage 2000 aircraft. Large numbers of the MiG 27 were licence manufactured in India by the HAL. The HF 24 *Marut* fleet was unfortunately wound down prematurely, a step that dealt a devastating blow to the indigenous effort to design and build combat aircraft. The MiG 23 BN and the Mi 25 Attack Helicopter were inducted for battlefield air support role. The MiG 23 MF replaced the Gnat in the air defence role and the MiG 29 Air Superiority Fighter introduced a qualitative change in the air defence capability as also the tri-sonic MiG 25 took over the role of strategic reconnaissance from the subsonic Canberra. The ageing piston-engined Packet C 119G fleet was replaced by the turboprop AN 32 and strategic airlift capability was acquired through the induction of the four engine long range jet transport aircraft, the IL 76 from the USSR. The Otter was replaced by the Dornier DO 228. Mi 17 and Mi 26 helicopters were inducted to enhance tactical mobility and firepower for ground forces. The ADGES was strengthened with the induction of a family of SAMs such as SA 3, SA 16 and SA 18. The supporting infrastructure by way of additional air command headquarters, wings, stations, logistics and technical management organizations such as equipment depots and base repair depots were also established progressively in different parts of the country. This decade witnessed the emergence of the regional power status of India distinctly visible in the speedy intervention in Sri Lanka and the Maldives at the request of the respective governments. Part of the light helicopter fleet was handed over to the Indian Army for the establishment of the Army Aviation.

Lessons of Kargil

The decade of the Nineties was a period of consolidation and some more re-equipment. The major inductions were the Mi 35 Attack Helicopter to augment the Mi 25 fleet and the SU 30 MKI, perhaps the most potent combat aircraft in the world at that point of time, catapulting the IAF in to the status of one of the leading air forces in the world. However, the IAF together with the Indian Army and the Nation was taken by surprise by the discovery in 1999 of the large scale clandestine Pakistani intrusion into Kargil. The IAF went into action albeit with some delay and very soon, on account of the combined effort of the land and air forces, the peaks were vacated but at a painfully heavy price in terms of young lives lost on the ground and in the air. As important as the successful eviction of Pakistani forces was the fact that the IAF learnt some important and vital lessons from the somewhat brief experience with air operations in the high mountains of Ladakh.

The New Millennium

The new millennium began with the focus shifting to the acquisition of force multipliers such as UAVs, in-flight refuelling aircraft the IL 78, Prithvi SAMs and Airborne Warning and Control System (AWACS) built on the IL 76 platform mounting a Phalcon radar. The first decade of the new millennium will witness selection of a new fleet of Multi Role Combat Aircraft (MRCA), mid-life upgrade of practically all existing frontline aircraft except for the SU 30 MKI, the induction of the indigenous Advanced Light Helicopter (ALH) and the Light Combat Aircraft (LCA). In the middle of the first decade of the new millennium, the IAF stands as the fourth largest in the world with over 10,000 officers, 120,000 airmen and a 1,500-aircraft inventory.

In consonance with the new found regional status, the IAF, in major departure from insular policies followed in the past based on archaic notions of secrecy, opened up to the outside world in a big way. Apart from exchange programmes, a number of joint tactical exercises have been held in the new millennium with the air forces of France, South Africa, USA and Singapore. IAF combat aircraft were flown halfway across the globe to Alaska and South Africa for the joint exercises with foreign air forces, accompanied by in-flight refuelling aircraft and duly supported by its own strategic airlift capability. The IAF aerobatic team, the *Surya Kiran*, participated in the international air show in Singapore in 2004 and put up aerobatic displays in Thailand and Myanmar. Ironically, more than six decades ago, IAF aircraft had visited Myanmar (then Burma) to drive out the Japanese forces! Indeed the wheel has turned a full circle for the IAF, and, to witness this is Arjan Singh, the officer who as squadron leader, commanded No. 1 Squadron in the Burma Campaign and is now in uniform as Marshal of the IAF.

18
ROLES OF THE IAF

Air power provides a nation with the ability to safeguard vital interests and on account of its enormous reach and capability of swift response, the means to project its will, not only within its boundaries but in areas of concern outside as well. The IAF as the primary component of air power is quite literally the spearhead of the armed forces of India. The IAF is most effective when it is the first to go in to action at the start of any conflict. Although wars are fought jointly by the three services, each service has been assigned clearly defined roles by the Government. The roles assigned to the IAF are:-

- To defend the motherland against air attack and to prevent violation of her airspace.
- To build up and maintain long range strike and interdiction capability against enemy forces, installations and targets of economic importance.
- To provide offensive air support to surface forces on land or at sea.
- To provide strategic and tactical air mobility to the Indian Army.
- To provide logistic support to the Indian Army and the Navy.
- To carry out strategic and tactical reconnaissance.
- To undertake disaster relief operations.
- To undertake any other task assigned by the government.

Force Structure

In order to be prepared at all times to carry out the assigned roles, the IAF needs to maintain the correct mix and force level consisting of aircraft and other weapon systems. Modern combat aircraft combine the attributes of interceptor and strike aircraft and hence are referred to as MRCA. A comprehensive force mix for a potent air force is as under:-

- Long range interceptor aircraft for area air defence.

- Long range combat aircraft for deep strike and interdiction of strategic nature.
- Medium range interceptor aircraft for area and base air defence.
- Medium range combat aircraft for battlefield air support and battlefield air interdiction.
- Wide range of terminally-guided aerial weapons such as air to air missiles, ASMs, anti-radiation missiles, smart bombs and maritime strike weapon systems with stand off capability, air-launched cruise missiles, runway denial weapons, cluster weapons, fuel-air explosive bombs, napalm, conventional unguided bombs and rockets.
- SSMs systems for short and medium range strike.
- Long range, heavy lift transport aircraft and medium range/capacity tactical transport aircraft capable of aerial delivery of paratroopers, supplies and heavy equipment and helicopters for strategic and tactical mobility for the Indian Army.
- Reconnaissance systems such as satellites, UAVs and fixed-wing aircraft equipped with appropriate sensors.
- A network of high, medium and low level SAMs for the AD of vital areas (VAs) and vital points (VPs).
- A comprehensive network of radars with command, control and communication systems to detect, activate and guide air defence weapon systems against intrusion in to Indian airspace.
- EW equipment for electronic suppression of enemy air defence systems.
- Force multipliers such as in-flight refuelling aircraft, aerostats, AWACS and network-centric operating environment.

Integrated HQ of MoD (Air Force): Organizational Structure

To exercise control over a diverse mix of role oriented forces and coordinate their activities to optimize output in both war and peace, there is a hierarchical command and control structure in place with Air Headquarters (Air HQ) at the apex. Air HQ is located in New Delhi from where the head of the IAF designated as the CAS exercises authority vested in him, formulates policy and long-term plans for the growth and development of the air force to meet with challenges of the future, periodically reviews progress of plans, monitors performance of the various elements of the organization and provides the necessary wherewithal and budgetary allocation for the efficient and effective functioning of the IAF. The CAS is answerable to the Government of India through the *Rakhsha Mantri* and is responsible for rendering professional advice on matters concerning national security. At Air HQ the CAS is assisted by six PSOs of the rank of Air Marshal. These are as under:-

- Vice Chief of Air Staff (VCAS): Next in seniority after the CAS, he is responsible for operational matters.

- Deputy Chief of Air Staff (DCAS): Responsible for drawing up long-term plans for acquisition of equipment, progressing cases with the Government and interaction with indigenous aerospace industry in respect of the requirements of the IAF.
- Air Officer in-charge of Personnel (AOP): Responsible for personnel policies, manpower planning, cadre management and training.
- Air Officer in-Charge of Administration (AOA): Responsible for general administration including works services and welfare activities.
- Air Officer in-charge of Maintenance (AOM): Responsible for technical and logistic support.
- Director General in-Charge of Flight Safety and Inspection (DG FS&I): Responsible for inspection of all units for operational and functional efficiency and macro management of flight safety in the IAF.

The PSOs are assisted by one or more senior staff officers designated as Assistant Chief of Air Staff (ACAS) in the rank of Air Vice Marshal. In all departments put together, there are 19 posts of ACAS at Air HQ.

Air Command Headquarters

The next rung in the organizational structure are the air command headquarters. For the conduct of air operations, the country is divided into five regions. Each region has its own air command headquarters whose jurisdiction extends over a defined geographical area as under:-

- Western Air Command (WAC). Located in Subroto Park in New Delhi, WAC is responsible for the conduct of air operations over Delhi, Punjab, Himachal Pradesh and J&K. It functions in close coordination with Western Army Command located at Chandimandir near Chandigarh.
- South Western Air command (SWAC). Located at Gandhinagar, it is responsible for air operations over Rajasthan, Gujarat, Maharashtra and Goa. Till recently, HQ SWAC functioned alongside HQ Southern Command, Army. However, a new army command, named South Western Command has been set up at Jaipur and will have an area of responsibility partly congruent with that of SWAC. HQ Southern Command Army will continue to coordinate with SWAC for operations in some areas under its jurisdiction.
- Central Air Command (CAC). With its HQ at Bamrauli near Allahabad, CAC is responsible for the Central Sector i.e. UP, MP, Uttrakhand, Chhattisgarh, parts of Maharashtra, Bihar and Jharkhand. CAC functions in coordination with HQ Central Command of Army located at Lucknow.
- Eastern Air Command (EAC). Located at Shillong, its jurisdiction extends the entire north-eastern region of the country and coordinates operations with Eastern Command of Army located at Kolkata.
- Southern Air Command (SAC). Located in Thiruvananthapuram, its jurisdiction extends

over the whole of South India and the Lakshadweep islands and functions in coordination with HQ Southern Command of Army located in Pune.

Training and maintenance are two vitally important support functions to enable the IAF maintain a credible operational status. These responsibilities are vested in two functional commands as under:-

- Maintenance Command (MC). With its HQ located at Nagpur, it is responsible for all logistics management and technical support. HQ MC exercises functional control over all its units irrespective of their location.

- Training Command (TC). The second functional command, located at Bangalore, HQ. TC exercises control over all training establishments conducting basic training in all disciplines i.e. flying, technical, ground duties and paramedical both in the officer and airmen cadres, irrespective of their location. HQ. TC is also responsible for a number of specialized in-service courses.

An air command HQ is headed by officers of the rank of Air Marshal designated as Air Officer Commanding in Chief (AOC-in-C) and functions on a three-pronged system consisting of operations, maintenance and administration. The AOC-in-C is assisted by three Senior PSOs. These are designated as Senior Air Staff Officer (SASO) heading operations, Senior Maintenance Staff Officer (SMSO) heading maintenance and the Senior Officer in Charge Administration (SOA) heading administration.

Wing/Station

In the jurisdiction of each command HQ there are a number of air bases designated as Wings. These are static by nature and are generally commanded by officers of the rank of Air Commodore designated as Air Officer Commanding (AOC). Smaller bases are called stations, are commanded by Group Captains and have an organisation similar to that of a wing. In line with the three-pronged system at command HQ the AOC of a wing too has three PSOs under him heading operations, maintenance and administration. Wings are serially numbered and at each of these are located operational units such as fighter, transport or helicopter squadrons, missile and radar units. The operational units are mobile and capable of being relocated at short notice in accordance with operational requirements. Wings have the infrastructure, vehicles and manpower to provide the necessary maintenance, logistic and administrative support to operational units. There are other static units such as training establishments, equipment depots, base repair depots and air force hospitals. Static units may be placed under wings, air command HQ or be administered directly by Air HQ.

Squadron

A squadron is the basic combat or operational unit be it a fighter, transport, helicopter, missile squadron or a radar unit. Such units are usually commanded by an officer of the rank of Wing

Commander. Some larger units are however commanded by Group Captains. A combat or operational unit has bias towards operational and maintenance elements and has a minimal administrative element as the bulk of the administrative support is provided by the wings where they are located. A fighter squadron is roughly equivalent to an infantry battalion or an armoured regiment in the Indian Army, except that a squadron is less manpower intensive, is more technologically oriented, has greater reach, more firepower and is heavily dependent on the infrastructure and support services of a base to operate from.

19
TYPES OF AIR OPERATIONS

Air Defence

The first and foremost responsibility of the IAF is to have a strong air defence capability. In simple terms it implies that in the event of hostile intrusion by enemy aircraft into Indian airspace, the IAF should have the capability to inflict crippling damage on the intruders which would serve as a deterrent against such adventure in the future. The other important aspect is that the air defence system should be able to neutralize intrusion well before enemy aircraft are able to release their weapons. This is becoming more and more difficult with increasing stand-off ranges of precision-guided munitions, air-launched nuclear weapons or long range SSMs. However, integration of AWACS aircraft and aerostats with ELINT/ COMINT facilities into an air defence organization helps extend detection range considerably enhancing early warning and consequently the reaction time for the air defence system. A network-centric environment facilitates speedy processing of information, threat analysis and positive identification. Capability of early detection and positive identification of the intruder are key elements in an effective air defence organization.

The basic sequence of actions by an air defence organisation can be summarised as:-

- Detection.
- Positive Identification.
- Interception.
- Destruction.

Weapons of Air Defence

An air defence organization employs a combination of interceptor aircraft, long range SAMs systems, quick reaction air defence missiles and radar- guided air defence artillery to provide defence in depth. Air defence aircraft armed with Beyond Visual Range (BVR) AAMs, short range close combat AAMs and guns are responsible for providing area defence covering VAs and form the outermost segment of the multi-tier deployment of air defence weapon systems. Aircraft such as the Mirage 2000 and the SU 30 MKI are suitable for the tasks related to area defence. Long range SAMs are employed in the next tier to engage intruders that escape destruction by interceptor aircraft. Finally, short range quick reaction missiles and radar-controlled AAD weapons are deployed as the last line of defence to secure VPs against the unlikely event of an intruder breaching the outer and middle tier of defences.

Air defence radars are also deployed in tiers to cover every segment. Forward most tier consists of a chain of early warning radars that provide gap free cover against low level intrusion. The chain of early warning radars are augmented by teams of observers called Forward Observation Posts deployed in multiple rings to cater for possible gaps in the detection capability, temporary or permanent. Radars deployed in the second tier, apart from the ability to detect intrusion, are capable of guiding air defence aircraft for interception of hostile track. These are called Ground Control Interception (GCI) radars and are manned by specially trained officers of the Administration or Flying branch called Fighter Controllers. The entire sequence of air defence operations are controlled by a centralized agency called Air Defence Direction Centre (ADDC) where information from all sources is collated in real time and a continuously updated comprehensive picture of the developing situation is presented at all times for the benefit of the decision makers who are required to act within minutes. Integration of AWACS and aerostats into the air defence system enhances the range at which the intruder can be detected and coupled with networking and automated data handling systems, the capability of air defence systems to respond to threats can be enhanced considerably. Given the criticality of an air base where there is a large concentration of aircraft and other expensive assets, a degree of autonomy is provided in respect of their own air defence. The local commander is vested with the authority to launch aircraft against threat to his base. In such an arrangement the system is called Base Air Defence and the local commander is designated as the Base Air Defence Commander. Needless to say the air defence organization in India is on round-the-clock alert not only during war but in peacetime as well. Few air defence aircraft fuelled and fully armed for the air defence role are parked close to one end of the runway in use with fighter pilots resting in the vicinity ready to take to the skies within minutes of warning by day or night. This arrangement is termed as Operational Readiness Platform (ORP) duty and the process of quick take off is called 'Scramble'.

Long Range Strike

Given the enormous reach of combat aircraft that can be further enhanced with in-flight refuelling, facilities and installations of strategic, economic and military importance to the enemy constitute the target systems for the long range strike elements of the IAF. The aim of such operations is to strike at the heart of the enemy to weaken him economically and militarily as also prevent vital supplies from reaching the theatre of war by disruption of rail and road communication. Aircraft such as the Jaguar, MiG 27, Mirage 2000 and the SU 30 MKI are well suited to undertake such tasks. In view of their large radius of action, these aircraft operate from the sanctuary of airfields located in depth. Forward airfields are used by long range aircraft for staging through, should the need arise or in an emergency.

At the start of a full scale war, it is necessary to inflict on the enemy air force a high level of damage to seriously erode the capability of enemy air power to interfere with the operations of our land forces. This objective is the best achieved by use of long range strike aircraft and long range SSMs missiles to simultaneously attack enemy airfields, radar installations and communication centres. Such attacks can also be carried out by SSMs if the targets are within range. Operations to neutralize the enemy air force are collectively termed as 'Counter Air Operations' and are aimed at achieving control over the airspace. This condition is also described as 'Air Superiority'. A higher degree of control of the air is described as 'Air Supremacy' or in the best case, 'Command of the Air'. When the warring sides are evenly balanced, it may be difficult to establish air supremacy or even air superiority. In such a case, all efforts must be made to establish at least a modicum of control of the air described as 'Favourable Air Situation' without which it would be extremely difficult if not impossible for surface forces to conduct operations successfully. One should expect the enemy to have the capability to quickly recover from damage caused through counter air strikes and therefore, disruption of enemy air operations may only be temporary. As such, for any degree of control of the air to be durable, it is necessary to sustain counter air operations albeit with somewhat lower intensity in comparison with the initial onslaught. A substantial proportion of long range strike element have to be set aside for this all important task, the benefits of which are indirect and hence not easily perceived or appreciated by surface forces.

Offensive Air Support

In keeping with the mandate, IAF aircraft can be employed to attack target systems such as tank harbours, troop concentrations, armoured thrust, vehicle columns, supply dumps, artillery positions, etc. in and around the battlefield which can be neutralized effectively through attacks by short range combat aircraft operating from forward airfields. Offensive air support tasks are performed by aircraft such as the MiG 21 Bis, MiG 27 and attack helicopters. These operations can be divided broadly into two categories, Battlefield Air Support (BAS) which involves attacks near the front line in close proximity of own troops and Battlefield Air Interdiction (BAI) which involves attack on supply lines immediately outside the battle zone with the express purpose of preventing supplies reaching the enemy troops deployed on the frontline in offensive or defensive posture. This type of air operations are very popular with surface forces as they are relatively more visible to the troops and results are immediate with profound and positive effect on morale. However, the battlefield environment is becoming increasingly lethal for combat aircraft owing to heavy infestation of quick reaction, short range terminally-guided SAMs and radar-controlled air defence weapons, making especially BAS operations more and more difficult, challenging and prohibitive on account of the possibility of high attrition rates which may be unaffordable. BAI is relatively better option as the environment outside the battle zone is relatively less lethal and there is only a minute lag in the impact on the course of the battle.

Aerial Reconnaissance

Aerial Reconnaissance is an important function that is carried out for obtaining intelligence on economic and military target systems, enemy disposition and his Order of Battle (Orbat), infrastructure and assessment of post-strike damage. Intelligence gathering operations could be of strategic nature, carried out by satellites with cameras capable of high resolution photography or high speed high flying aircraft such as the MiG 25 which is fitted with high powered cameras that can photograph not only the ground below but can look sideways and cover a wide area. The MiG 25 aircraft was retired from the service of the IAF in 2006 after serving for over 25 years. Tactical reconnaissance involves similar activity in and around battle areas and is carried out by low flying fixed-wing fighter aircraft equipped with cameras or infrared imaging equipment carried in under-wing pods. UAVs with day or infrared cameras or a variety of sensors or synthetic aperture radar (SAR) whose operations are not inhibited by weather, are effective instruments for aerial reconnaissance. With appropriate equipment onboard and data link, intelligence information can be made available to the user in real time. The use of electronic devices for intelligence gathering has now become an important component in the regime of aerial reconnaissance. Intelligence information is vital prerequisite in the planning and conduct of all types of military operations on land, sea and in the air.

Air Transport Operations

The IAF maintains a fleet of transport aircraft and helicopters to provide strategic and tactical mobility to the land forces with the aim to provide the capability for swift response in changing situations. The IAF and the Indian Army train jointly to insert combat forces by way of paratroopers and their equipment behind enemy lines. These are called 'Airborne Assault Operations' and are meant to open a new front or bring about a collapse of enemy resistance through surprise attack from the rear. Such forces invariably need to be supplied by air. Airlift capability is used to redeploy large ground forces from one theatre of war to another and to maintain forces deployed in far flung areas in the mountainous regions not easily accessible by other means of communication. Military transport aircraft are designed to operate from semi-prepared short runways called Advanced Landing Grounds (ALGs) in forward areas and helicopters operate from helipads at altitudes of around 21,000 ft. Casualty evacuation and disaster relief are two important functions carried out by the transport and helicopter fleet as a matter of routine. Transport aircraft and logistic helicopters are unarmed and as such need a high degree of control of the air to be able to operate with a reasonable degree of safety in a hostile environment that obtains over enemy territory.

Electronic Warfare

The vulnerability of aircraft on missions inside enemy airspace has been increasing progressively with improving capability of defensive systems such as ground based surveillance radars, GCI radars and fire control radars, as also infrared heat seeking terminal-homing missiles. Strike aircraft rely heavily of countermeasures to erode the detection capability by electronically flooding the radars with spurious signals. This causes enough confusion in the radar picture, reducing considerably the possibility of detection by surveillance and GCI radars and missile guidance by fire control radars. This in simple terms is called 'jamming of the radar' and in more sophisticated terms is called 'defence suppression'. The range of activities of this character is collectively called 'Electronic Warfare' (EW). Strike aircraft have inbuilt electronic warfare equipments such as Radar Warning Receivers (RWR) and Automatic Self Protection Jammers (ASPJ), that provide limited protection. Strike formations therefore need to be escorted by aircraft that carry more powerful jamming devices in under-wing pods and are dedicated to the EW role to enlarge the protection envelope of the strike formation. EW aircraft must match the strike aircraft in range and speed to be able to function effectively especially in missions against targets deep inside enemy territory. Needless to say that radars too have capability such as 'Frequency Agility' to reduce the debilitating effect of jamming. Thus, there is constant race between the development of new offensive and defensive capability in warfare.

Training Philosophy

The IAF has a number of institutions that develop human resources necessary for a technology intensive service that demands high threshold of professional knowledge and skills before entering the main stream. The training institutions of the IAF focus on acquisition of knowledge, development of skills and inculcation of value systems and orientation of attitudes. It is of utmost importance that individuals joining the service must have the right mix of intellectual attributes, physical attributes and the correct mental orientation referred to as 'attitude'. A career in the IAF is not merely an honourable means of livelihood but a lifetime commitment of complete dedication and sacrifice. While there is considerable emphasis on the development of the individual, the best results can only be achieved through teamwork. Training philosophy in the IAF is therefore structured not only to focus on individual development but also to promote deep understanding amongst the various branches and disciplines. The effort is to develop strong bonds of friendship and the spirit of camaraderie that promote a smooth work environment and facilitate teamwork.

In pursuance of the training philosophy, basic training, whether for officers or airmen, male or female, is divided broadly into two phases. In Phase I, trainees of all branches and disciplines are trained together to study subjects of common interest which deal with the fundamentals of the organization. This is called the 'Joint Basic Training Phase'. Apart from an academic curriculum related to general service knowledge, trainees participate jointly in drill, team games, competitive sports, outdoor exercises, camps and cultural pursuits. The wide range of activities helps in character building and developing esprit de corps, vital prerequisites for a fighting force. After one semester of joint training, trainees branch off to respective institutions or establishments for Phase II which includes branch or trade specific training before they proceed to operational units for field service.

The training curriculum and methodology at the various training institutions are reviewed periodically on the basis of changing paradigms in the organization, equipment, technology and doctrines. Institutions are provided with the best infrastructure, the latest training aids, networked environment and selected high profile instructional staff. It is only through competent instructors who can function as role models that a subtle influence can be exerted on the minds of trainees to inculcate the right value systems and thereby mould attitudes.

SU 30 K in formation

AN-32

A huge IL-78 covers the horizon

MiG 21 Bis

MiG 29 Turning Left

A Paradrop in progress

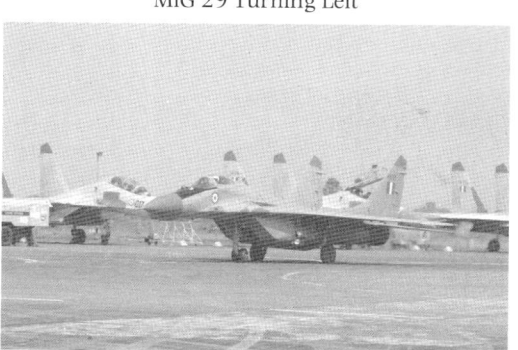

MiG 29 in the foreground

Mirage 2000

SU-30MKI

A Jaguar

Mirage 2000

MiG-29 Flying over mountains

AN-32 on the tarmac

MiG-29

MiG 21 in formation

HAL Druv Army Version

Mirage-2000

SU-30 MKI

An IL-78

SU 30 K in a dive

Small Boy Formation - AN 32 in the lead flanked by two Dorniers

In-flight refueling of two Mirage 2000 by IL 78

SU 30 MKI

MI 17 under maintenance

Mixed Formation : SU 30 K leading, MiG 21 just behind, flanked by two Mirage 2000, MiG 29 on far left and behind, MiG 23 far back and right

Mirage 2000

A Jaguar

IL 76

MiG 29 lined up on tarmac

SU 30 MKI landing

MI 17 Disgorging troops while hovering

SU 30 MKI

Jaguars flying in a formation

SU 30 K landing

Mixed Formation – two M 2000 in centre row flanked by two SU 30 K.

Jaguar – tail chute deployed after touch down while landing

SU 30 MKI in air display

Tejas: the Light Combat Aircraft

Tejas – underbelly exposed

MI 17 Slithering Operations

SU 30 MKI

IL 76 lined up at Air Force Day Parade

SU 30 MKI trailing smoke during air display

MI 17 on tarmac

20
IAF: Meeting The Challenges of The Twenties

Planning for Modernization of the IAF

Festivity during the 75th anniversary of the Indian Air Force in October 2005 was overshadowed by the concern over its depleting combat power. Obsolescence appears to be overtaking the IAF as several components of its combat and supporting assets are reaching the end of technical or calendar life and need replacement very soon. The Government appeared to be seized of the problem as a few days later at a Combined Commanders' Conference held in South Block, came the assurance from the highest level that modernization of the armed forces was a matter of high priority and that the required resources would be made available.

Modernization of the IAF involves acquisition of expensive capital equipment that has a life span of three to four decades. Acquisition of equipment for the IAF in the past has generally been characterized by slow decision making and complex procurement procedures leading to delays in the operational integration of the equipment with the organization. The procurement process is long drawn and in the best case may take seven to ten years to fructify. As such, plans drawn up today must remain valid in the decade of the twenties by which time changes in the operating environment could well render decisions of today irrelevant. Modernization plans must therefore take in to account the challenges of the evolving scenario in the geo-political, geo-strategic, technological and operational environment in the region and the world as these would impact on the role and responsibility of the IAF as also its shape and size. It is therefore necessary to reflect on the historical perspective of regional equations and visualize the scenario that is likely to prevail in the twenties before undertaking plans for modernization of the IAF.

Conflict and the Developing World

In the first half of the 20th century the world went through the convulsions of two major wars that apart from wreaking widespread death and destruction, divided the world in to two distinct camps hostile to each other and ushered in an era of the Cold War and global peace, essentially on account of a balance of power arising out of superpower rivalry. While the two superpowers maintained a balance of terror, conventional proxy wars continued to rage and were confined largely to the developing world. These wars served the political and economic interests of the superpowers as they helped perpetuate strategic relationships and turn the wheels of the military industrial complex of the developed world.

Sino-Indian Relations

Emerging as a dismembered but independent nation in the middle of the 20th century, India inherited several thousand kilometres of land borders that had a potential for conflict whose origins lay in the flawed policies of the British Government. The border between India and Tibet had been defined unilaterally by the British Government during their reign in India without any formal agreement with China who constantly maintained that in the first place, there was no need for a redefinition of borders as the traditional boundaries were well known and that there was no need to indulge in the exercise at all. At no stage did the Chinese endorse or accept the British action with regard to the delineation of the border with Tibet. The alignment of the traditional boundaries perceived by China were also not universally known except perhaps to the Chinese themselves.

The unresolved legacy inherited from the past left an unwary nation traumatized in 1962. More than four decades later, efforts are now on to resolve the fundamental dispute and notwithstanding the inspiring rhetoric emanating from the political establishment of both India and China and the somewhat regimented bonhomie at the military outpost at Nathu La beamed on the visual media occasionally, the ground situation has not changed in favour of India. In fact, in some ways it has indeed worsened as in the intervening years, the Chinese have only consolidated their gains of 1962 in Ladakh and are continuing to develop regions bordering Arunachal on a scale that cannot be justified for economic reasons alone. It would be imprudent to believe that it is possible only through dialogue to alter the age old position held by China regarding the alignment of international borders between India and Tibet. But in the absence of any other option, the dialogue must continue. We ought not to ignore the fact that it is more important for us to come to an amicable settlement of the border dispute than it is for China. As per a renowned Chinese leader, it may be desirable to shelve the problem for now and leave it to the future generations who may be wiser to find a solution. A politically weak position combined with a visibly weak military posture on our part therefore could seriously undermine the process of the ongoing dialogue as also impinge on the fragile relationship that we believe to have succeeded in building in the recent past.

Apart from the ongoing border dispute, the economic rivalry that is building up slowly but surely between the two of the fastest growing economies in the region, has the potential for conflict arising out of clash of vital interests. While India aspires to emerge as a regional power, China is emerging as a global economic power house and her sights are set on superpower status. China would not have failed to notice the shift in India's foreign policy aimed at strengthening the strategic relationship between the two largest democracies in the world. China acquired nuclear power status several years ahead of India to achieve a credible deterrent against a perceived threat from a superpower. China has also successfully completed her second space mission and in the next decade and a half, is planning to despatch a manned mission to moon as also build a space station. Clearly, China is ahead in the race with India. Then there is the long standing relationship with Pakistan wherein apart from supply of conventional military equipment, China has played a key role in transforming Pakistan in to a nuclear weapon state, a step that has only accentuated the tension and served to complicate the security equations in the sub-continent.

Indo-Pak Confrontation

On the western front, the status of Jammu and Kashmir, truly the only cause of conflict, is a legacy of the colonial past. In the wake of super-power rivalry, Britain was replaced in the region by the USA, and while Pakistan was drawn quite readily in to the American camp, India adopted a philosophy of non alignment opting for a diverse inventory of military equipment i.e. British and French. However for strategic, economic and political reasons India had to subsequently lean heavily on the Soviet Union for military hardware to meet with the demands of national security. Even though formally not allied with the USSR, India was seen by the USA as being squarely in the Soviet camp and was treated with extreme suspicion and unconcealed disdain. Nearly six decades and four major conflicts later, there appears to have been some qualitative change in the equation between India and Pakistan. People to people contact, exchange programmes in a variety of fields, restoration of rail and road transport, liberalization of visa regimes, trade both official and unofficial and cooperation in the wake of the disastrous earthquake in the recent past have rekindled hopes for peace between the two adversaries. The media has also by and large played a very constructive role in exposing the reality of India to the several brainwashed and misled generations of Pakistanis. All these developments have served to weaken the anti-each-other platforms that the political establishment on both sides have so far thrived upon.

However, there are other factors and deep seated ant-India sentiments that militate against normalization of relations. In the Pakistani mindset, India is a hegemonic power that poses a constant and potent threat to her very survival. The corporate aim of the Pakistani establishment has been to exploit the vulnerabilities of India, weaken her from the inside and 'to bleed her with a thousand cuts'. The situation with regard to the status of Kashmir has not changed, and like a persistent virus, resurfaces with irritating regularity, seemingly frustrating efforts at forward movement. In spite of all noble intentions, it appears difficult if not impossible for the Pakistani establishment to retreat from or significantly alter their long held position vis-à-vis Kashmir as it would amount to political suicide for the leadership whether military or civilian. As for the Indian view, it is only for Pakistan to demonstrate flexibility which the leadership is not prepared to do. And then there is the unfinished business of POK. Also, as it appears, the maximum that India can concede on Kashmir is less than what would be acceptable to Pakistan. In view of the inflexible position on both sides, Kashmir will continue to be a major impediment in any effort at securing the western borders from the possibility of conflict. Nothing short of reversing the process of partition leading to the reunification of India and Pakistan can help resolve the dispute over Kashmir. Solution to the Kashmir problem will therefore remain as much in the realm of fantasy in the foreseeable future as the suggestion to reunite the two nations.

Apart from the Kashmir issue, there are problems on other fronts as well. The population of Pakistan is growing at roughly 2.6% annually and is not matched by its economic growth. Pakistan will therefore continue to be in a dysfunctional state and would have to depend heavily on foreign assistance for survival. The growing economic disparity between India and Pakistan could aggravate the sense of insecurity that a small nation perceives from a bigger and more prosperous and powerful neighbour with whom there are deep ideological differences and a long history of turbulent relationship. The sense of insecurity may be further aggravated if our western neighbour finds her position vis-à-vis Kashmir weakening. Under such circumstances, for Pakistan, a conflict may appear to be an inevitable and desperate option. Under the shadow of the nuclear threat, in all likelihood, Pakistan may avoid an all out war and prefer to sustain low intensity conflict in the valley and undermine our interests through covert support to insurgency in other parts of the country bordering Nepal and Bangladesh. This certainly would be a more convenient and cost effective option for Pakistan.

Prospects of Peace

It should be clear from the preceding that India cannot rest on its oars and take permanent peace in the subcontinent for granted. Perhaps peace can only be ensured if one is well prepared to meet with any conceivable threat to national security by all the means at its disposal, be it political, economic, diplomatic, or military. Encouraging progress in efforts at settlement of disputes with both China and Pakistan ought not to be assumed as good enough reason for scaling down military capability. Besides, in future conflicts with either or simultaneously with both the neighbours, India needs to be prepared to manage conflicts at the conventional level as also fight and survive in a nuclear environment. In the ultimate analysis, a nation is respected for its strength, political, economic and military.

India as a Regional Power

The last decade of the 20th century witnessed a set of three major events that had a profound effect on the destiny of many nations as also on that of India. The first of these was the collapse of the Soviet Union which seemed to have severed India's moorings to set it a drift for a while. The second major event was the uncaging of the Indian economy and the process of economic reforms and liberalization that thrust India on to the global scene. The third and most significant event was the explicit assertion in 1998 of the nuclear status by both India and Pakistan. Thus in the new century, the situation for the nation and her armed forces is qualitatively different in a number of ways. In the emerging scenario and the rapprochement with the USA, India could well be drawn in to a US led security arrangement for a new power balance in the region. The

USA regards India as one of the power centres that can exercise a stabilizing influence in the region and can be relied upon. High levels of investment notwithstanding, containment of China will remain a major concern for the USA. In her own perspective, on account of India's energy security needs, so vital for sustained economic growth, India's zone of interest transcend her geographical boundaries extending from South East Asia to the Central Asian Republics and the Gulf. India conveyed to the world a subtle message by of her swift response to the Tsunami in December 2004. In the evolving geopolitical situation and economic growth sustained at 8%, conditions are favourable for India to assume the role of a regional power in not too distant a future.

India would be expected to shoulder higher levels of military responsibility consequent to her evolving regional power status. In addition, the fundamental reasons for conflict with China and Pakistan continue to linger vigorous political and diplomatic efforts notwithstanding. The search for solutions to disputes rooted deeply in history require prolonged and complex negotiations. However to be successful on the political and diplomatic fronts, one needs to negotiate from a position of strength. India is well on the way to becoming an economic power. It is incumbent on the leadership to ensure that there is no dilution of military capability if the equation with our traditionally hostile neighbours is not to be compromised. Rhetoric, assurances and promises must not lull the nation in to complacency and risk a replay of the 1962 debacle.

Security Environment in the Twenties

To summarize, in the geopolitical, geostrategic and security environment that is likely to prevail in the 2020s, the dictates of national security would place the following demands on armed forces of the nation:-

- To be prepared for a prolonged and widespread multi front border war with China with only a remote possibility of employment of nuclear weapons.

- To be prepared for a short and intense conflict with Pakistan with the real possibility of the first use of nuclear weapons by the adversary.

- To be prepared for simultaneous conflict with both the potential adversaries acting in collusion.

- To sustain the capability to fight a prolonged low intensity conflict in Kashmir and other sensitive regions of the country in the pursuit of internal security.

- To develop and maintain the capability for rapid strategic intervention and power projection in the region extending from the Strait of Malacca to Central Asia and the Gulf to safeguard and promote national interests.

- To play a dominant role in the management of disasters and natural calamity in the region of interest.

While considerable progress has been made on the political, economic and diplomatic fronts, the overall security situation continues to remain fraught with uncertainties. India's growing political and economic stature in the world and commitments of national interests necessitate a move away from the traditional defensive mindset. India must acquire the capability for power projection in the area of interest which will require a qualitative change in the operational philosophy of the armed forces especially of the IAF. Within the broad structural framework that has evolved over the last five decades, there is a need to modify the composition and character of the various constituents of the IAF to provide extended reach and staying power. The focus must shift from the 'Tactical' to the 'Strategic' as also on 'Force Multipliers'. The IAF must also integrate fully with the sister services as also aim to develop interoperability with other friendly powers in the region and the world for furtherance of mutual interests.

The armed forces of India have matured through a number of major conflicts with our neighbours in the last five decades. The IAF in particular has benefited from the lessons learnt in these conflicts and has been quick to absorb the technological advances witnessed elsewhere in the world. Undoubtedly, in the military dimension of national security, the IAF would be called upon to shoulder enhanced levels of responsibility and would have a critical role to play both during peace and war especially in situations demanding swift response. The IAF needs to draw up plans to acquire the wherewithal to meet with the challenges of the 2020s. As the pace of change is slow, radical change in the framework is neither desirable nor possible in the timeframe under consideration. However, there is imperative need to introduce qualitative change in the capabilities of the IAF driven by the technological revolution in Air Power.

Aerial Reconnaissance

In peacetime, apart from training for war, an important mission of the IAF would be the acquisition of strategic and tactical intelligence through technical means. Strategic reconnaissance by fixed wing aircraft would have to be replaced by space based platforms equipped with a wide variety of powerful sensors. Tactical reconnaissance would be assigned to a family of Unmanned Aerial Vehicles (UAVs) even over long range through the use of high endurance machines controlled remotely from thousands of miles away with the aid of satellite based data links. Employing a variety of photo, infrared and comint sensors, it would be possible to counter the element of surprise by maintaining continuous surveillance to assess intent through changes in enemy orbat and relocation of forces. Surveillance systems will be employed to map and update information on strategic target systems and provide highly accurate data necessary for precision attacks by smart weapons particularly in the opening stages of any conflict. Assurance levels of smart weapons are contingent on the accuracy of target data and hence the critical importance of the capability of intelligence gathering platforms and airborne sensors.

Strategic & Tactical Strike Capability

To develop a credible deterrent as also meet with its commitments of power projection in the region, the IAF would have to have a fleet of potent, long range, nuclear capable, multi role strike aircraft that would have the capability to neutralize any target system in the area of interest. The strike force must have at its disposal a variety of smart weapons with sizeable stand-off range, air launched cruise missiles and versatile electronic warfare suites to defeat known detection devices and fire control systems. The IAF is in the process of inducting 190 (ten squadrons) of the state of the art, 40-ton class SU30 MKI multi-role aircraft. With in-flight refuelling, this fleet would have the attributes essential to fulfil the strategic commitments of the nation. With a lifespan of at least 30 years including a mid-life upgrade of avionics, the fleet of SU30 MKI would remain in service though the 2020s. However, the IAF would have to reassess the requirement of the size of the fleet periodically vis-à-vis changing scenario and constantly upgrade its weapon systems for the fleet to retain its front line status.

The IAF would also need a fleet of medium range Multi-Role Combat Aircraft (MRCA) in the 20-ton class. Moves are already afoot to acquire 126 (six squadrons) of MRCA for air defence and strike tasks of tactical nature. With in-flight refuelling this fleet could also be used to augment the long range strike force. If the IAF is able to overcome the bureaucratic and procedural impediments and make the fleet operational in the next five years, this fleet too would remain in service well beyond the 2020s. The current fleet of Mig 21, MiG 27, MiG 29, Jaguars and Mirages will largely be obsolete by the 2020s and only a handful of upgraded aircraft may remain to undertake second tier tasks. The effective strength of the IAF is likely to deplete rapidly as we approach the 2020s. The IAF must therefore draw up concrete plans and take urgent steps to ensure that the fixed wing combat element of the IAF is restored to at least 40 squadrons if not more. The LCA is a possible answer but only partly. Also, the uncertainty that has plagued the LCA project over the last two decades does not inspire much confidence. Acquisition of aircraft from foreign sources is a complicated process and cannot be conducted as a fire fighting exercise. Presently there is at least a five year gap in the assessment by the IAF and the Indian Aerospace Industry of the timeframe in which to expect the LCA to be available. In any case, the rate of production may not be adequate to close the gap of 24 squadrons in a respectable timeframe leaving the IAF with no option but to search for solutions elsewhere. Given the size of the deficit, the investment would involve an outflow of resources to the tune of billions of dollars if aircraft are to be acquired from foreign sources. The IAF may run in to affordability barriers and may be compelled to stretch the ageing fleets through expensive upgrades and suffer erosion of capability. The IAF must find answers to this challenge in the context of the security concerns and the emerging regional power status of the nation.

Air Defence

Apart from the combat fleet, the IAF would need to put in place a gap free and responsive automated air defence surveillance system comprising an overlapping integrated network of low, medium and high level radar coverage. In a nuclear environment, an air defence system must be totally impregnable as even a single aircraft or missile armed with a nuclear weapon could be catastrophic. Besides, own nuclear second strike capability must be protected against an attack by the enemy. Efforts to acquire AWACS and Aerostats even though in small numbers, are steps in the right direction but more needs to be done. Our scientific establishments need to move ahead quickly in their ambitious project to develop a space based reconnaissance and surveillance system to cover the airspace over the entire country. The existing ground based surveillance assets are woefully inadequate for even the current level of responsibility and need total revamp. Given the extent of our frontiers, infrastructure for total coverage solely through ground based surveillance systems would be prohibitively expensive and possibly unaffordable. The AWACS aircraft would be a more cost effective option as it would also provide low level cover deep inside enemy territory not only to direct own forces but also to track hostile aircraft departing for missions from their bases thus facilitating positive identification and increasing substantially the reaction time available to the air defence system.

While there is no debate over the necessity of AWACS aircraft, the question is that of numbers. In the event of imminent or outbreak of hostilities, AWACS aircraft would have to be 'on station' round the clock in adequate numbers to cover the entire length of hostile borders. Given the limitations of endurance of the aircraft and the crew, serviceability considerations of an infinitely complex machine and the volume of the airspace to be scanned, the IAF would have to reassess the size of the fleet required to be procured. The fleet of Phalcon equipped IL 76 aircraft being acquired in the next two to three years, will only provide a learning experience. To meet with needs of the 2020s, the size of the AWACS fleet would have to be significantly larger and hopefully augmented by the DRDO developed Embraer based system. Integrating the AWACS in to the Air Defence System, developing the technical skills to maintain and operate the platform and finding the resources to procure these machines in the requisite numbers would be some of the major challenges for the IAF and the nation. To exploit the advantage of extended low level cover provided by the AWACS, air defence aircraft must be armed with BVR missiles with range long enough to intercept hostile targets well before they are in a position to pose any threat.

Strategic & Tactical Airlift Capability

The emerging regional power status requires the nation to have the capability to intervene in the region to preserve peace and stability. Action of this nature was witnessed in the late eighties on a small scale in Sri Lanka and the Maldives. Operations of this nature may have to be conducted on a larger scale in the future. The existing strategic airlift capability structured around the IL 76 fleet acquired in the mid-eighties is grossly inadequate for the perceived strategic role for reasons such as fleet size, poor state of serviceability and low residual calendar life of the fleet. The IAF must have strategic airlift capability to move at least a Brigade Group along with their combat equipment in a single wave over extended range to cover the area of interest without the need for intermediate refuelling stopover. The IAF needs to reassess the shape and size of strategic airlift fleet and plan the induction of the replacement aircraft within ten years from now. Updated versions of the American C 17 and the C 130 or the European A400 could be some of the possible options. Contingency plans must include employment of the huge civil air fleet as well. In view of their larger reaction time however, the civil air fleet will be useful not for initial response but for induction of larger formations and for supporting operations that follow.

In addition to the strategic airlift capability, the nation will also need a sizeable tactical airlift capability which must combine medium tactical transport aircraft and heavy lift helicopters.

Plans by HAL to develop a medium tactical transport aircraft in collaboration with renowned international partners, is yet in a nascent stage and need to be pursued with singular focus as the AN 32 fleet will have to be phased out in a decade or so. Tactical airlift capability will be required for inserting a battalion group directly into battle in airborne assault operations or for air mobility of ground forces for inter-theatre operational redeployment in response to rapid changes in the situation, for a variety of internal security tasks as nearly 30 per cent of the districts in this country are naxalite infested in addition to insurgency in J & K and the north eastern regions and the management of disaster. The IAF needs to build up heliborne forces trained for operating both by day and night obtaining real time intelligence information from UAVs for vertical envelopment in counter insurgency operations in all types of terrain. Action is in hand to acquire 80 helicopters of the MI 17 class which will meet with current requirements. For the 2020s, a fresh assessment would be necessary.

Battlefield Strike

The constantly rising and prohibitive cost of fixed wing combat aircraft presently to the tune of Rs 200 crore or more apiece and the increasing lethality of the battlefield, it is becoming more and more difficult to employ fixed wing combat aircraft against low value targets in the battlefield. The responsibility to engage targets in the battlefield could shift to Battlefield Support Missiles which for enhanced accuracy, will be programmed with target information obtained in real time from UAV operating over or in the vicinity of the battle area. Low value targets could be engaged more effectively, efficiently and economically by Unmanned Combat Aerial Vehicles (UCAV). Helicopters too may be employed for battlefield support in conjunction with real time intelligence information from UAVs. But in the battlefield of the future, helicopters would be highly vulnerable.

In-flight Refuelling

A force multiplier acquired in the recent past is the fleet of six IL 78 In-flight Refuelling Aircraft. Its rapid integration in to the IAF has been a remarkable feat by any standard. In-flight refuelling capability helps enhance the radius of action of combat aircraft and given the size of the combat fleet and the intensity of operations, the fleet of force multipliers acquired recently, is clearly inadequate. In-flight refuelling can also enhance the range and radius of action of medium tactical transport aircraft as well and help augment airlift capability. Thus apart from providing support to combat elements, this capability will have a crucial role in the security of the EEZ and the island territories as also in the discharge of responsibilities related to regional power status.

Exploitation of Space

One dimension that the IAF would need to exploit is that of space. The intent to do so is evident in its pronouncement to create an IAF Aerospace Command. While the concept of using space based lethal weapon systems may yet lie in the realms of imagination, considerable progress has been made in the regime of communication and surveillance by space based platforms using optical, IR sensors and radar. The scientific establishments in India have made impressive strides in the field of space technology. It would be the responsibility of these organizations to provide the IAF with new capabilities in its drive to be an Aerospace Power.

Training

Perhaps the weakest area that afflicts the IAF today is the inadequacy of training infrastructure. A fighting force equipped with the most sophisticated aircraft, smart weapon systems, complex sensors, space based surveillance & reconnaissance systems, a network centric environment needs to be supported by an equally advanced and sophisticated training environment with computer based training systems, elaborate simulation devices for all disciplines, automated distance learning and evaluation systems, all designed to train for the next war and not the last one. In this respect, the IAF is at the bottom of the hill. Human resources must be trained well enough to be able to meet with the challenges of new technology and concepts. Not only the training systems and methodology need to be upgraded, the entry thresholds and service conditions also need to be redefined and upgraded significantly to meet with the qualitative requirements of human resources of the future.

Technological Revolution

The closing years of the last century witnessed rapid changes in technology which will have a profound impact on the methodology of air warfare in the future. Emergence of digital and nano-technology will revolutionize military equipment by way of miniaturization and automation. Many of the tasks now performed by humans will shift to machines rendering it possible to reduce manpower in a technology intensive force such as the IAF. Also the pace of change in technology is increasing rapidly. The type of technological development that took ten years earlier may take perhaps two years in the future. This also means quicker obsolescence. Advances in technology will also enhance the accuracy and lethality of weapon systems that could translate in to the overall reduction in the size of the force for the same level of commitment. Advances in Information Technology will transform the battlefield of the future in to a Network Centric Environment wherein information from a variety of ground based, airborne or space based sensors would be collected, processed and disseminated to end users in real time and easily comprehensible formats. Network Centric Environment will facilitate speedy decision making at command & control centres, quicker response by forces and better accuracy in weapon delivery. It will be a major challenge for the IAF to remain abreast of technology and reorient doctrine, strategy and tactics to operate in and exploit fully the new environment.

Conclusion

The evolving geo-political and go-strategic situation combined with rapid economic growth has placed India on track to emerging as a regional power with consequent enhanced level of responsibility. There is however no perceptible change in the overall security situation in the subcontinent. Internal security also continues to remain a major challenge for governance. Meanwhile, on account of obsolescence which is inevitable in a rapidly changing technological environment, it is necessary for the IAF to take stock and adopt appropriate measures to ensure that the IAF remains fully prepared to undertake a new range of tasks in its expanded envelope of responsibilities. The IAF needs to redefine priorities and restructure itself to upgrade to the strategic level. As technology will be the force that will drive change in the future, the IAF cannot afford to lag behind. But most important of all, change of mindsets would be a prerequisite for any modernization plan to be meaningful. This perhaps would be the greatest challenge for the leadership.

21
Officers' Cadre: Rank Structure

Before proceeding further, it is necessary to understand the rank structure in the officer cadre of the IAF and their equivalents in the Indian Army and the Indian Navy as tabulated below. On completion of training for the officer cadre, the Air Force trainee receives the President's Commission in the rank of Flying Officer. Thereafter the officer has a clearly defined promotional ladder as listed below in the column on the left :-

IAF	Army	Navy
Flying Officer	Lieutenant	Sub Lieutenant
Flight Lieutenant	Captain	Lieutenant
Squadron Leader	Major	Lieutenant Commander
Wing Commander	Lieutenant Colonel	Commander
Group Captain	Colonel	Captain
Air Commodore	Brigadier	Commodore
Air Vice Marshal	Major General	Rear Admiral
Air Marshal	Lieutenant General	Vice Admiral
Air Chief Marshal	General	Admiral
Marshal of the IAF	Field Marshal	Admiral of the Fleet

    The rank structure is common to all branches in the officer cadre of the IAF. Also, in accordance with the new promotion policy, with effect from 16 December 2004, there is accelerated and assured promotion up to the rank of Wing Commander. Promotion to the rank of Group Captain can also be effected on the basis of selection much earlier than that under time scale. Promotion to the rank of Air Commodore and above is by a rigorous selection process. An officer holding the rank of Air Marshal retires in the normal course at the age of 60 years. Officers lower in rank retire at an age lower by two years for each rank if not selected for promotion to the next higher rank. So far, Arjan Singh is the only officer of the IAF to be appointed as Marshal of the Indian Air Force. He also had the distinction of heading the IAF in the sixties as the Chief of the Air Staff and was also the first Chief to hold the rank of Air Chief Marshal.

Entry Conditions: Officers' Cadre

All trainees for the officer cadre must be at least a graduate except for a few who are selected from amongst serving airmen who may not have a degree. Candidates for Education and Meteorological branches must have a post graduate degree. Officer trainees of the technical branch receive provisional commission and are granted rank of Flying Officer on the day of joining the training establishment. They are granted Permanent Commission on probation only after successful completion of training. Officer trainees for flying and ground duty branches are commissioned after successful completion of one year of training. All officer trainees receive a handsome package of remuneration and perks while under training. Airmen selected for training for the officer cadre continue to draw salary as applicable to their rank as airmen.

Entry in to the flying branch is either through the National Defence Academy, Pune after completion of class XII or directly into the Air Force Academy after graduation through a Combined Defence Services (CDS) examination conducted by the UPSC. Entry into the other ground duty and technical branches are through Combined Entrance Tests (CET) conducted by Air HQ. Entrance examinations are conducted every six months and are duly advertised with all relevant details in the leading national dailies.

Induction of Women in the Officers' Cadre

Traditionally, the IAF has employed women as permanent commission medical and nursing officers. However, a decision was taken in the early nineties to open doors to women as commissioned officers in the other ground duty branches. Consequently, the first batch of women officers were commissioned into the Administration and Education branches on June 1993. Soon thereafter women were inducted to cover all ground duty branches and finally the first batch of women pilots was commissioned in December 1994. At this point of time, in the year 2005, women officers other than those in the medical branch, are entitled to hold Short Service Commission (SSC) for a maximum term of 15 years and are not entitled to pension on retirement. Also women pilots are restricted to flying transport aircraft and helicopters only. However, these terms and conditions could change with time. Today there over 500 women officers in the IAF this is approximately 5 per cent of cadre strength. A woman officer married to a male IAF officer can expect postings at the same station as her husband for a substantial part of her 15 year service career. Although here are no guarantees, the IAF has been particularly considerate and has a respectable record in this regard.

Branches

The officer cadre comprises a number of specialist branches and sub branches. These are as under:-

- Flying
  - Flying Pilot
  - Flying Navigator
- Technical
  - Aeronautical Engineer (Electronics)
  - Aeronautical Engineer (Mechanical)
- Administration
- Accounts
- Logistics
- Education
- Meteorology
- Medical

Officers of the flying branch function as aircrew on board IAF aircraft and have a central role in the conduct of air operations. Officers of the Aeronautical Engineering branch perform technical, managerial and R&D functions. Officers of the Administration branch provide complete spectrum of administrative support as also perform duties of Air Traffic Controllers and Fighter Controllers in air defence organizations. Officers of the Meteorological branch are responsible for providing meteorological services. As weather phenomena can prove to be a major impediment in air operations, support by efficient meteorological services is a vital prerequisite for safe and successful flying operations. Officers of the Logistics, Accounts, Education, and Medical branches provide services relevant to their areas of responsibility. Incidentally, the IAF is the only one amongst the three services to have an integral Accounts branch. Having accounts personnel in uniform makes the accounting system in the IAF highly efficient and facilitates matters immensely for personnel.

Entry Criteria: Officers' Cadre

Flying Branch

To obtain a Permanent Commission (PC) in the flying branch, one must be unmarried and follow the route as under:-

- **National Defence Academy (NDA):** Entry into NDA is open to male candidates only and is through a competitive examination conducted by the UPSC twice in a year. The advertisements inviting applications appear in the media in March and October. To be eligible to appear for the examination, one must be between 16 ½ and 19 years of age on the day of commencement of training at NDA. He should have completed Class XII with Physics and Mathematics. Candidates who pass the written examination are subjected to a six-day testing schedule including a once–in-a-lifetime Pilot Aptitude Battery Test (PABT) by one of the Air Force Selection Boards (AFSB) located at Dehra Dun, Varanasi or Mysore. Candidates successful at AFSB, are required to undergo a stringent medical examination at Air Force Central Medical Establishment, Subroto Park, New Delhi or at the Institute of Aerospace Medicine (IAM), Airport Road, Bangalore. Vacancies at the NDA are filled from the final all India merit list prepared based on the results of all three tests. Those who successfully complete the three year training and a simultaneous JNU sponsored BSc graduation curriculum at the NDA, join the Air Force Academy at Dundigal, Hyderabad as pilot trainee and are designated as Flight Cadet After the first semester, pilot trainees are assigned to fighter, transport or helicopter streams for further training. The President's Commision is granted in the rank of Flying Officer on probation (equivalent to Lieutenant in the Army) after successful completion of one year of training as a pilot.

- **Combined Defence Services Examination (CDSE):** Male candidates with a graduate's degree in any discipline but with Physics and Mathematics in Class XII or with B.E/ B .Tech between 19 and 23 years of age on the day of commencement of training at AFA, are eligible to appear for the written examination conducted by the UPSC twice a year. The advertisement appears in the media in April and September. Thereafter the process is common with candidates for the NDA.

- **National Cadet Corps (NCC).** Male candidates with a graduates degree in any discipline with Physics and Mathematics in Class XII or BE with a Senior Division NCC 'C' Certificate and age between 19 to 23 years on the day of commencement of training at the AFA, may apply through the Commanding Officer of the NCC Air Squadron at their Institution in April and October each year. Candidates through NCC are not required to appear for the UPSC examination. They are tested directly by the AFSB and medical establishment after which they are placed on common merit list.

Aeronautical Engineering Branch

The Aeronautical Engineering (AE) Branch of the IAF is subdivided into two sub-branches, Electronics and Mechanical referred to as AE (L) and AE (M). Male candidates between 18 and 28 years of age on the day of commencement of training at AFA are eligible to apply to appear for Combined Entrance Test conducted by Air HQ twice a year. Applications are invited in April and October. Candidates must have a minimum aggregate of 60 per cent in the qualifying examination for being eligible to apply. First division with GATE score of 70 per cent or above are preferred. Educational qualifications for the two sub-branches are as under:-

- **AE (L):** B.E/ B.Tech Electronics/ Telecommunications/ Electrical/ Electrical Communication/ Electronics and Communication/ Instrumentation/ Computer Science and Engineering or a combination of these subjects. OR

   Diploma in Electronics of Madras Institute of Technology. OR

B.Tech in Radio Physics and Electronics/ Optics and Opto- Electronics. OR

M.Sc. in Physics with Electronics/ Electronics/ Computer Science/ Computer Science/ Computer Application/ MCA with Mathematics, Physics and Electronics at Graduation Level/ M.Sc. Tech in Electronics and Radio Engineering. OR

Section A&B Examination of the Associate Membership Examination of the Institute of Engineers (India) in Electricals, Electronics or Telecommunication Subjects.

Graduate Membership Examination of the Institute of Electronic and Telecommunication Engineers with Subjects of Section A and full Subjects of Section B by actual studies (Mathematics, Applied Electronics and Circuits, Principals of Communication Engineering, Transmission Lines and Networks). Section A&B of Examination of Aeronautical Society of India by actual studies in Avionics and Communication streams.

- **AE (M):** B.E/ B. Tech in Aeronautical/ Mechanical/ Production/ Industrial Production or combination of these subjects. OR

Section A&B of Associate Membership Examination of Institution of Engineering (India) with Mechanical/ Aeronautical subjects by actual studies. OR

Section A&B Examination of the Aeronautical Society of India with Group I (Design & Production) or Group II (Maintenance, Repair and Overhaul) subjects by actual studies.

Ground Duty Branches

Entry in to the Ground Duty branches for both PC and SSC (Women), is through a Combined Entrance Test (CET) conducted by Air HQ twice a year. Applications are invited in May and November. Entry criteria for Permanent Commission into the various Ground Duty Branches are as under:-

- **Administration & Logistics.** The age bracket is between 20 and 23 years for graduates, 20 to 25 years for post graduates. The upper limit of age is relaxed up to 26 years for those holding a Law Degree of a three-year-course. The aspirant must be a graduate or a post graduate with 60 per cent or above or an MBA/ Post Graduate Diploma in Business Administration with minimum of 60 per cent marks from Institutes recognized by All India Council for Technical Education (AICTE).

- **Accounts.** The minimum age limit is 20 years with the maximum limit at 23 years for graduates, 25 for post graduates and 27 for holders of CA/ ICWA etc. The candidate must have a minimum B.Com/ B.Com (Hons) or M.Com with a minimum of 60 per cent marks. Additional advanced qualifications would be preferred.

- **Education.** The minimum age limit is 20 years with the upper limit at 25 which can be relaxed up to 27 years for those holding MEd or PhD. The minimum educational qualifications are M.A/ M.Sc. with 60 per cent or above in English/ Psychology/ defence Studies/ mathematics/ Physics/ Statistics/ Computer Science. The candidate may have an MBA or

PGDBA with 60 per cent marks (two year full-time or three year part time course) from Institutes recognizes by AICTE with a combination of minimum two subjects out of Physics, Mathematics, Statistics, English, Psychology or Defence Studies at B.A/B.Sc. level.

- **Meteorological Branch.** The candidate must be between 20 to 25 years of age on the first day of training at AFA. He must have at least a M.Sc. in Physics/ Applied Physics/ Meteorology/ Geophysics with Meteorology and Oceanography/ Oceanography with specialization in Meteorology/ M.A or M.Sc. in Mathematics or Applied Mathematics/ M.Tech in Atmospheric Science from IIT, Delhi with a minimum of 60 per cent marks.

Entry Criteria for Women

Unmarried women candidates may apply for Short Service Commission (SSC) in all branches of the IAF. They are eligible to serve for an initial term of 10 years extendable to 15 years subject to availability of vacancies and suitability report based on their performance. Age and educational qualification required are as stipulated for male candidates in the different branches except that for the flying branch, the upper age limit can be relaxed up to 25 years for those women candidates who are in possession of Commercial Pilots' Licence (CPL). Applications for SSC (Women) for the flying and ground duty branches are invited in May and November and for the technical branch in October only.

22
Personnel below Officers' Rank/ Airmen Cadre

Unlike officers, airmen are categorized not as branches but as trades related to their vocational skills and are grouped into three broad categories as under:-

- Group X: Technical trades with a minimum entry qualification at Class XII and Education Instructors with graduate's degree.
- Group Y: Technical & Non Technical trades with a minimum entry qualification at Class X.
- Group Z: Musician trade only with expertise in music and proficiency on musical instruments as the only qualification required.

Recruitment to the PBOR cadre is controlled by the Central Airmen Selection Board (CASB) under Air HQ located at Delhi. Entry criteria for PBOR/Airmen and Trade Structure is discussed subsequently.

The PBOR

This expression covers all ranks of airmen, Senior Non Commissioned Officers (SNCOs), Junior Warrant Officers (JWO), Warrant Officers (WO) and Master Warrant Officer (MWOs). This category of personnel is also commonly referred to as 'Airmen'. The rank structure of PBOR/Airmen is as under:

- Aircraftsman
- Leading Aircraftsman
- Corporal
- Sergeant
- Junior Warrant Officer

- Warrant Officer
- Master Warrant Officer

Policy governing promotion of PBOR is under review and a revised policy incorporating accelerated time scale promotion up to the rank of Corporal in five years, Sergeant in 12 years and JWO in 17 years is expected to be approved by the Government in the near future. The proposal under consideration includes promotion on the basis of selection to the rank of JWO failing which time-scale promotion would be available in this rank on completion of 22 years of service. PBOR may look forward to improved career prospects under the new dispensation.

Entry Criteria

Group X (Technical Trades)

- **Age Group 16 to 22:** Passed Class XII or equivalent examination with English Physics and Mathematics with a minimum aggregate 50 per cent marks. OR

    Three-year Diploma in Engineering (Mechanical/Electrical/Electronics/Automobile/Computer science/Instrumentation Technology) from a Government recognized Polytechnic/ Institute.

- **Age Group 20 to 25:** Graduation with a teaching degree or diploma from a recognized Education Instructor University with a minimum of 50 per cent aggregate marks in each qualification. OR

    BA (Hons)/BSc (Hons)/BCA with minimum 50 per cent marks.

- **Age Group 20 to 28 :** A minimum second class Masters Degree in Education Instructor English/Mathematics/Physics/Computer Science/ Computer Application.

Group Y (Technical/Non-Technical Trades)

- **Age Group 16 to 20:** Passed Matriculation/equivalent with minimum aggregate marks of 50 per cent in English. OR

    Passed Intermediate/equivalent examination with minimum aggregate marks of 50 per cent with pass marks in English in either Matriculation or Intermediate.

Group Y (Musician Trade only)

- **Age Group 17 to 35:** Should be able to read and write English and has knowledge of elementary arithmetic. Should be proficient in playing at least one musical instrument out of Trumpet/Bass/Saxophone/Clarinet/Euphonium/Jazz/Drum/Picolo/BassTrombone/KeyBoard/Guitar/Sarod/Violin/Viola/Cello/String Bass.

Trade Structure : PBOR (Airmen)

Group X

Technical Trades

- Airframe Fitter
- Engine Fitter
- Electrical Fitter
- Instrument Fitter
- Missile Fitter (E), (L), (M)
- Radar Fitter
- Radio Fitter
- Plant Maintenance fitter (E), (M)
- Weapon Fitter
- Workshop Fitter (B), (C)

Non-technical Trade – Education Instructor

Group Y

Technical Trades

- Air Defence System Operator
- Machinist
- Mechanical Transport Technician
- Photo technician
- Radio Technician
- Safety Equipment Worker
- Meteorological Assistant

Non-technical Trades

- Aircraft Hand and General duties
- Airfield Safety Operator
- Catering Assistant
- Clerk Equipment Accounting
- Clerk General Duties

- Clerk Pay and Accounting
- Equipment Assistant
- Ground Training Instructor
- IAF (Police)
- Mechanical Transport Driver
- Medical Assistant
- Radio and Telephonist Operator

Group Z - Musician

Airmen Selection Centres in India

No 1 Airmen Selection Centre
48 Mansfield Road
Ambala Cantt 133001
Tel: 0171-2634980

No 2 Airmen Selection Centre
412 Air Force Station Race Course
New Delhi 110003
Tel: 011-23010231 Extn 7652

No 3 Airmen Selection Centre
Air Force Station Chakeri
Kanpur 208008
Tel: 0512- 2451730

No 4 Airmen Selection Centre
Air Force Station, Barrackpore
(Near Palta Gate)
West Bengal l743122
Tel: 033-25921251 Ext 6391

No 5 Airmen Selection Centre
Old Pali Road
Jodhpur 342011
Tel: 0291-2511516 Extn 2435

No 6 Airmen Selection Centre
411 Air Force Station Cotton Green
Mumbai 400033
Tel: 022-23714982 Extn 251

No 7 Airmen Selection Centre
No 1 Cubbon Road
Bangalore 560001
Tel: 080-25592199

No 8 Airmen Selection Centre
413 Air Force Station Tambaram
Chennai 600046
Tel: 044-22395553

No 9 Airmen Selection Centre
Near Rajdhani College
Baramunda
Bhubaneshwar 751003
Tel: 0674-2561336

No 10 Airmen Selection Centre
Air Force Station Bihta
Patna , Bihar 801103
Tel: 0612-2235502
0615-252234 Extn 4340

No 11 Airmen Selection Centre
Borjhar
Guwahati 781015
Tel: 0361-2840976 Extn 333

No 12 Airmen Selection Centre
Air Force Station Bowenpally
Secunderabad 500011
Tel: 040-27753551 Extn 267

No 13 Airmen Selection Centre
VII/302 B, Vayu Sena Road
Kakkanad
Kochi 682030
Tel: 0484-2427010

Indian Coast Guard
By
Vice Admiral (Retd) GM Hiranandani, PVSM, AVSM, NM, PhD

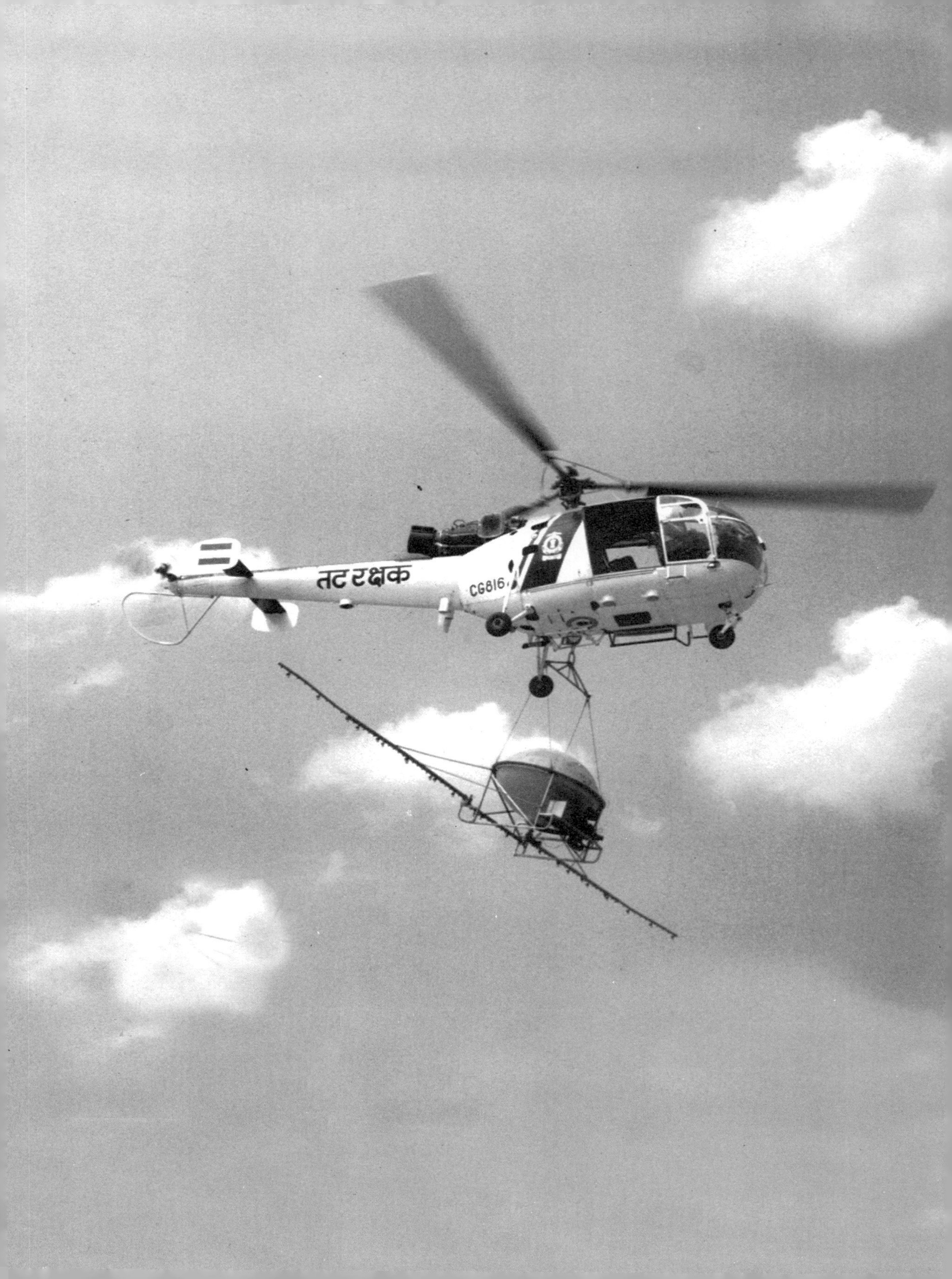
तट रक्षक
CG816

23
Indian Coast Guard

The deliberations, in the 1970s, of the United Nations Conferences on the Law of the Sea led to the establishment of India's Exclusive Economic Zone (EEZ).

On 25 August 1976, India passed the Maritime Zones Act which claimed a 12- mile territorial sea, a 24-mile contiguous zone, a 200-mile EEZ and a continental shelf up to 200 miles or the outer edge of the continental margin, whichever was greater.

This in turn led to the need for a force for safeguarding this zone.

An interim Coast Guard was constituted on 1 February 1977 with two frigates and five patrol boats transferred from the Navy. Its tasks were to enforce India's laws in the field of customs, immigration, poaching, and pollution at sea. It functioned under the aegis of the Navy until 1 August 1978.

The permanent Coast Guard was constituted as an armed force of the Union on 19 August 1978, under the Coast Guard Act - 1978, which came into force on that day.

The Coast Guard Act - 1978

The Act specified the Coast Guard's duties and functions:

- It shall be the duty of the Coast Guard to protect by such measures, as it thinks fit, the maritime and other national interests of India in the maritime zones of India.
- Without prejudice to the generality of the provisions of sub-section above, the measures referred to therein may provide for:
  - Ensuring the safety and protection of artificial islands, offshore terminals, installations and other structures and devices in any maritime zone.
  - Taking such measures as are necessary to preserve and protect the maritime environment and to prevent and control marine pollution.

- Providing protection to fishermen in distress at sea.
- Assisting the customs and other authorities in anti-smuggling operations.
- Enforcing the provisions of such enhancements as are for the time being in force in the maritime zones and
- Such other matters, including measures for the safety of life and property at sea and collection of scientific data, as may be prescribed.

* The Coast Guard shall perform its functions under this section in accordance with, and subject to such rules as may be prescribed and such rules may, in particular, make provisions for ensuring that the Coast Guard functions in close liaison with Union agencies, institutions and authorities so as to avoid duplication of effort.

The Maritime Zones of India (Regulation of Fishing by Foreign Vessels) Act 1981

Poaching is prevalent in the waters around the A&N Islands, in the approaches to the Hooghly River at the head of the Bay of Bengal, along the East coast between Visakhapatnam and Chennai, in the Palk Strait between India and Sri Lanka, along the West coast between Kochi and Mumbai and in the waters off the Gulf of Kachch.

The Regulation of Fishing by Foreign Vessels in the Maritime Zones of India Act came into force on 2 November 1981. It laid down the procedure to regulate fishing by foreign vessels in India's EEZ and provided for deterrent punishments like levying fines, confiscation of craft, etc. for illegal fishing in the EEZ.

Concurrently, notifications were issued extending the provisions of the Criminal Procedure Code and the Indian Penal Code over the EEZ.

The Coast Guard thus became the principal organization for enforcing all national legislation in the Maritime Zones of India, and the policing, surveillance and patrolling of:

- ***The EEZ*** of 2,013,410 sq kms that extends 200 miles from the shoreline (1,418,193 sq kms EEZ of the mainland and Lakshadweep and 595,217 sq kms EEZ of the A&N Islands). The EEZ is expected to increase by about one million sq kms when the Legal Continental Shelf regime comes in to force.

- ***The Coastline*** comprising a total of 7,517 kms (5,423 kms of the mainland, 1,962 kms of the A&N Islands and 132 kms of the Lakshadweep Islands).

- ***The Island Territories*** (598 islands near the shore, 572 islands in the Andaman & Nicobar Group and 27 islands in the Lakshadweep Group).

- ***The Offshore Installations*** off Mumbai and the Tamil Nadu coast to ensure their security and, to avoid duplication of work, working in close liaison with other Government authorities

- **The Territorial Waters** that extend 12 miles from the shoreline and the 155,889 kms of the shoreline's gulfs, bays, creeks, inlets and swampy marshy areas.

  In the implementation of the above, the Coast Guard is:

- The national coordinating authority for Maritime Search and Rescue in the Indian Search and Rescue Region (ISRR). This region extends from longitude 60Ú East in the Arabian Sea to longitude 97Ú East in the Bay of Bengal down to latitude 6Ú South in the Indian Ocean and covers a region of over six million sq kms.

  India shares Search and Rescue boundaries with:-

- Pakistan and Somalia in the West,
- Seychelles, Mauritius, Maldives and Sri Lanka in the South and
- Bangladesh, Myanmar, Malaysia and Indonesia in the East.

Coast Guard Resources

Surface Vessels

From 1983 onwards, in successive 5-year Plans, the Coast Guard has built up its resources in indigenously constructed offshore, inshore and fast patrol vessels, interceptor boats, interceptor craft and hovercraft. It has inducted Seaward Defence Boats, Offshore Patrol Vessels (OPVs) with Chetak helicopters embarked, Fast Patrol Vessels, Inshore Patrol Vessel and Interceptor Boats. It also operates and mans the Indian Oil Corporation's fast interceptor boats at Vadinar.

The Coast Guard's Air Wing

A helicopter squadron was commissioned in 1982 and a maritime surveillance squadron was commissioned in 1983.

Regional Organization

The structure that has evolved over the years is:

- Coast Guard HQ is at New Delhi.
- Three 'Regional Headquarters' at Mumbai, Chennai and Port Blair of the Western, Eastern and A&N Regions respectively. Each regional headquarters has under it 'district headquarters', Coast Guard Stations, Coast Guard Air Stations and Coast Guard Air Enclaves, Refit & Production Teams, Store Depots, etc:-
  - The Western region comprises the coastal states of Gujarat, Maharashtra, Goa, Karnataka, Kerala and the union territories of Daman & Diu and Lakshadweep. The locations of the respective Coast Guard District Headquarters are Porbander in Gujarat, Mumbai in Maharashtra, New Mangalore in Karnataka, and Kochi in Kerala. Gujarat has a Coast Guard Station each at Vadinar and Okha.

- The Eastern region comprises the coastal states of Tamil Nadu, Andhra Pradesh, Orissa and Bengal. The locations of the respective Coast Guard District Headquarters are at Chennai in Tamil Nadu, at Visakhapatnam in Andhra Pradesh, at Paradeep in Orissa and at Haldia in Bengal. Tamil Nadu has a Coast Guard Station each at Tuticorin and Mandapam.
- The A&N Island region comprises these two groups of islands. The Regional Headquarters at Port Blair has under it the District Headquarters at Diglipur in the Andaman Islands and at Campbell Bay in the Nicobar Islands.
- The Coast Guard Air Station (West) is located at Daman, Coast Guard Air Station (East) is located at Chennai. There are Coast Guard Air Enclaves at Mumbai, Goa, Kolkata and Port Blair.
- There is a Coast Guard Berthing Jetty, a Base Maintenance Unit and a Stores Complex at Chennai and a Berthing Jetty at Visakhapatnam.

Activities in Peacetime

In peacetime, Coast Guard vessels

- Participate in the joint Navy-Coast Guard patrols in the Palk Bay, off the Maharashtra and Gujarat coasts and around the A&N Islands.
- Assist in cyclone, flood and earthquake relief operations.

The Coast Guard participates in a number of peacetime activities in these maritime zones which include joint Search and Rescue exercises and conferences on issues like piracy and Search and Rescue.

Over the years the Coast Guard has undertaken joint exercises with foreign Coast Guards:

- Coast Guard ships and aircraft have exercised with ships of Indonesia, Italy, Japan, Mauritius, Maldives, Seychelles, Singapore, Sri Lanka and Thailand.
- Since 1991, regular training exercises named 'DOSTEE' (Friendship) have been carried out with the Maldives Coast Guard to help enhance confidence levels and understanding on joint law enforcement, oil pollution response, search and rescue, etc.

The Coast Guard has interacted also with maritime organizations like the ASEAN Regional Forum Workshop on Maritime Piracy and the International Maritime Search and Rescue Conference.

In 2001, the Coast Guard reached out as far as Japan to participate in an Indo-Japan Coast Guard Exercise.

Overview of Achievements

The evolution of the Coast Guard has been remarkably cost effective. Most of its ships and aircraft are indigenous. With the Navy's help, its manning and training have been extremely economical. Its anti-poaching operations, its anti-smuggling assistance to the Customs, its pollution-control operations, its protection to endangered marine species like the Olive Ridley turtles on the Orissa coast, its Search and Rescue Operations, its sustained round-the-clock surveillance in the shallow waters of the Palk Bay between Tamil Nadu and Sri Lanka, all have been invaluable.

From the time of its inception in 1978, the Coast Guard had, in round figures:

- Seized contraband worth over 300 crores of rupees.
- Apprehended over a hundred smuggling vessels, over eight hundred foreign poaching trawlers and over 8,000 of their crew.
- Responded to over 50 oil spill incidents and undertaken 30 oil spill operations.
- Interdicted over 20,000 illegal immigrants/infiltrators.
- Flown over 1,100 Search & Rescue sorties and saved over 1,500 lives at sea in over 750 missions.

Activities during Hostilities

As is done by other Coast Guards of the world, India's Coast Guard would during hostilities, function under the overall operational command of the Navy.

During the Kargil War in 1999 and during Operation Parakram in 2002, Coast Guard vessels and aircraft provided invaluable support to the Navy's operations in the Arabian Sea.

Directors General of the Coast Guard

To ensure the closest possible interaction between the Navy and the Coast Guard, the Directors General of the Coast Guard have been senior Vice Admirals, except briefly on two occasions in 2001 and 2005.

INDEX

A

Afghanistan, 71, 77
Africa, 1, 73, 77, 99
Ahmedabad, 73
Ahmednagar, 22, 74
Akhnoor, 81
Allahabad, 126
All India Radio, 81
Ambala, 119
Amritsar, 81
Anantnag, 67
Andaman and Nicobar Islands, 77, 80, 83, 100, 101, 102, 105, 106, 158, 159, 160
Andhra Pradesh, 24, 102, 160
Arabian Sea, 73, 80, 83, 99, 100, 105, 159
Arakkonam, 101
'Army Day', 2
Arunachal Pradesh, 43, 67, 138
Asia, 73, 77
Assam, 3, 43, 46

B

Baghdad, 73
Bangalore, 127
Bangladesh, 3, 70, 85, 121, 140, 159
Banihal, 67
Baramulla, 2, 66
Basra, 73
Battle of Cambrai, 22
Battle of Kanwah, 24
Battle of Panipat, 24
Battle of Somme, 22
Battle of Trafalgar, 77
Bay of Bengal, 75, 76, 80, 81, 82, 83, 84, 90, 100, 101, 105, 158, 159
Bengal, 1, 35
Berar, 74
Bidar, 74
Bihar, 11, 126
Bijapur, 74
Bikaner, 38
Bombay, 1, 35, 81, 83, 84, 86, 90
Braches of Army, 18-38
    AMC, 35-36
        advice on medical matters, 36
        evacuation of casualties, 35
        health services, 36
        maintenance, 35
        nursing and dental services, 36
        supplying medical stores, 36
    AOC, 33-34
        ammunition, mines, grenades and demolition explosives, 34
        technical stores, 34
        transport, general stores, clothing, 34
        warlike stores and equipment, 34
    armoured corps, 22-23
        regiments, 22
    army air defence, 26-27
        radars, 26
        communications equipments, 26
    army aviation corps, 28
    arms and services, 18
    artillery, 23-26
        field branch, 24
        surveillance and target acquisition branch, 24
    ASC, 32-33
        air dispatch platoons, 33
        animal transport company, 33
        heavy truck platoons, 33
        light truck platoons, 33
        supply platoons, 33

tank transporter platoons, 33
corps of engineers, 28-30
   Bengal Engineering Group, 28
   Bombay Engineering Group, 28
   Madras Engineering Group, 28
corps of signals, 30-31
   channeling equipment, 31
   line equipment, 31
   radio relay, 31
   radio sets, 31
   teleprinters, 31
EME, 34-35
   fitness of vehicles and equipments, 35
   inspection, 35
   maintenance, 35
   recovery and repair, 35
   technical training, 35
infantry, 18-21
   infantry units, 19
   mechanized infantry, 19
   parachute infantry, 20
   special units, 20
minor corps/services, 36-37
   AEC, 37
   APS, 37
   CMP, 37
   military farms, 36-37
   remount and veternity corps, 36
rashtriya rifles, 31-32
territorial army, 37-38
Brief History of Wars and Conflict after Independence, 65-71
   First Indo-Pak War, 1947-48, 65-67
      background, 65
      raider's attack, October 1947, 65-66
   Second Indo-Pak War, 1965, 68-69
      battle in Rann of Kutch, 68-69
      Operation Gibralter: Armed Infiltration in J&K, August 1965, 69
   Sino-Indian War, 1962, 67
   Third Indo-Pak War, 1971, 70-71
      course of operations, 70-71
Brigadier Ranjinder Singh, 66
Britain, 1, 77, 78, 79, 80, 83, 96, 104, 139
Burma, 1, 85, 119

C

Calcutta (Kolkata), 1, 11, 76, 86, 90, 91, 126, 160
Calicut, 74
Canada, 120
Career Opportunities, 108-09
   educations branch, 109
   electrical branch, 109
   engineering branch, 108-09
   executive branch, 108
Ceylon, 75
Chambal, 38
Chandigarh, 11, 126
Chattisgarh, 11, 126
Chamb, 70, 81
China, 1, 2, 67, 79, 104, 138, 139, 141
Cho La, 44
Cochin, 74
Colombo, 77, 99
Command and Control Structure of Army, 8-17
   chain of command, 10-11
      army vehicle flags, 11-13
      areas and divisions, 13
      commands, 12
      corps, 12
      sub-areas and brigades, 13
   field formation, 10
      brigade, 15
      corps, 13-14
      divisions, 14-15
   static formations, 10
jawans, 9
JCOs, 9
NCOs, 9
rank structure, 8-9
   brigadier, 8
   captain, 8
   colonel, 8
   general, 8
   jawan or sepoy, 9
   JCO, 8
   lieutenant colonel, 8
   lieutenant general, 8
   lieutenant, 8
   major general, 8
   major, 8
   NCO, 9
Congo, 2
Contemporary Naval Warfare, 88-96
   anti submarine tactics, 93-95
      antisubmarine ships and their ASW helicopters, 94-95
      MRASW Aircraft, 94
      sound propagation under sea, 93-94
      submarine search and kill submarines, 95
   augmenting India's warship building capacity, 91-92
   Goa Shipyard Limited (GSL), 91
   India's warship building yards, 90
   innovation in warship design and indigenous research

    & development, 89-90
        APSOH, 89
        hybridization, 89
    Navy's submarine arm, 96
    post independence acquisition of Mazagon Docks Limited (MDL) and Garden Reach Workshops GRW, 91
    role of Navy's Air Arm, 96-97
    submarines & anti submarine warfare, 92-93
        stealth and snorting, 92
        submarine tactics
    surface ships, 88-89
        roles, 88-89
Coast Guard, 157-161
    Coast Guard Act 1978, 157-58
    Coast Guard Resources, 159-61
        activities during hostilities, 161
        activities in peacetime, 160
        coast guard's air wing, 159
        Directors General of Coast Guard since its Inception, 161
        overview of achievements, 161
        regional organisation, 159-60
        surface vessels, 159
    Maritime Zones of India (Regulation of Fishing by Foreign Vessels) Act 1981, 158-59

D

Dakotas, 2
Delhi (*see* New Delhi)
Daman & Diu, 159
Devlali, 24, 28
Dwarka, 82, 83

E

East India Company, 1, 24, 35, 74, 75, 77, 90, 103
Egypt, 74
England, 76, 77
Europe, 104

F

Field Marshal Auchinleck, 65
Field Marshal Ayub Khan, 68
First World War, 1, 22, 56, 77
Foreseeable Future, 103-04
France, 1, 76, 104, 122

G

Gangtok, 44
Gaza, 2
Ghazi, 82, 84
General Thimayya, 67
Germany, 86, 87

Gandhinagar, 126
Gilgit, 66
Glimpse of Life in Army, 39-46
    life in field areas, 43-44
        hard field areas, 44
        soft field areas, 44
    life in peacetime location, 39-40
        normal working day, 40
            driving, 40
            education classes, 40
            parade, 40
            physical training, 40
            sports, 40
            weapons training, 40
    high altitude areas, 45-46
        routine in field, 45-46
        siachen glacier, 45
    unit institutes, 41-43
        family welfare centre, 43
        officers' mess, 41
        recreation room, 41-42
        religious institutes, 42-43
        unit medical inspection room, 42
        unit quarter guard, 41
        unit sanik sammelan, 43
        unit school, 42
Goa, 74, 75, 86, 91, 106, 126, 159, 160
Godwin Austen, 45
Golconda, 24
Gujarat, 15, 74, 99, 126, 159
'Gunners Day', 24
Gurez, 66

H

Himachal Pradesh, 38, 126
Himalayas, 3, 14, 43, 44, 45
Historical Overview, 1-4
History of Indian Air Force (IAF), 119-123
    Burma campaign, 119-20
    decade of sixties, 120
    foundation, 119
    lessons of Kargil, 122
    liberation of Bangladesh, 121
    new millennium, 122-23
    pangs of partition, 120
    post-1971: emergence of regional power, 121-22
    transition to jet age, 120
Holland, 76

I

Ibrahim Lodi, 24
India, 2, 3, 24, 56, 65, 66, 67, 68, 71, 76, 77, 79, 80, 81,

82, 103, 104, 120, 124, 138, 139, 140, 141, 157, 158
Indo-Pak War, 66, 70, 83
India's maritime background, 73-78
    Anglo-French Contests on East Coast 1740 to 1815, 76
    European contests for naval dominance of East Coast, 74-75
    Maratha Navy in 17th and 18th Centuries, 75-76
    millennia prior to Europeans, 73-74
Indian Air Force, 5, 28, 70, 81, 82, 85, 119
    history of, 119
    meetings challenges, 135
    officer cadre, 146
    PBOR, 152
    role of, 124
    types of operations, 129
Indian Air Force: meeting challenges of twenties, 135-145
    aerial reconnaissance, 140
    air defence, 141-42
    battlefield strike, 143
    conclusion, 144-45
    conflict and developing world, 135-36
    exploitation of space, 143-44
    India as regional power, 138-39
    Indo-Pak confrontation, 137-38
    in-flight refueling, 143
    planning for modernization of, 135
    prospects of peace, 138
    security environment in twenties, 139-40
    Sino-Indian relations, 136-37
    strategic & tactical airlift capability, 142-43
    strategic & tactical strike capability, 140-41
    technological revolution, 144
    training, 144
Indian Armed Forces, 3, 5, 100, 101
    air force, 5
    army, 5
    navy, 5
Indian Army, 1, 3, 5, 23, 28, 31, 35, 36, 37, 43, 65, 66, 67, 68, 69, 70, 101
    branches of, 18
    brief history of wars and conflict, 65
    command and control structure of, 8
    glimpse of life in, 39
    historical overview, 1
    recruitment in, 56
    role of armed forces, 5
    traditions and customs of, 47
Indian Coast Guard, 157
Indian Navy, 5
    career opportunities, 108

contemporary warfare, 88
development after independence, 79
foreseeable future, 103
India's maritime background, 73
officer entry, 110
operations after 1971, 98
today, 105
Indian Navy Today, 105-07
    best support, 106
    command and control, 105-06
        eastern, 105
        southern, 105
        western, 105
    training, 106-07
Indonesia, 73, 81, 102, 159, 160
Industrial Revolution, 76
'Infantry Day', 2
Iraq, 1
ISI, 3
Italy, 1, 160

J

Jaipur, 11
Jaisalmer, 38
Japan, 77, 104, 160
Jammu and Kashmir, 2, 3, 14, 16, 31, 38, 44, 45, 46, 65, 66, 68, 69, 70, 71, 100, 119, 120, 126, 139, 142
Jaywardene, 98
Jelep La, 44
Jhangar, 67
Jharkhand, 11

K

Kanhoji Angre, 75
Kannanur, 74
Karachi, 84, 119
Kargil, 3, 67, 69, 81, 100
Karnataka, 160
Kashmir, 2, 3, 66, 67, 68, 70, 71, 81, 100, 139, 140, 141
Kerala, 159
Khukri, 84
Kirpan, 84
Kochi, 102, 105, 106, 158, 160
Korea, 2
Kotli, 66, 67

L

Ladakh, 3, 14, 44, 45, 67, 68, 138
Lahore, 1, 3, 69, 81, 82
Lakshadweep Islands, 106, 127, 158, 159
Leh, 3, 66, 100
Lieutenant Colonel D. R. Rai, 66
Lieutenant General K. M. Cariappa, 2

Line of Control (LoC), 3, 44, 100
Lord Mountbatten, 66
Lord Kitchener, 1
Lovji Nusserwanji Wadia, 90
Lucknow, 11, 126

M

Madhya Pradesh, 11, 38, 126
Madras, 1, 35, 75, 76
Maharashtra, 22, 24, 28, 99, 126, 159
Major General Akhtar Hussain Malik, 69
Major General T. E. Rees, 1, 2
Major Somnath Sharma, 66, 67
Malabar Coast, 74, 75
Malaya, 73
Malaysia, 159
Maldives Islands, 99, 101, 102, 122, 142, 159, 160
Manipur, 43, 46
Mauritius, 78, 159, 160
Ministry of Defence, 10, 35, 60
Mirpur, 66, 67
Mizoram, 43
Mount K2, 45
Mugal King Babur, 24
Mumbai, 80, 82, 85, 86, 87, 91, 96, 99, 100, 105, 106, 158, 160
Mussoorie Hills, 38
Muzaffrabad, 66
Myanmar, 67, 119, 123, 159
Mysore, 84

N

Nagaland, 3, 43, 46
Nagpur, 127
Nasik, 28
Nathu La, 44, 138
National Defence Academy (NDA), 37
Naval Operations after 1971, 98-102
  anti-militant operations in Andaman islands, 100
  assistance rendered by Navy in peace time, 101
  deployment of fleet in north Arabian sea during Kargil War 1999, 100
  deployment of fleet in north Arabian sea in 2002 after Pakistan-based terrorists attacked India's parliament in December 201, 100-01
  deployments in supports of United Nations Humanitarian Operations in Somalia September 1993 to December 1994, 99-100
  evacuation of civilians from Lebanon, 102
  Indian Ocean Tsunami of December 2004, 101-02
  operations in support of Indian Peacekeeping Force (IPKF) in Sri Lanka, 98
  operations in support of Maldivian Government in 1988, 98-99
  patrols along Gujarat and Maharashtra Coasts, 99
Navy's Development after Independence in 1947, 79-87
  1965 war, 80-82
  1971 war, 84
  acquisition of British anti submarine helicopters, 82-83
  acquisition of Russian anti ship missiles, 83
  acquisition of ships from Britain, 79
  after China's intrusion in 1962, 79-80
  arrival of Russian acquisitions, 82
  changeover to Russia Naval Acquisitions, 80
  Leander Frigate Project, 80
  lessons of 1971 war, 85
  Operations in Arabian Sea, 84
  Operations in Bay of Bengal, 84-85
Nepal, 140
New Delhi, 2, 10, 36, 38, 60, 66, 84, 100, 105, 106, 125, 126, 159
Northeast, 31, 38, 39

O

Officer cadre: Rank Structure, 146-151
  branches, 147-48
  entry conditions, 147
  entry criteria, 148-51
    Aeronautical Engineering Branch, 149-50
    entry criteria for women, 151
    flying branch, 148-49
      Combined Defence Services Examination (CDSE), 149
      National Cadet Corps (NCC), 149
      National Defence Academy (NDA), 148-49
    ground duty branches
      accounts, 150
      administration & logistic, 150
      education, 150-51
      meteorological, 151
  induction of women in, 147
Officer Entry, 110-118
  sailor entry, 114-117
    artificers, 114
    electrical branch, 115
    engineering branch, 115
    list of recruiting offices, 116-17
    logistics cadre, 115
    medical branch, 115
    sailors for submarine arm and flight crew of Naval Air Arm, 115-16
    seaman branch, 114
  terms and conditions, 113-14

166　Indian Coast Guard

Operation Gibraltar, 81
Operation Grand Slam, 81
Operation Gulmarg, 66
'Operation JAK', 66
Operation Parakram, 161
Operation Sukoon, 102

P

Pakistan, 1, 2, 3, 44, 65, 68, 69, 70, 79, 80, 81, 85, 120, 121, 139, 140, 141, 159
    Indo-Pak War, 66, 70, 83
Pakistan Air Force, 70, 84, 85
Pakistan Army, 67, 68, 70, 81
Pakistan Occupied Kashmir (PoK), 2, 3, 44, 139
Pathankot, 67
Persia, 73
Personnel below Officer Rank (PBOR), 152-156
    airmen selection centres in India, 155-56
    entry criteria, 153
    PBOR, 152-53
    trade structure, 154-55
Pithoragarh, 38
Pondicherry, 76, 102
Poonch, 66, 67
Portugal, 76
Pune, 11
Punjab, 2, 3, 14, 38, 68, 70, 81, 101, 126
Punjab Boundary Force, 1

R

Rajasthan, 14, 16, 38, 70, 101, 126
Rajauri, 67
Rajiv Gandhi, 98
Rana Sangram Singh
Rann of Kutch, 3, 68, 73
Recruitment in Army, 56-64
    officers' selection system, 56-58
        final selection, 58
        interview, 58
        medical examination, 58
        selection organisation, 57
        tests at SSBs, 57-58
            GTO tests, 58
                command task, 58
                extempore lectures, 58
                group discussion, 58
                group planning, 58
                obstacles, 58
                progressive group tasks, 58
            psychological tests, 57
                Situation Reaction Test, 58
                Thematic Appreciation Test (TAT), 57-58
            Word Associate Test (WAT), 58
    pay and allowances, 62-64
        fair and assured promotion, 63
        group insurance, 63
        officers, 62-63
        other benefits, 63-64
    recruiting organisation, 56
    recruitment of other rank, 60-62
        physical fitness tests, 61
        written examination, 62
    women's special entry scheme, 58-60
Red Sea, 73, 74, 77
River Saraswati, 73
Role of Armed Forces, 5-7
    main braches of, 6
Roles of India Air Force, 124-128
    air command headquarters, 126-127
    force structure, 124-25
    organisational structure, 125-126
    squadron, 127-128
    wing/station, 127

S

Samba, 38
Second World War, 1, 56, 77, 119, 120
Sheikh Mujib-ur-Rehman, 70
Shimla, 11, 43
Shivaji, 75
Siachen, 44, 45
Sikkim, 43
Singapore, 77, 122, 123, 160
Skardu, 66
Somalia, 99, 100, 159
South Africa, 122
Soviet Union (USSR), 77, 78, 79, 80, 83, 120, 122, 139, 140
Squadron Leader Arjan Singh, 119
Squadron Leader K. K. Majumdar, 119
Squadron Leader Mehar Singh, 119
Squadron Leader P. C. Lal, 119
Sri Lanka, 98, 101, 102, 122, 142, 158, 159, 160, 161
Srinagar, 2, 66, 69, 100, 120
Subroto Mukherjee, 120
Surat, 1, 75, 90

T

Taditions and Customs of Service, 47-55
    battle cry, 48
    battle honour, 50
        honour title, 50
        particular operation, 50
        theatre honour, 50

Distinguished Service Medals, 52-55
   Ati Vishisht Seva Medal (AVSM), 53
   Jevan Raksha Padak, 54
   Nau Sena Medal (NM), 54
   Param Vishisht Seva Medal (PVSM), 52-53
   Sarvottam Jeevan Raksha Padak, 53
   Sena Medal (SM), 54
   The Parakram Padak (Wound Medal), 55
   Uttam Jeevan Raksha Padak, 53-54
   Vayusena Medal (VM), 54-55
   Vishisht Seva Medal (VSM), 53
drills and ceremonial parades, 48
Gallantry Awards, 50-52
   Ashok Chakra (AC), 51
   Kirti Chakra (KC), 51
   Maha Vir Chakra (MVC), 50-51
   Param Vir Chakra (PVC), 50
   Shaurya Chakra, 52
   Vir Chakra (VrC), 51
military etiquette, 47
officers' mess, 47
saluting, 47-48
   jai hind, 48
   ram-ram, 48
turnout and smartness, 48
War Medals, 52
   Sarvottam Yudh Seva Medal (SYSM), 52
   Uttam Yudh Seva Medal (UYSM), 52
   Yudh Seva Medal (YSM), 52
Tamil Nadu, 158, 160, 161
Thailand, 123, 160
Thiruvananthapuram, 126
Tibet, 43, 44, 67, 77, 138
Tithwal, 66, 67
Trincomalee, 77, 98
Tripura, 3
Tsunami, 101
Types of Air Operations, 129-134
   aerial reconnaissance, 132
   air defence, 129
      destruction, 129
      detection, 129
      interception, 129
      positive identification, 129
   air transport operations, 132
   electronic warfare, 132-33
   long range strike, 130-31
   offensive air strike, 131
   training philosophy, 133-34
   weapons of air defence, 129-30

U

Udhampur, 10
United Nations (UN), 2, 79, 99, 157
Uri, 67
U S (USA), 68, 77, 78, 80, 82, 101, 103, 104, 122, 139, 140, 141
   US Navy, 83, 103
Uttar Pradesh, 11, 70, 126
Uttrakhand, 38, 44, 67, 126
Uttranchal, 11

V

Vijayanagar, 74
Visakhapatnam, 77, 83, 85, 101, 105, 106, 160
V. K. Krishna Menon, 91

W

Wagah, 81